PSYCHOANALYTIC REFLECTIONS ON THE FREUDIAN DEATH DRIVE

Psychoanalytic Reflections on The Freudian Death Drive is a highly accessible book that investigates the relevance, complexity and originality of a hugely controversial Freudian concept which, the author argues, continues to exert enormous influence on modernity and plays an often-imperceptible role in the violence and so-called "sad passions" of contemporary society. With examples from cinema, literature and the consulting room, the book's four chapters – theory, the clinic, art and contemporaneity – investigate every angle, usually little explored, of the death drive: its "positive" functions, such as its contribution to subjectification; its ambiguous relationship with sublimation; the clues it provides about transgenerational matters; and its effects on the feminine. This is not a book about aggression, a type of extroflection of the death drive made visible, studied and striking; rather, it is about the derivatives of the pulsion that changes in the clinic, in life, in society and in artistic forms. With bold and innovative concepts and by making connections to film and books, Dr. Rossella Valdrè unequivocally argues that the contemporary clinic is a clinic of the death drive.

Psychoanalytic Reflections on The Freudian Death Drive seeks to relaunch the debate on a controversial and neglected concept and will appeal to psychoanalysts and psychoanalytic psychotherapists. Today's renewed interest in the Freudian death drive attests to its extraordinary ability to explain both "new" pathologies and socio-economic phenomena.

Dr. Rossella Valdrè is a psychiatrist and psychoanalyst of the Italian Psychoanalytical Society and International Psychoanalytical Association. Her interests include Freudian metapsychology, as well as cinema and psychoanalysis and their extension to the world of culture and society.

PSYCHOANALYTIC REFLECTIONS ON THE FREUDIAN DEATH DRIVE

In Theory, the Clinic and Art

Rossella Valdrè

Routledge
Taylor & Francis Group

LONDON AND NEW YORK

First published 2019
by Routledge
2 Park Square, Milton Park, Abingdon, Oxon OX14 4RN

and by Routledge
52 Vanderbilt Avenue, New York, NY 10017

Routledge is an imprint of the Taylor & Francis Group, an informa business

British Library Cataloguing in Publication Data
A catalogue record for this book is available from the British Library

Library of Congress Cataloging in Publication Data
Names: Valdrè, Rossella, author.
Title: Psychoanalytic reflections on the Freudian death drive :
in theory, the clinic, and art / Rossella Valdrè.
Description: Abingdon, Oxon ; New York, NY : Routledge, 2019. |
Includes bibliographical references and index.
Identifiers: LCCN 2018036534| ISBN 9781138353572 (hardback :
alk. paper) | ISBN 9781138354340 (pbk. : alk. paper) | ISBN 9780429756245
(epub) | ISBN 9780429756238 (mobipocket/kindle)
Subjects: LCSH: Death instinct. | Psychoanalysis. | Freud, Sigmund, 1856–1939.
Classification: LCC BF175.5.D4 V35 2019 | DDC 150.19/52—dc23
LC record available at https://lccn.loc.gov/2018036534

ISBN: 978-1-138-35357-2 (hbk)
ISBN: 978-1-138-35434-0 (pbk)
ISBN: 978-0-429-42485-4 (ebk)

Typeset in Bembo and Stone Sans
by Florence Production Ltd, Stoodleigh, Devon, UK

To my son

CONTENTS

Hirst
1160

FOREWORD

Dr. Laura Ambrosiano

I'm very pleased to refer here to a dialogue between Rossella and myself. This dialogue started some years ago through an exchange of papers and ideas.

Recently psychoanalysis seems to have returned to what can be called Freud's original proposal: a discipline *included* in the world of the events occurring "outside of the setting." For some decades, in particular around the '80s of the previous century, psychoanalysts dealt much more with the internal world and its vicissitudes than with the external one in which things occur. Now we find ourselves thinking that what is outside is also inside and this influences our theories, patients and clinical attitudes. What is outside seeps through psychoanalysis itself, as well as through philosophy and research in general.

This book of Rossella's on the death drive is the fruit of contact with an external world characterised by violence, which makes it difficult to make sense of the events of the world in which we live. The death drive (similarly to sublimation, which Rossella addressed in a previous work) is an old-fashioned concept, rare in contemporary psychoanalytic literature, except the French one, to which Rossella refers. This is an intriguing and ambiguous concept, as the author underscores, and thus it is a perfect example of those psychoanalytic concepts that Rossella invites us to *reflect upon* and to avoid defining as obsolete and "too metapsychological." The point is that metapsychology has a crucial role in psycho-analysis because it is what permits us to approach reality.

I do not intend to make a presentation of the book here: Rossella does this in her excellent introduction. Rather, I intend to focus on some keywords that have continued to fascinate me throughout the years.

Rossella probes the reasons why psychoanalysts lost interest in the death drive, a controversial concept since its introduction. She argues that this loss of interest is curious: death and life are not antithetic but rather different dimensions charac-terised by a conflicting and complementary dialectic. She reminds us that in many cases death and life are combined, for example in the phenomenon of cell suicide, or apoptosis, described by the immunologist Ameisen in 1999, or in some amazing artistic works. Rossella writes that without the epistemophilic drive, the creative act *per se* would not exist; but without the death drive, there would not exist those inquiries on human pain to which we must open our eyes and that only some great artists can give us. And this, I stress, does not apply only to artists or geniuses, but also to all of us. In fact, the death drive permits us all to love and to work and to individuate and to be subjective.

Death is not an exception or a simple event: it is the line marking our personal horizon. Death as a defined event and its presence inside of us as a drive disturbs us. This is clearly exemplified by many of our patients who wonder: why should we grow up, develop, work hard, if at the end we must die?

The death drive is entrenched in both our body and mind. It is the hard and unavoidable feature of our contact with reality, which makes us face our grief over our limits and our need for illusions in the face of the fact of our eventual death. Freud chose as a criterion for distinguishing between sanity and insanity the acceptance or refusal of reality: such a criterion does not allow us to make a clear distinction because acceptance and refusal are always combined in our relationships with people and things. These relationships are based on perceptions and illusions and thus our cultural development, that is, our constructions, options, creations, sublimations and all the things through which we try to give a meaning to our experiences.

I think that a first attempt to answer Rossella's question of why the concept of death drive is controversial lies in the fact that Freud was skeptical of individual and collective progress and of a happy ending, of a harmony between physical things and human beings. The idea of progress is based on the illusion that human beings, individually and collectively, will finally find a balance and that violence and unhappiness are transformed in order to build a better world, characterised by peace and well-being for everyone. This idea, which is typical of both Catholicism and the Enlightenment, is entrenched in us even when we rationally criticise it. Even progress seems to be an illusion that we need in order to stay alive, Rossella argues: that to take illusion away from human beings is tantamount to stripping them of every expectation of well-being and happiness. Assuming that death or our tendency towards destruction is a drive inside human beings undermines our faith in progress and reveals the illusory character of progress. The death drive stresses the inevitability of violence in human affairs, both individual and historical. It also stresses the need to start a work on violence: violence must be elaborated, thought, transformed throughout life. As Freud writes to Einstein, we cannot eliminate violence by delegating it to law and the judicial system because law and the judicial system can only contain, not eliminate, it.

Every time Freud was about to show that something was actually an illusion, he became unhappy and hesitant. Thus, he always avoided demonising illusions. In 1927 he argued that they are not lies or delusions but rather forms of needs and protection towards a reality that we cannot directly approach, otherwise our head could explode. That is why we need a bandana-like illusion to keep our head together, as Rossella beautifully reminds us by citing David Foster Wallace's explanation of why he always wore a bandana. If we take a look at artists, we have the impression that sublimation (a mechanism with a clear illusory feature) is different from the bandana-illusion, which allows us to approach the sense of things without defences and thus with so strong an intensity and such close proximity that it does not provide us with peace. A writer cannot feel safe far from her sheets, the painter far from her canvases, it is as if sublimation is pressing them . . . because every creation or work of art has an untranslatable aspect. So much so, as Rossella describes in her beautiful chapters dedicated to the arts, that we feel the need to weaken, to slow down, to find some peace in that daily undulating rhythm made of thinking/non-thinking, creation/repetition compulsion, search of the meaning/rejection of the meaning.

Today Auschwitz is not only a memory of terrible historical facts, but also the measure of the limitation of our capacity to give meaning. After Auschwitz, it has been said, philosophy should stay quiet.

These days we are witnessing the invasive presence of violence in both its noisy form (i.e. bombs, massacres, assassinations, etc.) and mute form (i.e. suicides, addictions, self-injurious behaviours, etc.), characterised by *disinvestment*, which Rossella defines as the disease of our age.

Disinvestment is our disease. It is not an evasion of reality based on redemptive illusion. It is a mental state according to which reality cannot reach or touch the individual. I agree with Rossella that it is not a form of sadness or depression but a pervasive feeling of helplessness and uncertainty, of a threat originating from the world and others. It seems impossible to libidically invest in something, in some features of reality or in some object. In these mental territories the need for protection cannot be satisfied with a bandana. It fosters the fantasy of an unaltered calm, an undisturbed daily routine. In this disinvestment psychic reality is massacred: neither the fight between our drives nor conflict can occur because the psychic place in which they take place is destroyed.

Thus, we find ourselves in the paradox of being immersed in a culture that forces individuals to realise themselves and to be creative but, as Rossella writes, does not provide or suggest the psychic means necessary for doing so. The path to subjectivisation is blocked.

The pressure of the neo-liberal ideological *apparati* appears to increase uncertainty and anxiety. These seem to consider the post-modern individual as a smooth surface composed of modules that sometimes must be perfected because they do not work well. The individual is nothing but a *performance machine* that is unable to understand why it must find the meaning behind its anguish (Benasayag, 2015).

Ultimately, it seems that the radical movement of post-modernism aims at deconstructing the internal world of the individual, who is lost, composed of isolated traits, without qualities, a quasi-individual.

The illusion that capitalism would have brought greater wellbeing and greater equality for all has fallen. These days we have to deal with so many lost illusions and with our apparent inability to create new ones. We have lost our illusory faith in linear and good progress, in the possibility of creating a better, more ethical and egalitarian world. We have lost the faith that the individual can stop violence and create a peaceful world. We have even lost the illusion of a transgenerational relationship characterised by *pietas* and love: in its place we find a landscape full of hatred and killer instincts among generations ready to explode.

The fall of the great ideological illusions has led to a feeling of defeat that has yet to be elaborated.

Subjectivisation collapses in the search for distinction in social behaviour: having tattoos, the latest cell phone or the most transgressive dress. "What does the Ego want? To be left alone and in peace." Here Rossella refers to Green (1990) in order to underline how the death drive sometimes aspires to a state of non-excitability, in a search for freedom from desire and thus from those objects that can stir emotions. The death drive is the de-objectualising drive.

The question is: could disinvestment mean a rebuttal of the dominant ideologies and values? Balsamo (2014) interprets the character of Bartleby invented by Melville as a potential discoverer of alternatives, of other ways of living, of other shared values. Momentarily silent, the only thing he says is "I would prefer not to." But from here we can discuss the alternative meanings of the death drive. In fact, as Rossella points out, as with every drive, the death drive can have different fates. A fundamental move towards subjectivisation and personal growth resides in the ability to break up. The rejection and the breaking of the link can foster our curiosity and compel us to search for more intimate meanings. Even repetition compulsion, perhaps the most evident signal of the death drive, can bring about elaboration and lead to a tenacious search for those split aspects and personal instances that are silent for now, waiting to be recognised and heard.

One of the most painful tasks of every new generation is to emancipate itself from what has been transmitted to it. This means accepting and renewing some aspects of the tradition that has been handed down and refusing and abandoning other ones. This involves freeing itself not only from beliefs, ideas and memories, but above all from the *mental functioning* of the past generations, which is transmitted through the rhythms and the modalities of care in the early phases of development. In fact, the parents, extended family and circle of friends transmit to newborns their psychic functioning, that is, their way of dealing with, elaborating and eluding pain, limitations, lacks, needs and the universe of desire. First of all they transmit the value they attribute to psychic life in order to face reality and the ways to circumvent and reject reality. Sometimes it seems that they transmit a dead world, or at best one in agony, that *covers* the child from the beginning and becomes an essential part of her. As Freud writes about Dostoevsky in 1927, in his love-hate for him, the son identifies himself with the dead father. From Ferenczi to Green (1990) we have many descriptions of these configurations in which the dead areas of the previous generations are transmitted silently like holes, like nuclei suspended outside time, to the new generations which subsequently experience them as intimate but unknown aspects of themselves. It is important to emancipate themselves and to do so, one must have at one's disposal aggressive resources – anger and hatred and the vital ability "to say no." This is but one of the fates of the death drive.

Here the "to say no" expresses itself as a willingness to betray familial intimacy, as Badoni (2016) writes. It is a painful route on which we can feel abandoned and isolated. On this route we can see the subjectivating function of the death drive. Rossella takes us there so we can discover through fascinating examples of artists and patients the pain, repetition, compulsion and masochism that occur when emancipation seems impossible.

In the absence of psychic work, the individual's *critical thinking* disappears. The subject is alone in front of the fall of illusions and must deal with an excess of reality without any means of containing it or elaborating possible meanings.

In this situation the future disappears. In fact, no tribe in the West or East seems to have the means to give hope to the world. The prospect of a future is neither possible for Westerners, who appear to be able only to mimic it, nor those Muslims who try to find their place in the world by attaching themselves to an idealised past and who believe that the ideal world is already here. In a sort of "political incest" (Benslama, 2009 p. 26) Muslims define themselves as the only ones to have achieved *umma* the community of the righteous. The word *umma* has its roots in the word "mother" ("*um*"). Thus, we can hypothesise that this community is based on the nostalgia of the union with the mother, full and round, able to protect from evil and despair.

Isn't the expectation of young Westerners for a peaceful world, in which they can be safe and undisturbed, similar to that of Muslims?

The problem is that at a certain point of de-subjectivisation the tendency to destroy or, in Rossella's terms, the noisy death drive, explodes and someone starts to shoot, to plant bombs and to kill.

In this state of de-subjectivisation and disinvestment, in which we are almost-individuals, a widespread feeling of inertia and psychic passivity promotes corruption and increases anger and hate and blazes the trail to corruption and to attacking the community and oneself. Violence seems like an alternative to a lack of personal identity. In fact, because individuals are unable to use words, they prefer to act and erase the faces and words of others, especially those who are different from them or strangers. The loss of the political word risks dropping individuals into a desperate torpor from which it seems attractive to die, dragging all the world with them; all are *witnesses* to their failure, as with young Westerner suicide victims and Muslim terrorists. Killing all witnesses is felt as a way to defend oneself and lost illusions.

So even the encounter with the stranger, Moses of Egypt, tribes from the other side of the Mediterranean, under these conditions does not favour the exchanges, surprises, helpful conflicts or critical discussions that are necessary for creating culture. The meeting is based on closure and immunity. Each tribe wants to protect itself from the contagion of the problems and difficulties of the others. The meeting, determined by a big immigration of masses fleeing war and famine, does not produce any shared project, only violence.

In order to escape this indifferent and violent confusion we are living in, we should find a space in our individual and collective minds in which we can again create an intimate and shared inner work so we can deal with the lacks, the incompleteness, the meaning of illusions and disillusions. This is inner work capable of indicating the needs and desires expressed in our illusions and the possibilities we can achieve.

Contrary to any spiteful reaction or behaviour, the work of mourning starts with thought and returns the word not only to the individual but also to the community. In order to start this work we need individuals who are able to take on the task of individuation, of starting from their own specificity. As Žižek brilliantly argues (2014, pp. 33, 34): "(. . .) one should value above everything else freedom, equality and crab soup," rather than, I add, freedom, equality, couscous or *orecchiette alle cime di rapa* (ear-shaped pasta with turnip greens). We should try to reduce our abstract ideas in the particular circumstances, individual idiosyncrasies and specific cultures.

Capitalism has shown itself able to overcome all ideologies. Thus, to repopulate public spaces we cannot wait for new ideologies.

Rather, we must find or invent new places for humanity (Donaggio, 2016, p. 144) where minorities and small groups can escape the isolation of an ego-system and engage gestures, ideas and emotions that are different from the mainstream. Small places where we can meet others in order *to do something different*, to share and not conform, stories and gestures; small places where *to say no*. For me Rossella's book presents a possibility to exchange ideas, to find ways *to do things in an alternative way*, to avoid those implicit ideologies that had been perpetuated only in order to sustain frail individual and collective identities, to propose a dialogue between psychoanalysis and the external world, to find partners outside our fields of expertise. These small places can foster experiences of reciprocal hospitality that do not lead to conformity, homogeneity or integration-assimilation. By reviving the disturbing notion of the death drive, this book encourages us to strike out for truly blasphemous, lively and thought-provoking directions (Gaburri, 1999/2015).

References

Ameisen, J.C. (1999). *La sculpture du vivant. Le suicide cellulaire ou la mort créatrice*. Paris: Editions du Seuil: Paris.

Badoni, M. (2016). Tradimento e corruzione. Sul potere corruttivo dell'amore materno e sul buon uso del tradimento. In L. Ambrosiano and M. Sarno (Eds.), *Corruttori e corrotti* (Ed. L. Ambrosiano and M. Sarno). Milan: Mimesis: Milan.

Balsamo, M. (2014). Avrei preferenze di no. Letture di Bartleby lo scrivano: una storia di Wall Street di Melville. Psiche, 2:, 395–420.

Benasayag, M. (2015). *Clinique du mal-être*. Éditions La Découverte: Paris: Éditions La Découverte.

Benslama, F. (2009). *Psychoanalysis and the challenge of Islam*. University of Minnesota Press: Minneapolis: University of Minnesota Press.

Donaggio, E. (2016). *Direi di no. Desideri di migliori libertà*. Feltrinelli: Milan: Feltrinelli.

Freud, S. (1927). *Dostoevsky and parricide, S.E. 21*. Hogarth: London: Hogarth.

Freud, S. (1927). *The future of an illusion, S.E. 21*. Hogarth: London: Hogarth.

Gaburri, E. (2015). *Per un'etica profana, Scritti Scelti*. Mimesis: Milan: Mimesis. (Original work published 1999).

Green, A. (1990). *La folie privée. Psychanalyse des cas limites*. Gallimard: Paris: Gallimard.

Lipsky, D. (2010). *Although of Course You End up Becoming Yourself: A Road Trip with David Foster Wallace*. Broadway Books: New York: Broadway Books.

Valdrè, R. (2014). *On Sublimation*. Karnac: London: Karnac.

Žižek, S. (2014). *Event*. Penguin: London: Penguin.

ACKNOWLEDGEMENTS

I wish to thank everyone who has generously given their help towards the publication of this book. I wish to thank my translators in particular, Flora Capostagno, Kathryn Haralambous and Giuseppe Lo Dico.

I am also grateful for the permission given to publish excerpts from:

Appetites: Why Women Want, by Caroline Knapp. Copyright © 2003, reprinted by permission of Counterpoint Press.

Holy Hunger, by Margaret Bullit-Jonas. Copyright © 1998, reprinted by permission of Penguin Random House.

Although of Course You End up Becoming Yourself, by David Lipsky. Copyright © 2010, reprinted by permission of Penguin Random House.

Fat Girl, by Judith Moore. Copyright © 2005, reprinted by permission of Penguin Random House.

Tutte le poesie Tomo I and Tomo II (All poems, Volume 1 and Volume 2), by Pier Paolo Pasolini. Used by permission of his heir, Maria Grazia Chiarcossi, Garzanti Editore and Archinto Editore.

The Selected Poetry of Pier Paolo Pasolini: A Bilingual Edition, by Piero Paolo Pasolini. Used by permission of his heir, Maria Grazie Chiarcossi, University of Chicago Press.

Roman Poems, by Pier Paolo Pasolini, translated by Lawrence Ferlinghetti and Francesca Valente. Translation Copyright © 1986, by City Lights Books, reprinted by permission of The Permissions Company, Inc., on behalf of City Lights Books, www.citylights.com.

The Poems of Emily Dickinson: Variorum Edition, edited by Ralph W. Franklin, Cambridge, Mass.: The Belknap Press of Harvard University Press. Copyright © 1998, by the President and Fellows of Harvard College. Copyright © 1951, 1955, by the President and Fellows of Harvard College. Copyright © renewed

INTRODUCTION

The silent drive: death inside life

Over and over again we find, when we are able to trace instinctual impulses back, that they reveal themselves as derivatives of Eros. If it were not for the considerations put forward in *Beyond the Pleasure Principle*, and ultimately for the sadistic constituents which have attached themselves to Eros, we should have difficulty in holding to our fundamental dualistic point of view. But since we cannot escape that view, we are driven to conclude that *the death instincts are by their nature mute and that the clamour of life proceeds for the most part from Eros.*

(Freud, *The Ego and the Id*, 1923, p. 45, my italics)

I am among those who believe in the concept of the death drive as Freud, beginning with the well-known watershed of the 1920s and *Beyond the Pleasure Principle*, originally formulated it and essentially never abandoned it. I agree with the general theoretical scheme because, above all, it seems to me to recognise the death drive's obvious presence and vividness in manifestations both in the clinic and in life, so heavily imbued with destructiveness and unbinding; perhaps it outright fascinates me, like other great Freudian conjectures. I am also, however, among those who far from wanting to make the death drive an idealised fetish, recognise all the ambiguities, the generality, the extreme difficulty (if not impossibility) of concretely demonstrating its existence. We are aware that the death drive is one of the most controversial concepts in psychoanalysis, frequently mentioned but equally frequently denied (rather curious, this: why is there so much talk about something that is not believed?), debated since its coming to light and yet, precisely for this reason, the source of one of the aporias that I find to be the most interesting, perturbing and intriguing in psychoanalysis – in psychoanalysis as a whole, not only in the Freudian school.

So I decided to write this book, fully aware that I would be putting a thorn in the side that many see as bleeding unnecessarily, or that many simply ignore, because if you talk and debate, then the extraordinary fruitfulness of Freudian thought, be it hidden or awkward, is preserved. Because we should avoid being tempted by trivialisation and the clinic of the obvious, that, as we shall see, easily confuses the silent drive with aggressiveness, and we should not forsake once again (after a recent glimmer on the horizon) metapsychology's richness and central role, as I have often had occasion to stress, in the identity of psychoanalysis.

I will proceed on this journey as I usually do. First I present a theoretical part that reviews the concept in Freud and after Freud, presenting a paper that appeared in the *Italian Journal of Psychoanalysis* in 2012, extensively revised and expanded; a second clinical part where we see "death at work" (Pontalis, 1988, p. 98) in its most typical expressions in masochism, self-sabotage, coercion to repeat and negative therapeutic reactions, at an individual level and in the collective with destructiveness and violence; a third part that digresses into art and the countless examples it offers, choosing some recent films – *Blue Jasmine, Anomalisa* – and a group of writers who share, I believe in a specific way, not so much destructiveness itself but the simultaneous presence from the *fusion* I would describe as all-consuming between the maximum of vitality and the maximum of the drive force to die: Pasolini, David Foster Wallace, Richard Yates and others of the American generation between the 1940s and the 1980s. This specific choice presupposes the theoretical assumption coming up shortly. In this study "pure" expressions of the death drive do not move us much and are, by definition, extremely rare or impossible, whereas its unbreakable bond with life does. In these great and troubled minds and in their written testimony, we have the opportunity to see the death drive with particular clarity, illuminated by the universal light of art. The book concludes with a reflection on contemporaneity, defined with good reason as "the era of sad passions" (Benasayag and Schmit, 2003), attributing Spinoza's famous definition to today. What distinguishes a sad passion? It is not so much sadness raising its head or the mark of pain in the acceptance of suffering authentically lived, but the opaque sadness of *disinvestment*, resulting in not only the pathologies that are virtually the only ones entering our analysis rooms, but also the more general social and cultural climate[1]. Could the voice of psychoanalysis have a role in all this, in those vast marshlands that I feel are muddier than in the past, in the pervasive and underground spread of precisely that *silent drive* identified by Freud? Recognise it anyway, and deal with it not only in individual clinical cases but in a more ambitious *Veltenshaung* of *Kultur* that too often, as also in the case of this successful book, is taken from us by other disciplines. This already constitutes a psychoanalytical vocation. The sad passion is *our* specific field of investigation, if we recognise all the surprising modernity of Freudian intuitions. On the other hand, this is a very delicate and slippery area that requires us to keep a balance, always oscillating between the Scylla of pure sociology (everything is due to society) and the Charybdis of the empire of isolated psychism (everything comes from inside). If as early as 1920, not an era of *evident* sad passions but still contained and reassured by the great ideologies despite the devastation of the First World War, Freud formulated this concept, it is to be considered that, despite the post-modern and ambiguous fluidity of his values certainly providing a contribution in favour of disinvestments and renunciation of conflict, the problem is much more ancient. It is rooted in man, in the human being itself, the unconscious bearer within an apparently paradoxical instance: to operate against life, against his own Good.

Clinical considerations aside, recent reflections lead me to write these sentences, or rather to give full shape to an observation that I have been pondering over for some time now, stimulated by the clinic and from an observation on life: can it be said (today?) that women's bodies – or the body in general – are a particularly fertile ground for the death drive understood as an *aversion to desire* in its different forms, as seems to be shown by the spread of *all* (and not only anorexia) the disorders in eating behaviour, but also the invasion of cosmetic surgery even in extreme and debilitating forms and in women's frequent (more than you would think from superficial observation) withdrawal from pleasure and enjoyment? I know this is not a new observation from a psychological point of view, but I intend to contribute to it from an *experiential* perspective through the stimulating reflections of some American academics, first among them Caroline Knapp with *Appetites* (2003)[2], who helped me to find common *threads* in favour of hypotheses that for now I tentatively and freely put forward.

Even at a collective and group level, up to the large masses, the death drive in its everted form of destructiveness and hetero-destructiveness has already been widely studied and documented, so we will therefore only make brief references. Evil projected towards the other has always been present in history. In every age it has found free ground to manifest itself and modernity is no exception. As is known, *Beyond the Pleasure Principle* is also born out of bitter considerations on human nature, of questioning not only the primacy of pleasure but also the confidence that until then Freud had enlightenedly put in reason. Yet we cannot forget the role of the Great War, the upheaval in the heart of Europe that had such an impact on Freud, contributing to the new topic that would be theorised, five years later, in *Beyond the Pleasure Principle*. Incessant wars, a taste for evil and cruelty even gratuitously perpetrated may not only have contingent reasons. From then onwards for Freud, the task of psychoanalysis would become to thoroughly investigate the unconscious roots not only of pleasure, life's undisputed driving force, but of hatred, too. In proceeding we should always remember that there is an *active, noisy, destructive* perspective to the death drive, one for which peoples and people die just as, even gratuitously, states are mobilised and we organise study groups. But aggressiveness is not the subject of this book, it is not what clothes are worn on the outside; rather it is the silent drive, the skeleton inside. We will try, therefore, not to omit the importance of destructiveness in clinical practice and in social issues but to explore its unconscious drive roots, submerged underground, not accepted by everyone, the common stock from which life and death originate. We will not see the branch, but the darkness of the root. As this is an ambitious and conjectural process, I am aware I am risking slips, partial and personal readings, interpretations that must necessarily refer to Freud, to *that* Freud who from the 1920s onwards had to deal with a spanner in the works. Pleasure has no primacy in psychic life; life does not tend to its own Good.

What I particularly wish to emphasise in this book is the far from being resolved and infinite complexity of the drive interweave: we are used to thinking about life and death as antithetical, one opposite to the other, but a more in-depth reading of Freud opens up a far more complex and disturbing scenario.

Death and life are bound – as we will see, even inside our bodies. One is not the simple *opposite* of the other, but their interweaving, something more mysterious and specific to the traditional *fusion* that sees the two drives always linked in sustaining life, their interweaving appears more interdependent. "One always travels together with the other" (Resta, 2016, p.105, translated for this edition). This interweaving, this absurd simultaneous presence in the eyes of reason, the drives moving our lives, is this book's subject. Deridda coined the apt expression *life death (la vie la mort)*, a daring formulation of the two terms that juxtaposes without the conjunction "and" and without punctuation, to forcefully emphasise this indefeasible commixture, we would say *contiguity* and not only continuity: the irreducibility of life to Good. So if Freud has made it a precise psychoanalytic instance, the concept of the existence of death inside life is not new to thought. Going a step further, as we will see in the theoretical part, not only are the two drives mixed, but life *needs* death. The death drive is entrusted with the paradoxical task of defending life at that moment in which, externally discharged in the form of aggressiveness, it causes the death of the other while preserving its own. Is this too pessimistic a vision, a universe too marked by *mors tua vita mea*? Such a scenario may cause anguish and repudiation, but reality appears to confirm this.

The libido has the task of making the destroying instinct innocuous, and it fulfils the task by diverting that instinct to a great extent outwards – soon with the help of a special organic system, the muscular apparatus – towards objects in the external world. The instinct is then called the destructive instinct, the instinct for mastery, or the will to power. A portion of the instinct is placed directly in the service of the sexual function, where it has an important part to play. This is sadism proper. Another portion does not share in this transposition outwards; it remains inside the organism and, with the help of the accompanying sexual excitation described above, becomes libidinally bound there. It is in this portion that we have to recognise the original, erotogenic masochism (Freud, 1924, pp. 162–163).

Thus Freud did not fail to emphasise the indispensability, the "positive" role of the death drive (to be found again in more recent authors, such as Zeltman), when putting itself at the service of Eros and the drive for self-preservation, discharging in part externally preserves the life of the self, giving death to the other. What I wish to emphasise, in short, is not the opposition between the two drives but their *intrinsic bond*, their sly *complicity*, that sees them not only act together – one noisily, Eros, and the other silently – so that "the death instincts seem to do their work unobtrusively" (Freud, 1920, p. 62) – but also as allies, each in the service of the other, to a different extent in individuals, in the phases of life and in historical moments. As Lispector writes, in her poetic remembering of her childhood, evil was her calling; however she also felt goodness was lukewarm and light, not entirely rotting (1943, pp. 9, 10).

Life death will therefore be the underlying theme of this book, not life _and_ death. I suggest that it was this disturbing contiguity, that subverts the usual antinomy that is much more reassuring for thought (Western thought in particular, always dichotomous, is the only one we deal with here) and has contributed to making the concept so confusing and ill accepted, since its exordium, in part of the psychoanalytic community: how to accept the perturbing hypothesis that death is contained in us, that it works silently on the side of life and that life has absolutely no primacy, just as reason proved to be miserably fragile and conscience an appendix, how to accept being bearers of death, inevitably destined to aggressive movements towards the object or towards the self to survive? It is something more than a simple theory, acceptable or not. It is a radical vision of existing aimed in a direction with no escape that nevertheless psychoanalysis must deal with, without judgement or moralism. We do not like the idea of containing all this in us. We would like to be more intrinsically good, more tied to life – _evil is my calling_, writes Lispector's little Joana[3]. Without abandoning renunciation, Freud has had the courage to demolish this unrealistic vision of human drives.

Allied, accomplices, mixed: _life death_. There is no escape.

The relationship between drive fusion and defusion provides a good indication of the way in which the life drives and the death drives have succeeded in blending together internally, giving coherence to their union and according a certain homogeneity to the psychical organisation. Sometimes, both of these drives live in a state of mutual coexistence, without interpenetration and without imposing tensions on the mind that are too disorganising. In those forms where defusion seems to get the better of fusion, it is not always the unbinding of the destructive drives that prevails, but sometimes the coexistence of the two groups of drives living side by side without reciprocal exchange. Just as the manifestations of erotic seem to have no link with the destructive manifestations, so, too, destructiveness seems to have no relation with the forms of erotic life [. . . .] Ultimately, when the work of defusion carries the day, it is the destructive impulses that prevail and the forces of defusion that dominate. But when defusion prevails, the cohesion of the psychic . . . the field left to destructiveness becomes ever wider. It follows that the forces of the instincts of life, which are believed to militate in favour of the bond, are no longer sufficient [. . .] (Green, 2010, p. 67).

We will often come across these terms, binding and unbinding, objectivising and de-objectivising, coined by Green, who has, I believe, best sought to deepen and _actualise_ Freudian discourse, remaining substantially faithful but attempting a courageous declination in contemporary clinical practice.

In short, we can find expressions of the silent drive everywhere, in the subject, in groups, in society, never pure but always mixed with Eros in varying degrees, if we are not too or solely distracted by the bustle of life, by the noise of the libido, or too anchored to negation and to fear. We can recognise the strength of an antagonist drive that, silent by definition, underhandedly works for betrayal, a solitary boycotter who puts a bomb right there, in the midst of a crowd's energised vitality. As I have already mentioned, in fact, I intend to specifically investigate the clearest expressions of destructiveness and violence, a far from resolved thorny question both on an individual and a social level in particular, as many studies and much psychoanalytic literature already exist on this matter. Manifest aggressiveness and violence are evidence and concepts that, unlike the death drive, are obviously agreed on by all, albeit with different theoretical shades ranging from Bergeret's (1994) fundamental violence to destructiveness and bond attachment as interpreted by the School of Object Relations, to name just a few.

What I propose is something I find more intriguing both metapsychologically speaking and in concrete expressions: a journey not in modalities or territories where the death drive in the form of sadism or pure hetero- or self-aggressive defusion is easily evident, but where it keeps silent, where you cannot see it, where mute and undisturbed it works in depth. In the cracks of disinvestments, in the crenels of desire, in *oblomovian* apathy, in the thousand Nirvanas with which we seek to subdue psychological pain and life's cumbersome wearisomeness, using drugs and substances of any form, including lethal relationships, soporific gregariousness, recourse to the consumption of something – an object or a person or a psychic instance – that puts the vital drive to sleep and anaesthetises it, tames it, extinguishes it. Personally, I come up against this with unprecedented, though silent, frequency.

So this is the territory, the "marshy sod" (Falci, 2005) wherein we sink without realising and, ambivalently, without wanting to, the type of shifting sands of individual and collective psychism that I suggest we investigate. There are also the ambiguous and often controversial metapsychological *border* territories that we will try to shine light on, first and foremost the relationship with sublimation. As already discussed in my previous work dedicated to it (Valdrè, 2015a), the relationship with sublimation, so little explored post-Freud (and left totally unsaturated by Freud himself) constitutes another conceptual node apparently of pure theoretical speculation, but looking more closely we see it is deeply connected to life and death, the ever-impervious crossroads between pleasure and pain. Could it be, as some have hypothesised, that drive defusion caused by the necessary desexualisation of drives to make them transformable and at the disposal of sublimation, to paraphrase Green (1993), may be paving the death drive's path of sublimation? We will certainly be returning to this further, intriguing aporia.

Literature and philosophy as well as other fields of knowledge have always, if not openly investigated, certainly intuited in advance of psychoanalysis, art *in primis*, but clearly there is no answer to these major issues arising from Freudian concepts, nor does this book aim to give one. Quite the opposite, this is a book of questions that wants to stimulate examination, reflection, curiosity; the presence of death inside life – whether it is called death drive or not, and also the abandonment, as many suggest, of the concept itself of the drive considered too tied to a presumed and indemonstrable outdated Freudian biologism – to this silently suicidal presence, there is no answer.

Recent acquisitions by neuroscience or, more precisely, in this case by *immunology*, are proof of how far-seeing Freudian intuition was. The immunologist Jean Claude Ameisen (1999) has given us what has been defined as the overwhelming, paradoxical and counterintuitive hypothesis of *cell suicide*, in medical terms the phenomenon of apoptosis whereby each cell, from the moment of conception, contains in itself the possibility, if it does not find a sufficiently suitable environment for its survival, to commit suicide, to produce weapons that allow them to self-destruct within just a few hours. The concept of apoptosis dates back, to tell the truth, to 1972 (Kir and Miller, cited in Doninotti, 2011) and corresponds exactly to what Ameisen later described more fully. But already in its first descriptions, apoptosis is described as a phenomenon of cellular implosion. Part of a cell triggers its suicide by disengaging from the neighbouring cells, fragmenting until enzymes are released that destroy the surrounding environment. Death at a cellular level is silent and sly as well, as Ameisen would say. Death provides neither lesions, nor scars, nor inflammation and the surrounding cells fill the void left by the dead cells.

We are sculpted[4], says Ameisen, literally from birth to death; life, you might say, occurs notwithstanding, the process is far from obvious, since the kingdoms of cell suicide know no borders (Ameisen, 1999).

Could a more extraordinarily evocative and precise metaphor and parallel of the Freudian death drive exist? Beyond the considerable medical therapeutic repercussions that this hypothesis has brought, by literally overturning the traditional scientific axiom that has always attributed a primacy to life that is also "moral" over death, a foreign and malignant entity to be fought against with every means, the similarity and the metaphorical scope of the concept to our discourse is clearly appreciable. If the living being tends to die (a linguistic paradox?), with the return to the inorganic and quietness, is not life then reduced to a pathetic, useless "disorderly parenthesis between the absolute quietness of before life and that of after," a "libidinised race towards a goal that would not be death exactly but the previous state of life"? (Preta, 2015, p. 126, translated for this edition).

Biology, as Green (2007) also recognises, seems to agree with what was a little simplistically, and wrongly in my opinion, defined as Freudian pessimism. It underlies instead, it seems to me, a clear and precise philosophy of the human paradox: we fight to defeat or to defer death, when we are made by death, "sculpted" in Ameisen's suggestive meaning, when it is actually death, self-annihilation, that resides at the heart of life. *Cell suicide* is connected, as in the subtitle, to *creative death*.

If we are to take it as a truth that knows no exception that *everything living dies for internal reasons* – becomes inorganic once again – then we shall be compelled to say that "*the aim of all life is death*" (Freud, 1920, p. 37, my italics).

The contemporary neurobiology of emotions today can tell us something about the complex pleasure/pain dynamics, intimately connected to the death drive. In addition to the phenomenon of cell suicide, we know that *pleasure*, life's drive force, is supported by dopaminergic systems and by endogenous opioids (*Seeking System* of studies by Panksepp, 2016)[5]. But we also know that life is not so simply solved like this and that, on the contrary, as a result of traumatic experiences or anti-vital movements the *Seeking System* "includes in its needs the search for *pain*" (Bastianini, 2016, my italics, translated for this edition). Although it is bold to make these discoveries (I would describe them as confirmations), they coincide exactly with the death drive as originally intended, and the topicality of the Freudian hypotheses is amazing! It is, however, not necessary to identify a perfect coincidence, it is enough to know that it has been established by sectors of the scientific world that are always less distant from and always less antithetical to psychoanalysis; that death and life are no longer opposite polarities and antonymous, but necessary, ambiguous and conflicting *cohabitees*. As inseparable spouses, *neither with you nor without you*, they cannot be conceived as stand-alones but always jointly at work and, veterans of every faith in the primacy of reason, not always does life get the better, nor do life and pleasure fare well alone, without the mixed contribution of the other partner, death. The revolutionary impact of the Freudian discovery is this and not its labile verification in the biological anchorage of the drives, which Freudian enlightenment and his determination to make psychoanalysis a science, would try to formulate.

In the course of the book, we will see the death drive at work in individuals and in society and on the latter front there are many paradoxes. Just as the organism, that believes itself to be built for life must instead address the tragic evidence that life is but an accident, a stumble compared to death, so, too, History, in particular in our current century and its predecessor, has some singular paradoxes.

The century that wants to confirm life indefinitely and pursues the maximum *intensity* of life, engaging in an endless war for life, sowing death wherever, offering wherever the cruel and seductive spectacle – like a *feast* – of a great slaughter, of an abattoir, of a death that dominates in close-up the early twentieth-century stage.

The historian Caterina Resta (2016, pp. 103, 104) not only writes of the inevitability of war and mass destruction even in the more "evolved" of eras so far known by man, in which we can go around with the world in our pocket enclosed in an iPhone, but she also underlines its more barbarously psychological aspect, the one that never goes away, the one that unites humans of every country, ethnicity, provenance: the pleasure of the *feast*, as understood by Nietzsche (1887)[6], the enjoyment of sadism.

Cruelty, writes the philosopher, is part of the festive joy of the ancients [. . .]. No cruelty, no feast.

And what is cruelty, sadism, if not one of the pure defused expressions of the death drive? It is known that the devastation that struck Europe, until then the cradle of civilisation, in the Great War made a strong impression on Freud, and that *Beyond the Pleasure Principle*, written a few years later, certainly expresses the effects of the bitter realisation that life, contrary to what he had previously believed, is not held up just by the pleasure principle, but that to justify a similar destructive wave a *beyond* had to exist in humans, an *other* land, antithetical, obscenely violent but therefore seductive, the inescapably attractive Evil. To this thrust, present in the world of human drives, not loud and evident like Eros but constantly active in various forms, Freud gave the name death drive: from there, from the so-called watershed of the 1920s, of this silent anti-vital presence, powerfully active in the human unconscious, psychoanalysis accesses the second topic and will always have to take into account this apparently illogical and paradoxical drive. Whether you believe in it, or not.

Typical of his procedure, after the 1920s watershed, not only will Freud not abandon the concept and will consequently have to reckon with its theoretical and clinical encumbrance, as well as the psychoanalytic technique (just think of the therapeutic negative reaction) that the death drive since then will imply, but he will never fail to underline the essential aspect, which is the subtitle of this book. We do not expect the death drive to be naive, to show itself equal to the commotion of Eros, or to show its self. We will only come across derivatives, secondary aspects. It is and remains, as its main characteristic, essentially mute, silent. Until *Civilization and its Discontent* (1930), Freud will recall the importance of this characteristic that also outlines the task of psychoanalysis, because only psychoanalysis can trace a drive in the unconscious that cannot be heard:

> [. . .] We can only suspect it, as it were, as something in the background behind Eros, and it escapes detection unless its presence is betrayed by its being alloyed with Eros.
>
> (Freud, 1930, p. 121)

We are not prejudicially loyal to the term drive. The purpose of my journey into the inaccessible territories of the silent drive is precisely to give it a voice, to dig it out, to see the surprising links with and *for* life, the paradoxical alliances. It is not my intention to defend the existence or otherwise of a concept whose evidence seems to me to be so continuous and macroscopic in the individual and in the world that it does not need to be defended, but to understand the unexpected interweaving with what was thought to be its opposite: life, Eros, sublimation. It seems to me that from the certainly mysterious, perhaps constitutional and irreducibly subjective nature of this interweaving, from its *quality* and *quantity*, from its projective outlets, evacuative or not in its expressions, the whole of human life depends. Therefore, beyond academic differences, the stakes are high.

We are not attached, therefore, to the word "drive", which I find fascinating and appropriate, because in recent times it arouses antipathy in psychoanalysis. It is deemed too anchored to so-called Freudian biologism (which we have just seen, however, confirmed at an immunological level). It certainly struggles to find proof and clinical confirmation (nor, I believe, should it find it), and is therefore deemed obsolete, part of that baggage of Freudian metapsychology wrongly considered as psychoanalytic archaeology. Because we are not prejudicially loyal to the name but to the concept then you could call it differently by a more "modern" version that I leave others to invent, but we are not equally easily disposed to abandon the concept rather to consider it, if anything, a great metaphor today, a "meta-drive." I would say that the whole drive theory and metapsychology, this fascinating shaping of the unconscious that Freud never renounced, may today be seen as a grandiose metaphor, a bold conjecture to help us to think, to feed visions of the mind – the famous "fantasise, translate, guess" already expressed to Fliess as the end of psychoanalysis in 1895, and apparently so modern (Lucchetti, 2002) – once these have been abandoned, as has happened with part of post-Freudian psycho-analysis. It is flattened out in the here and now, limited to the manifest and obvious and does not build theories of the mind any more. The psychic is certainly interwoven with the organic, in ways that are for the most part still mysterious. Death impregnates life. According to some, it sculpts it, governs it, it reduces life to a fortuitous and casual exception. Pleasure and Eros do not exist if not in fusion with their opposite, pain and Thanatos, and because no definition is peremptory, because even as psychoanalysts and researchers we become powerless and at risk of reductionism faced with so much mystery, I would suggest that while waiting it is better to maintain the old concept of drive, in the exquisite meaning given by Widlocher (2011), of a *pulsionnalité sans pulsions*.

> Bichat disait autrefois: "La vie est l'ensemble des fonctions qui résistent à la mort." Aujourd'hui, on plutôt aurait tendance à dire que "La vie est l'ensemble des fonctions capables d'utiliser la mort."
>
> (Ameisen, 1999)[7]

Notes

1. Although the book refers to the current clinic for adolescence above all, it adopted the title for pure assonance with what I wish to talk about.
2. Always ahead of its time and the land of every excess and its opposite, in the United States the presence of these texts shows the opening of a debate that in Italy, for example, is not yet explicit, but which I believe will soon be examined and studied over here as well.
3. The novel, published in Brazil in 1943, is considered to be largely autobiographical.
4. The original title is the most significant: *La Sculpture du vivant* (see References).
5. The theme of the 18TH SPI National Congress, Rome, 26–29 May 2016: "The logics of pleasure, the ambiguity of pain." Although indirectly, therefore, the question of the death drive was the subject, I would say the conceptual background of most of the interventions during the congress could be stated as: if the pursuit of pleasure is less in the delicate balance of a living being, and the search for pain prevails, we are in the territory of the death drive.
6. F. Nietzsche, *On the Genealogy of Morality*, 1887, (p. 42, 43).
7. Professor of immunology at the Université Paris VII, Centre Hospitalier Bichat. "Bichat once said: 'Life is a set of functions that are resistant to death.' Today, you would have a tendency to say that 'Life is a set of functions that are capable of using death'."

References

Ameisen J.C. (1999). *La sculpture du vivant. Le suicide cellulaire ou la mort créatrice*. Editions du Seuil: Paris.

Arendt H. (1963). *Eichmann in Jerusalem: A Report on the Banality of Evil*. Viking Press: New York.

Bastianini T. (2016). L'esperienza del piacere e del dolore nella costruzione intersoggettiva della vita psichica, paper given at XVIII SPI Congress, Rome, May 2016.

Benasayag M. and Schmit G. (2003). *Las pasiones tristes. Sufrimiento psíquico y crisis social.* Editorial Siglo XXI: Buenos Aires.

Bell D. (2008). La pulsione di morte: prospettive nella teoria kleiniana contemporanea, *Rivista di Psicoanalisi*, 54: 54–70.

Bell, D. (2015). The death drive: phenomenological perspectives in contemporary Kleinian theory. *International Journal of Psychoanalysis*, 96: 411–423.

Bonasia E. (1988). Pulsione di morte o terrore di morte? Una ricerca sul problema della morte in psicoanalisi. *Rivista di Psicoanalisi*, 34: 273–315.

Cimino C. (2011). Estasi e perturbante. Nei dintorni di Thanatos, Aut-Aut. 252: 103–111.

David C. (1998). Un aigle à deux têtes, sublimer mais à quelle fin?, *Revue Française de Psychanalyse*, 4: 1109–1122.

De Masi F. (2007). *La perversione sadomasochistica: l'oggetto e le teorie.* Boringhieri: Turin.

Fachinelli E. (1989). *La mente estatica.* Adelphi: Milan.

Falci A. (2005). Declinazioni del destino, *Rivista di Psicoanalisi*, 51: 799–822.

Fornari F. (1988). *Psicoanalisi della guerra.* Feltrinelli: Milan (Originally published 1966).

Freud S. (1985). *Letter from Freud to Fliess, May 25, 1897, The Complete Letters of Sigmund Freud to Wilhelm Fliess, 1887–1904.* Harvard University Press: Cambridge, MA.

Freud S. (1905). *Three Essays on the Theory of Sexuality. S.E.,* 7. Hogarth: London.

Freud S. (1910). *Leonardo da Vinci and a Memory of His Childhood. S.E., 11.* Hogarth: London.

Freud S. (1920). *Beyond the Pleasure Principle. S.E., 18.* Hogarth: London.

Freud S. (1923). *The Ego and the Id. S. E., 19.* London: Hogarth.

Freud S. (1924). *The Economic Problem of Masochism. Civilization and its Discontents. S.E., 21.* Hogarth: London.

Gaddini E. (1972). Aggressività e principio di piacere, *Rivista di Psicoanalisi*, 18: 139–153.

Green A. (1993): *The Work of the Negative (Le travail du negatif).* New York: Free Association.

Green A. (1995). *Seminari romani* (Ed. Chianese D.). Borla: Rome.

Green A. (2007). *Pourquoi les pulsions de destruction ou de mort?* Panama: Paris.

Green A. (2010). *Illusions and Disillusions of Psychoanalytic Work.* Karnac: London.

Guillaumin J. (2000). *L'invention de la pulsion de mort.* Dunot: Paris.

Knapp C. (2003). *Appetites.* Counterpoint: New York.

Kristeva J. (2008). *Thérèse mon amour.* Fayard: Paris.

Laplanche J. (1970). *Vie et mort en psychanalyse.* Flammarion: Paris.

Le Guen C. (2008). *Dictionnaire Freudien.* PUF: Paris.

Lispector C. (2012). *Near to the Wild Heart.* New Directions: New York.

Lussana P. (1972). Aggressività e istinto di morte da Freud a Melania Klein. Teoria e note cliniche. *Rivista di Psicoanalisi*, 18: 155–178.

Masciangelo P.M. (1988). Su Freud per il dopo Freud. Una riflessione metapsicologica, in *Trattato di psicoanalisi* (Ed. Semi A.A.). vol. 1. Cortina: Milan.

Nietzsche F. (2004). *On the Genealogy of Morality.* Cambridge University Press: Cambridge.

Preta L. (2015). *La brutalità delle cose.* Mimesis: Milan.

Resta C. (2016). Freud e la guerra: pulsioni di morte, in *La Filosofia e la Guerra.* Mimesis: Milan.

Ribas D. (2002). Chroniques de l'intrication et de la désintrication pulsionnelle. *Revue française de psychanalyse*, 66: 1689–1770.

Rosenfeld H. (1975). *The Negative Therapeutic Reaction.* vol. 2. Jaron Aronson: New York.

Schmidt-Hellerau C. (2000). Pulsion de vie, pulsion de mort. *Libido et Léthé.* Delachaux et Niestlé: Paris.

Séchaud E. (2005). Perdre, sublimer. . . . *Revue française de psychanalyse*, 69: 1309–1379.

Steiner J. (2008). The repetition compulsion, envy and the death instinct, in *Envy and Gratitude Revisited,* (Ed. Loth P., Lemma A.). IPA: London.

1

IN THEORY

Freud and after Freud, the destinies of a controversial concept

Death drives and their destinies: to relaunch a vexing topic[1]
L'è il dì di mort. Alegher!
(It is the day of the dead. Be happy!)

(D. Tessa, 1917)[2]

Despite all the controversy, are we witnessing a renewed interest in the death drive, perhaps in metapsychology in general as well? From its first appearance in 1920 in *Beyond the Pleasure Principle*, the concept of the death drive (*Todestrieb* in Freud's original German), in the precise Freudian meaning of the Nirvana principle (ibid., p. 241), has always evoked perplexity and divisions in the psychoanalytic community, although the term has somehow become common usage and part of the psychoanalytical lexicon. This reluctance is certainly not surprising: "how to admit that *death is actively at work in the living being*" (Le Guen, 1989, p. 536, translated for this edition), that the organism decides its own death from within, as we have also seen in Ameisen's studies, and wants to "die only in their own way" (Freud, 1920, p. 225)? It is as if life, in a perspective that is daring and overturned with respect to current (reassuring) thinking, were an exception, an *in spite of* occurrence, an accidental happening, a result that is never guaranteed or to be taken for granted, a difficult mix of libidinal and destructive drives, Eros and Thanatos in a potentially always precarious and fragile oscillation, susceptible to falls and regressions, succumbing to the seduction of a defusion or, according to more current terminology (which we will encounter often in this book) of *disinvestment*, of *unbinding* (Green, 1983), of *dé-liaison*.[3] For Freud, the living organism tends towards death not out of fury or desire, but as a sort of silent natural fate of drives, due not so much (or only secondarily) to direct attachment to self or to aggressiveness, but because staying alive, *l'être vivant*, is a kind of random accident or a misuse, as nature's programme has us born to die after having given us a mixed set of drives, libidinal and destructive, upon whose success and delicate balance depends our staying alive, both physically and psychologically, or our death. Such a concept, understandably, could not fail to rouse opposition, for now of a *theoretical* nature (to which we will return). And so we ask many questions, including these:

- Was a concept really necessary? Was not the sexual instinct enough?
- Freud sees the death drive as tightly tied to the biological, so how can we explain the jump to metapsychology?
- If life depends on the fusion of instincts it follows that a certain degree of death drive is needed *as well* for balancing, and this is a common thread or *fil rouge* of this book; then why use the word "death" for such a tendency (Penot, 2002, 2006) if it is also indispensable to psychic life?

Thus, far from constituting an outmoded or sterilely speculative concept, I believe that the death drive, both in its Nirvana form and as disinvestment, according to the original and more Freudian formulation, both in its most destructive and active form against self or object (a form more easily understood and observable), helps us today to understand contemporaneity without losing sight of metapyschology's compass (Di Chiara, 2009). It also helps us to understand history, as we have seen from Resta's studies (2016). Many, if not all, symptomatic expressions of the contemporary clinic that has become a *negative* clinic of disinvestment and confirmation of a fragile self, as we shall see, extending to social phenomena such as drug addiction (that has always existed but nowadays permeates every social class), visible phenomena such as the exhausting pursuit of pleasure and consumption, avoiding the weight of grief and responsibility at any cost – in this context it all can be a stimulating and unrivalled theoretical contribution. Careful rereading and updating that takes the Freudian framework into account leads us to ask ourselves, according to refined (but not unnecessary) reflections from various French-speaking authors as detailed in the endnote, if it is still a unique unitary concept, or if from the so-called death drive we can glimpse not one but *several destinies as well*, depending on the specific internal and external balance that occurs in the subject or in the social group in an equilibrium that cannot only be intended as purely subjective.

Yet another theoretical question: are we to deal with the death drive as a thrust that is only negative, deadly, anti-vital or, as viewed in the contributions that are the subject of my reflections and in my opinion, too, is it possible to recognise it as an element that is *also* positive, useful for a psychic life that is uncompromisingly not monotonous? So we can attempt a *partial* reassessment of one of the possible destinies of *Todestrieb*: that is to say, the need for an amount of unbinding that is indispensable to *subjectivation*, and therefore the basis of personal identity (Le Guen, 1989; Scarfone, 2004).

An exquisitely modern yet timeless concept, if viewed in this light, both for the theory as well as the psychoanalytic clinic and broadened into a wider reflection on the social sphere and culture poses the question of whether Culture, the Freudian *Kultur* of *Civilization and its Discontents*, is sufficient to *bind* aggressive drives that would otherwise be free and unbound, destined to discharge into pure destructiveness. Although the latest Freudian considerations, embittered by confirmation of the inevitability of war, do not appear to come out in favour, it is, however, legitimate and stimulating to investigate the inevitability of destruction, even from a theoretical point of view:

> Psychological—or, more strictly speaking, psycho-analytic—investigation shows instead that the deepest essence of human nature consists of instinctual impulses which are of an elementary nature, which are similar in all men and which aim at the satisfaction of certain primal needs. These impulses in themselves are neither good nor bad. We classify them and their expressions in that way, according to their relation to the needs and demands of the human community. It must be granted that all the impulses which society condemns as evil—let us take as representative the selfish and the cruel ones—are of this primitive kind.
>
> (Freud, 1915, p. 280)

The questions and the theoretical knots may be many, but they will not lead us further away from questions posed above. Indeed, our path winds through them: the death instinct can be the object of not one but *more destinies*; it also contributes to the vital construction of the individual. It is within this acceptation, to return to the book's opening, that I find myself among those who believe in the death drive, as a metaphor and a conjecture that has glimpsed a deep and tragic human truth, but believing its obliged biological derivation to be outdated or not clinically necessary, despite confirmation by recent research that must not, however, be given the value of a direct overlap. If, as it seems, we are facing a renewed interest, although beneath the surface, in a concept that is so controversial, crude, profoundly secular, that also calls into question the defences against the anguish of death that are present in all of us (Bonasia, 1988), I suggest that one of the reasons is the fact that the contemporary clinic as well as historical and social events have renewed the interest of Freudian speculation. Wars continue, the problem of destructiveness is far from being resolved and indeed today sees a particularly extensive expressive form, virulent and unpredictable, in the new radicalism that tears entire continents apart and, so, too, the individual cannot stop self-harming or fading away when faced with life.

Let us now briefly review the biographical, historical and cultural context in which *Beyond the Pleasure Principle* was born, the structure of the work, the fate of the concept after Freud until now, focusing in particular on some recent contributions that I find especially stimulating for our discussion and, in this part, giving prominence to the francophone psychoanalysis with a unitary and theoretical consistency with respect to both the clinical side as well as the more vast open side to which Freud never ceased to devote himself (and that actually characterises the late *outside the walls* Freud) that may today be construed as an attempt at a psycho-analytic reading of postmodernism.

Beyond the pleasure principle: the biographical, historical and cultural context

The death drive as a concept in itself appears organically described for the first time in Freud's work in 1920, *Beyond the Pleasure Principle*, a complex reformulation of theoretical speculation of the drives theory, as it was structured until then. The new concept, a key turning point in Freud's thoughts, and we could say in psychoanalysis, as the understanding of the human psyche, quite rightly defined as "the real cornerstone of metapsychology" (Couvreur, 1989), gave rise from the outset to divisions and disputes in the psychoanalytical world. It is the 1920 watershed.

Although in *Beyond the Pleasure Principle* the concept finds its full formulation, the idea of the existence of a death drive in psychic life, of a non-exclusivity of the pleasure principle, is traceable in Freud's thinking right from the start. He soon intuits that the pleasure principle is essential to keeping us alive, but that life does not end with its fulfilment: there is a *beyond*, a shadow zone, dark and silent.

Still from an economic point of view, in a *Project for a Scientific Psychology* (1895) a *search to reduce tension* is identified in the neuronal cell, in accordance with the *principle of constancy* to which psychic life aims. We find it again, indirectly, in the *Formulations on the Two Principles of Mental Functioning* in 1911, a short work but rich in insight that clarifies the relationships and the complex passage between the pleasure principle and the reality principle; then again in 1914, dealing with the vicissitudes of narcissism; and still more fully in the work that precedes *Beyond the Pleasure Principle*, in *Instincts and their Vicissitudes* in 1915. Here, while still lacking a full metapsychological system, Freud identifies the four possible destinies of the drive that, regardless of Eros, may: (1) be desexualised in sublim-ation; (2) turn towards the actual person of the subject; (3) move towards removal and (4) be converted into the opposite, from love to hate.

Hatred, in relationship with objects, is the oldest of emotions, *older than love*; love, if the environment is sufficiently inviting (as subsequent psychoanalytic developments will clarify) will enable the drives to mix in such a way that the libidinal drive *will prevail* over the death drive, without the latter disappearing from unconscious life, however. It is with a shout, and not with a smile, that we come into the world. Overwhelmed by needs (hunger, love), dependent, lost, still lacking in language: the prevalence of life, in Freudian man, the presence of pleasure, this must always be stressed, do not offer themselves up but *for negation*, for subtraction. There is life if the priority thrust towards death does not prevail; there is pleasure only in the absence of the primitive dis-pleasure. I think this is what is meant by so-called Freudian pessimism, a view I do not share. This vision of life and of pleasure not only as a struggle, but as a fortuitous negative, depending on the goodness of our first objects and of our drive constitution, seems to me to be a realistic, albeit bitter, assessment. We find the death drive once more in the form of one of its derivatives in *The Economic Problem of Masochism* in 1924, and we shall encounter this again in the clinical part, in which Freud postulates the priority of an *original* erotogenic masochism, essential and structural to being, and clarifies how sadism and destructiveness, that is to say phenomena that are more easily observable in external reality, are but *necessary* eversions of the death drive: without an outlet or an opening to the outside, onto the object, the drive would be destined – as sometimes happens – to turn solely against the self.

He will finally turn to the death drive in his mature work – in *Civilization and its Discontents* in 1930 and in 1938 in *An Outline of Psychoanalysis*, in which, if on the one hand he reiterates his own distance from an "oceanic feeling" (1930, p. 558) in himself, on the other hand he is now unequivocally certain of the death drive, investigating above all its manifestation in society and, last but not least, seeing it as the cause of human unhappiness. Thus Freud in one important piece of writing, systematises a concept that had already appeared in previous works and would never be abandoned but would be reviewed in the light of new discoveries, in 1920 urged by unexpected clinical discoveries and also for personal and historical reasons, matured a profound conviction that would accompany his thought from his initial intuitions up to the vast explorations of his mature years. Indeed, this provides the underlying theme not only of the development of psychoanalytic theory, but of the actual conception of humankind, of life and death. With the death instinct, as well as for the other "grand conjectures" (Conrotto, 2008) of Freudian thought, we leave the comfort of the psychoanalytical sofa to venture into human nature, the essence of life itself, *at the heart of life* as Ameisen puts it, whether or not one agrees with the correctness of the concept itself. This is, in my opinion, the greatness of Freud, so rare in subsequent psychoanalysis that has not been able to provide (with the exception, in part, of Bion and Green) equally strong, suggestive and large-scale theories of the mind.

The 1920s saw many losses for Freud, by now some 64 years of age: the death of his beloved daughter Sofia,[4] the suicide of his pupil Tausk in 1919, the death of his friend and benefactor Von Freund but especially the devastation left in Austria and Europe by the Great War, affording an opportunity not only to question himself on *why* humankind does not know how to evade wars, but also to observe more directly the *neurosis of war* and the paradoxical return, in the traumatised, of traumatic dreams. Where does all of this fit in? How can the books be balanced with the primacy of the pleasure principle? Why in the heart of the most evolved civilisation present on the world scene at that time, Europe, did people devastate an entire continent with a war and why, once it was over, did the war veterans not only fail to defensively jettison their painful memories, as the pleasure principle would hold, but continued to relive in their dreams the trauma suffered? It is necessary to call into question another drive adverse to pleasure, or at least distinct from it, even if "in the century that wants to maintain life to the bitter end, that engages in a never-ending war for life, that pursues the maximum *intensity* of life, it sows death everywhere [. . .]" (Resta, 2016, p. 103, translated for this edition).

I believe that out of the various personal events of the time, the Great War of the previous five years had the greatest impact. It crushed Freud's faith in progress and reason, and it forced him to investigate archaic, anti-vital drive impulses that operate in people. After this point of no return in history, for Freud it was psychoanalysis's task to investigate not only the individual psyche and its neuroses, but the collective psyche and the "psychotic," blind and destructive movements of the masses (reflections that would appear in *Group Psychology and the Analysis of the Ego* in 1921[5] and *Civilization and its Discontents* in 1930), to emphasise once again the fragility of human civil constructions, the paper castle of civilisation, fruit of a painful and not always possible drive renunciation, the ultimate goal of the drives for survival – paradoxically, the drive's goal would be its own demise, its renunciation. The last word on war will be entrusted to his 1932 correspondence with Einstein, *Why war?*, faced with an even more frightening abyss that will produce *the unrepresentable* Shoah, and in front of which Freud will reiterate his complete distrust in the goodness of human drives.

Within this historical-cultural context in which his work matures, in that same year he reads Schopenhauer, as evidenced by his letter to Lou Salomé on 1st August 1919, "For my old age I have chosen the theme of death; I have stumbled on a remarkable notion based on my theory of the instincts . . .",[6] and Nietzsche as well, the eternal return from the Nirvana side and the desire for power on the everted side of the drive. Darwin's theory of evolution was also present. On a *psychoanalytical level*, there are only two previous contributions to mention: that of Stekel in 1907 ("the sex-impulse is always accompanied by the instinct of self-preservation and its counter-impulse, the Death impulse" (Stekel, 1907, p. 3) not commented on by Freud)[7] and that of Sabina Spielrein in 1912, in *Destruction as a Cause of Coming into Being*, to which Freud will instead pay homage when he speaks of primary of masochism: "A considerable portion of these speculations have been anticipated by Sabina Spielrein (1912) in an instructive and interesting paper" (1920, footnote to p. 54).

We will see later how Freud not only through the dreams of traumatised war victims, but directly from the analysis room, comes to the bitter findings of *Beyond the Pleasure Principle*.

Let us now move on to the text.

Structure of the work

The debate on the issue that appeared in the *Journal of Psychoanalysis* in 2005 emphasised how the work has an essentially *dualistic* structure (Falci, 2005). The first part describes clinical facts (coaction to repeat, negative therapeutic reaction, fort–da game) and the second, starting from the fourth chapter, is purely speculative. Between the two, is what Falci a trite critically calls an "argumentative leap" (ibid., p. 804): in complete freedom, aware of performing a methodologically necessary leap rather than a release from the biological substrate, Freud infers the existence of *Todestrieb* by an apparently mysterious insistence with which the analysands seem to refuse to heal, to escape from wellness, to unconsciously search for suffering. The same suffering that led them to treatment at a certain point pushes to claim its rights and revolts, often successfully, against recovery. It is as if the essay opens with an underlying fundamental question: *Is the primacy of the pleasure principle still sufficient to explain human nature?* To briefly summarise, Freud reviews the conceptual baggage used until then, *pleasure-sorrow* dualism from an economic point of view, *free* or *binding* states of psychic energy and their consequences in terms of increased internal tension and therefore sorrow and pain if free; vice versa a decrease in tension with release; and pleasure, if binding. The aim of this balance that inhabits the psyche is to *maintain constancy, homeostasis,* to always return to *a zero level of tension.*

"What does the Ego want?" – asks Green (1990) – "That you leave it in peace . . ."

That is what Freud calls the Nirvana principle, at the heart of the Freudian death drive. The concept of Nirvana, coming from Buddhism and then adopted by other religions such as Hinduism, literally means extinction, cessation of breath. The significance will then be broadened in search of freedom from desire – "désir de non désir," says Aulagnier (1979). In *Beyond the Pleasure Principle*, Freud defines it in a manner identical to the principle of constancy, thus being able to create the ambiguity of considering as equivalent the tendency to maintain a certain level of energy and the tendency to reduce to zero every excitation (Laplanche and Pontalis, 1967). If it is true that only in 1920 was theorisation accomplished, "the aspiration to a state of total non-excitability – the non-excitability of non-invested systems to which he refers in the *Project* – is a constant thought of Freud" (Green, 1983, p. 103).

The fourth chapter sees the theoretical speculation begin, perhaps methodologically questionable, but which nevertheless remains a distinctive and still fascinating text with which Freud opens:

> What follows is speculation, often far-fetched speculation.
>
> (Freud, 1920, p. 34)

A note in the margin: if we want to read Freud in a modern way and grasp the whole revolutionary scope and relevancy, it is necessary, as Anna Freud said regarding sublimation and defences, *to take off your glasses to look at them, not put them on* (Sandler and Freud, 1985, p. 176). That is to say, we should read in depth but let us not get lost in the detail. Let us not insist in wanting to justify everything. Metapsychology is to be seen today as a great metaphor of the mind, and I would add as an unsurpassed one. Psychic life does not then tend only to pleasure – a positivist illusion that has proved insufficient – but first of all to *conservation,* that is to say that drives have a conservative character. They are opposed to change. Their goal is the restoration of the previous state, of non-tension, calm, inertia.

And lastly, of death: "The aim of life is death" (Freud, 1920, p. 224). It is an absolutely paradigmatic leap.

If life is the result of the pleasure principle not prevailing, but of the *balance*, of the *dynamic interplay of the two drives, of life and death* (and indeed, as seen, the two are secretly allied so death *serves* life), in the end it is the latter that prevails. The organism decides, from within, its own death. Staying alive is therefore the tiring outcome of *drive fusion*: if the drives unbind (the more one regresses then the more it is possible) the prevalence of a destructiveness that is primarily self-directed (masochism) or directed to the outside (sadism), kills the bond with life. But the death drive remains the core of these showy manifestations of Thanatos that bear different names, in fact: *Aggressionstrieb* for aggression (which, as we will see later, psychoanalysis *confuses* with the original Freudian death drive) and *Destruktionstrieb* for the destructive drive.

With the concluding chapter, the sixth, the circle closes and Freud returns to the universal, thus sealing the broad scope of *Beyond the Pleasure Principle*. He reviews the thinkers to whom he is, in part, in debt (firstly Schopenhauer, Plato) and closes by asserting that we have not so far, not even with psychoanalysis, reached certain knowledge about life and death or about the seeds of psychic life, and he trusts in science to fill these gaps (as we have seen in part with modern immunology).

It is from these Freudian speculations about the centrality of the dynamic equilibrium between *sexual impulses that bind and deadly impulses that unbind* that Green (1993) and contemporary French authors will process the concept that I view as the most original and most capable of synthesis today in the longstanding diatribe between drive and object. Thus, we find the "old" articulation of life and death drives – by now stigmatised as outdated and too "biological" – under the much more dynamic definition *objectualising drives* against or, better, *à coté*, that is, next to *dis-objectualising drives*.

The devil thrown out of the house has merely changed his attire, adapted to the times and crept back in through the side door.

After Freud: the "destinies" of the death drive

With respect to the drive theory, contemporary psychoanalysis can be roughly divided into two currents of thought: one has abandoned all reference to drives (and we will return to this when we discuss the relationship with sublimation),[8] starting with Klein and the school of object relations up to the psychology of self and inter-subjectivism, which has meant a certain indifference and decline for metapsychology in general; the other is livelier in France but also includes individual authors in the English-speaking world and in Italy, and continues to refer to the concept, thus enriching its elaboration over time. It must be said that a similar fate, regarding the drive theory in its general scheme, has invested other large Freudian concepts, the "great conjectures" of which we have spoken: the death drive has thus became aggression, sublimation has ended up overlapping with reparation and desire with need. That is to say, the *shift* is *generic* and it is not devoid of important implications – not just theoretical ones, but clinical and technical, too, that undermine the very *identity* of psychoanalysis, as I have pointed out on various occasions (Valdrè, 2015).

But let us stay with the death drive. Some rejection and weakening of interest towards metapsychology, springing mainly from English and North American psychoanalysis, has led in past years to a refusal, *tout court*, of the drive theory and therefore within this also of the death drive; or it can be assumed that puzzlement over the death drive provoked a more general rejection of the entire and, to the clinical Anglo-American eyes mysterious, drive scheme. As it is, if on the one hand the death drive remains the cornerstone of metapsychology and, in my opinion, there is no psychoanalysis without metapsychology, in agreement with the radical affirmation of Assoun, according to which metapsychology "is ultimately the other name of psychoanalysis" (1996, pp. 245–246, translated for this edition), the concept does not fail to ask thorny theoretical questions (Couvreur, 1989) that could be summed up as follows, and to which we shall return:

- What are its representatives: destructiveness, unbinding, repetition, Nirvana?
- Is it a counteracting force to Eros, autonomous, an extreme drive destiny, or should it be regarded as a released current, with a destiny of its own, of the *sole* existing drive, that is to say, the sexual one?
- Is it a principle of functioning without the possibility of representability, the most radical form of the negative?
- Do Eros and Thanatos belong to the biological and psychological categories rather than to philosophy and myth?

I have mentioned for the sake of completeness these intriguing theoretical points, considering them on the one hand to be fertile ground for reflection on a theme that can be infinite, but on the other hand this excessive peering *with glasses*, as Anna Freud puts it, can paradoxically cause us to lose our sight.

In the current state, we basically find three positions (Bokanowski, 1989): (1) those who completely reject the existence of an autonomous death drive and do not feel it has any use (Anglo-Saxon psychoanalysis, inter subjectivists); (2) those who recognise the existence of a true antagonist drive, complementary and mixed to varying degrees with Eros and deriving from Eros; for these, the work of Eros-Thanatos is fundamental (Laplanche and Pontalis 1967); (3) those who argue that it is a *founding principle* of drive life, of life and death, in the full meaning of the more speculative Freud (Green, 1983; Laplanche, 1970; Aulagnier, 1979).[9] The positions of Green and Laplanche and Pontalis are therefore subtly but decidedly discordant; Laplanche and Pontalis, within a careful and refined rereading of the Freudian text, recognises the importance of the *sole sexual instinct*: Eros, the only drive existing from which everything originates, branches out into a vital libidinal part and into a part that is defined as *demonic*, but always beginning from the sexual. The name he gives it is "sexual death drive" (Laplanche, 1970). Conrotto, among the Italians, not believing in a death drive in itself, believes that "the so-called death drive should not be regarded as an expression of biological functioning but a *metaphorical expression* that alludes to the thrust of the psychic apparatus to get rid of excess tension, and therefore an expression of the desire for calm" (2012a, p. 45, translated for this edition). These authors also emphasise how the death drive, seen as a thorny concept and viewed with mistrust even when it is understood, has tended to be distorted and "monopolized" (Borgogno and Viola, 1994), transforming and overlapping, in fact, with *aggressiveness*, which is conceptually quite different.

Among the post-Freudians, substantially only Klein and subsequently Lacan, within very different conceptualisations, seem to accept the existence of a death drive, but they both move away from the original Freudian intent. Since the publication of *Beyond the Pleasure Principle*, despite making continual references to the concept, no one has really remained on this terrain (Conrotto, 2008; Green, 1983). In fact it is rather the academics from other areas who have kept it alive and recognised it, such as the already mentioned historian Caterina Resta, 2016).

Whatever happened to the death drive? Klein and her school, initially at least, accept the concept, making it a strength of their clinic, but transforming it, as is typical of the Kleinian school, into being *eminently clinical*, superimposed and confused with aggression and identified with *primary envy*, that has nothing to do with the Freudian death drive – as Klein has no interest in metapsychological matters she uses, in fact, the term *instinct* rather than *Trieb*, drive – thus creating, as for other concepts (sublimation/repair, for example) as well, a sort of "semantic confusion" (Conrotto, 2008). Not everyone is of this opinion. While I share with Conrotto and others the idea that the paradigm shift made between the notions of the death drive and the death instinct has in fact eliminated the original Freudian concept to create another one that is more easily traceable in clinical practice, others (Hinshelwood, 1989) consider Klein as the author who developed most the concept of the death drive/instinct. Therefore, it is a question of diametrically opposed visions. It is the envious super-Ego, pre-genital in nature, that Klein holds is the primary manifestation of the death instinct. Present since birth, hostile to the presence of the other, but depending on it, it hinders each relationship and every learning. Only the progressive, oscillating and never definitive integration of the depressive position with the life instinct will give refuge from the destruction of the object and of the self. From the clinical point of view, however, the Kleinian school must be credited with having attempted to make full use of the metapsychological concept of the death drive, bringing it to the heart of clinical practice and analytical technique. Klein understands that the concept of the death instinct, although she lacks a precise theorisation, could be of great clinical use to explain the precocity and severity of the archaic super-Ego – a hypothesis that puts her in contrast with both Freud and his daughter Anna. Nothing at all is mute and silent, the death instinct is manifested therefore in the severe precocity of the archaic super-Ego. It is clear that we are faced with something that has nothing to do with Freud's thought.

Hanna Segal (1993), while part of the Kleinian strand, specifies that she does not agree with the translation of *Trieb* into *instinct* in English – the source of so much confusion, as we have already seen, but prefers either the French *pulsion* or the English *drive*. *Death drive* is used equally frequently, in fact, to indicate the death instinct. Metapyschological questions are of little interest to her, as is generally the Kleinian way, but Segal wonders about clinical utility, recognizing that Freud cared not so much about the biological origin of the problem but rather its disconcerting clinical evidence in masochism or coercion to repeat, negative therapeutic reactions, deadly aspects of the melancholic super-Ego. With respect to the difficulty Freud had in finding the death drive in a pure or nearly pure state, Segal holds that subsequently, with the treatment of psychotic disorders, this difficulty is removed. Psychosis is *also* death drive, annihilation of thought and of the whole thinking apparatus. An interesting observation of Segal's about the perception of pain: if the death drive is an extreme attempt to not perceive life's emotions, both painful and pleasant, through the return to zero tension, why is it that when the death instinct is *at work* we always feel great pain? It would be the libidinal Ego, wounded in this fight between pleasure and pain and pleasure *in* pain, that would suffer for the death threat. Pleasure in pain, for Segal, in addition to masochism, can also be linked to the triumph by the part of the self dominated by the death drive, as happens in negative therapeutic reactions. The fusion between life and death instincts can assume very different gradients, from healthy development in which life prevails, to the death drive thrust outwards in aggressiveness or, in cases in which the libido is put at the service of the death drive, perversions. Segal is in agreement with Klein in seeing envy as the main unconscious expression of attacks on life and its sources, the greatest manifestation of the death instinct: necessarily ambivalent, because it is born to defend itself from perceiving a need, it is a hostile but also painful feeling for whoever feels it because there can never be a total annihilation of need.

Lacan (1956), several years later and in the highly specific cultural climate of French psychoanalysis, welcomes the concept, too, and includes it in his personal theoretical elaboration. In the *Seminar on The Purloined Letter* (1956), inspired by a tale of Poe, he inserts the death drive into the conceptualisation of the unconscious structured as a language. With the death drive, however, *not everything* in the unconscious still belongs to the signifying chain, not everything refers to the symbolic order. The problem lies with Thanatos, the hardest part of the Freudian framework for Lacan to digest. Without entering into Lacan's complex theorisation, it is enough to say here that the death drive can be matched to that part of the concept of the unconscious that *subtracts itself from the symbolic order* and the word, its vector, succumbing to the *automatic* and *deadly thrust of enjoyment* (*jouissance*), the impossible enjoyment of the Thing (*das Ding*), the Thing for the mother, the Supreme Good, "desire that can never be satisfied because that would be the end, the termination of the whole universe of the demand" (Lacan, 1986, p. 84). The inertia of enjoyment, the irreducible *remainder* that exposes us to the perennial *lack* to which human beings are destined, approaches, at least theoretically, the Freudian Nirvana. Life does not tend to Good for Lacan either: the human being is paradoxically condemned to want to exist but as well to want a primary object, the Thing, unreachable by its very nature unless in madness. In Lacan, the terms of the question are therefore *das Ding*, "that binds to enjoyment (*jouissance*) as in *beyond the pleasure* (principle), and *real* (different from reality), an irreducible discard with respect to symbolization and language. [. . .] All these terms, closely connected, imply the Freudian discovery of a beyond the pleasure principle, of the death drive" (Resta, 2016, p. 100, translated for this edition).[10] In a more advanced stage of his thought, while he had initially linked the death drive to narcissism and the end of treatment to subjective resignification, Lacan sees the treatment process oriented to the assumption of this instinct, this reality that is not assimilable, always a *foreclosure, rejected* (the Freudian *Verwerfung, rejection*, already identified in 1894 and to which we shall return), humanly contained only in the universe of language or rather of the *discomfort of civilization*, of the necessary Freudian drive renunciation. The terms may change, but Lacan's thought is unerringly traceable to the Freudian structure. Nevertheless, Lacan, too, does not seem to continue with further insights and in fact according to some (Conrotto, 2008) he, too, matches the death drive with aggressiveness.[11]

It is important to emphasise once more that on a metapsychological level in the original Freudian formulation the death drive:

> . . . has nothing to do with aggressiveness, if not in that it makes use of it in its manifestations outside the subject (sadism) and Freud always refused to recognize the existence of a destructive autonomous energy, *destrudo*, an alternative to libido.
>
> (ibid., p. 134)

Aggressionstrieb and *Destruktionstrieb*, in other words, do not coincide but rather are derived from the primary *Todestrieb*. This is the Nirvana drive at the root of what is observed in destructive human behaviours. Therefore, although they are potentially confusing in practice and in the clinic, their needs are quite different. Aggression needs vital force to express itself – aggressiveness is *pulsional* – Nirvana inertia, at least apparently, no, it shuns all motion, all tension, as our clinical practice shows: the patient who attacks the object is different from the one searching only *to be left in peace* (although the outcome can be psychic death for both of them, and although in asking to be left in peace they are turning their backs on the object that is in some measure "violent" and active). The technique will vary as a result, with a subtly different intervention by the analyst, at least initially, in these different destinies of the *Todestrieb*, as we shall see in our first case study.

So, even if they are among the most faithful to the Freudian text heritage neither Lacan nor Klein will continue with the unsolved problems: as Le Guen (1989) succinctly puts it, the first gets by with *subterfuge* and the second with *concretization*.

To conclude this brief foray into Lacanian thought, I consider Lacan to be more faithful and incisive than Klein. Regardless of how he uses the concepts or

not, he is close to Freud in his attempt to give a broad human, social and philosophical conceptualisation where human development is rescued from both biological reductionism and psychological pedagogy. For Lacan as for Freud, life does
not tend to good. As Pontalis puts it so beautifully, inside life death "is at work"
(1988).

Among contemporaries of Freud, Eitingon subscribed to the concept, in part
Abraham, Numberg, Menninger, initially Alexander, Federn, in part Ferenczi (the
first person to read *Beyond the Pleasure Principle*); Jones, Fenichel, Loewenstein and
others[12] were critical. Gradually, from the Congress of Vienna in 1971 onwards,
while on the one hand all analysts have given increasing importance in clinical
practice to aggressiveness − the type of patient has also been changing, they are
ever closer to the *borderline* area − the metapsychological concept continues to be
"manipulated and misunderstood" (Borgogno and Viola, 1994).

The characterising element of post-Freudian psychoanalysis up to now is that
it greatly enhances the role given to the *environment* becoming the prime focus and
the theory of object relations prevails. Winnicott, Meltzer, Bion, while giving
much importance in their theorisation to destructive components of the personality,
do not feel the need to make them a precise metapsychological concept and they
are gradually cast aside and blurred, according to Rosenfeld, the discussed Kleinian
innate colouring is gradually blurred and abandoned. The relationship with the
object and its vicissitudes, the caregiver's capacity or lack thereof to receive,
respond, be empathetic with the child's needs, supersede the solitary Freudian
drive universe, implicitly accused of not taking due account of the object − this is
something I disagree with after careful reading of late Freud in particular. Winnicott
is particularly attentive, despite being the first to highlight environmental
deprivation and the environment–mother as a source of aggressiveness in a child,
while bearing in mind the importance of the coexistence of interior and exterior
reality, with harmonic and real sharing, as he writes:

> To be able to tolerate all that one may find in one's inner reality is one of
> the great human difficulties and an important human aim is to bring into
> harmonious relationship one's personal inner and outer realities. . . . When
> the cruel or destructive forces there threaten to dominate over the loving,
> the individual has to do something to save himself and one thing he does
> is to turn himself inside out, *to dramatise the inner world outside*, to act the
> destructive role himself and to bring about control by external authority.
>
> (2016, p. 69)

The technical repercussions are clear and impact the whole of the psychoanalytical
framework: reconstruction is replaced by the here-and-now relationship, the
importance of the field and so forth. If all this had the indisputable merit of putting
transference and also the countertransference to the fore and everything concerning
the analyst, removing it from the cult of neutrality that had become an exaggeration,
in my opinion recent decades have seen a sad overturning with a flattening of

psychoanalysis, or we are at risk of this happening, in a psychology of the obvious and the manifest, in an

> [. . .] Idealization of the clinic *simply* as a place of truth of the analysis (and that this) will contribute to the progressive divarication between a range of increasingly heterogeneous clinical experiences and a theoretical apparatus that increasingly has the task of probing the non-manifest levels, with the result of being once more at *ground zero* of psychoanalysis and at the rebirth of a "psychology of the obvious": the subject of conscience, the manifest plan, the facts, the real relationship, the real child and the mother [. . .]. Hence the contemporary translation of psycho-analysis to psycho-pedagogy.
> (Riolo, 2015, translated for this edition)

I have quoted this in full and agree with all its assumptions and the cry of alarm it contains, but it is also a cry of hope to young student-practitioners. All these shifts and changes have not always been in favour of integrity and psychoanalytic identity (Petrella, 2005; Valdrè, 2015).

Bion should be credited for a certain return to Freud and the construction of a personal but coherent theory of the mind. The death drive is contemplated, but not in the original Freudian sense of tension towards calm. Instead Bion remains in the Kleinian vein of aggressiveness and destructiveness, not only against the object but, in a psychotic person, against the thinking apparatus. Although they are two different conceptual actions I would also mention that perhaps a derived expression of the death drive in Bion is the attack on thinking, − K, a hatred of truth and thus of all the psychic apparatus that the psychotic carries out against himself: the death drive would express itself as hatred for reality and the impossibility of any transformation. In the split that sees the evacuation of the part of personality given to perception, the patient is moved by the death drive in that:

> The operation of expulsion is not aimed at the dispersion of the destructive drive, because destruction and evacuation occur *under the pressure of the death drive*, and are not necessarily aimed at liberation from suffering and pain; all the more so that, with the elimination of the perceptual apparatus, the psychotic finds himself in a condition that cannot be described *neither life nor death* [. . .].
> (Galimberti, 2000, p. 109, my italics, translated for this edition)

This moves towards, I would even say juxtaposes, Bion's conception for which there can be no life, mental life, if there is no *food for the mind* because it is absent or jealously refused; the digestive metaphor, mind-body as apparatus for receiving and ejecting, are a feature of Bion's work. He writes that in some personalities

> the superego appears to be developmentally prior to the ego . . . and to deny development and existence itself to the ego . . . the usurpation by the

superego [. . .] involves imperfect development of the reality principle, which is an exaltation of a "moral" outlook and lack of respect for truth. I am reminded that healthy mental growth seems to depend on truth, as the living organism depends on food.

(1965, pp. 37–38)

While referring to the psychotic personality and his hatred for the truth, using different, more drive-oriented language, we can suppose that people with an undernourished or poisoned mind orient more easily towards the death drive.

Thus, while Bion accepts its existence in psychic life, he, too, moves away from metapsychology and from drives to make a useful and interesting declension of the hatred that the psychotic mind nourishes for thinking and perception, in order to defend itself from pain. This is clinically challenging terrain that has opened many perspectives, but once more it is one that moves away from the Freudian sense of the concept. Central to Klein and Bion's re-elaboration of the Freudian death drive is the essential role of the archaic or primitive super-Ego, in charging itself with the death drive. It will be love and the vital drives that will decontaminate the super-Ego, to make it protective and non-destructive, to allow life. Among Italian authors, Giaconia (2005) reaffirms on several occasions how, in order not to succumb to the remaining destructiveness in a paranoid-schizoid position, it is important to renegotiate the depressive position and to access the possible elaboration of the destructive drive or, better still, its *reclamation*. "Do you really need to diversify the death drive from the life drive?" she asks. "I have come to hypothesize that the unelaborated drive itself is deadly" (Giaconia 2005, p.11, translated for this edition).

Post-contemporary Kleinians retrieve in part the death drive, making primarily psychological use of it and making important contributions, any of which would be the subject of a book on its own (Bell, 2008; Feldman, 2000; Segal, 1993; Steiner, 2008). Feldman's position is particularly noteworthy. Differing from Segal, he maintains that the purpose of the death instinct (we have seen that from Klein onwards it will be called *instinct* and not *Trieb*) is not "literally to kill or to annihilate," but "the patient feels impelled to maintain a link with the object that often has an evidently tormenting quality [. . .]. In the clinical examples I have quoted, it is significant that the objects are not dead but poisoned, weakened, immobilized and, one suspects, (*forever dying*)" (2000, pp. 53–56).

Hinshelwood (1989), to remain in the vein of clinic and destructiveness, recognises three expressive modalities. In the first, the death instinct merges with that of life and is projected in *an object* with a willingness to kill it, and this is the basis of acute paranoia. In the second mode, in my opinion the most frequent one, residual elements of the death instinct, always fused with the libido, occur with anger and aggression against *the subject*, who lives it in a persecutory manner as a threat from the outside. In the third mode, a residual element of the death instinct can, in the long term, destroy the self or the *perception* of objects. In the latter, the *killing of perception*, I find an interesting link with Bion and his theory of psychosis.

With regard to *envy*, that for Klein represents the maximum expression of the death instinct, as an unconscious instance that aims to destroy all the good part of the object and the self, for post-Kleinians the concept is refined and becomes more ambivalent, as an expression of the recognition of *need* and its satisfaction. Envy thus understood envisages not only the death instinct, but a function (we are therefore closer to Freud) between the life and death instincts where these latter ones predominate: when a need demands to be satisfied, a defence is erected where death prevails and the need is attacked and fought off.

As is well known, Rosenfeld (1975) starts from Freud but broadens the clinical complexity so not only is there an internal force to the personality unconsciously tending to destruction, but *an organisation*, a veritable band, attacks the good parts of the Ego. Again, we see that the concept of the death drive circulates between the lines. I would say that it is *necessary* to sustain the existence of aggression, but it presents in clinical aspects and relationships with objects of deadly destruction, certainly enriching psychoanalysis with new contributions. These depart from the Freudian framework, despite the latter seeming indispensable to all these successive formulations: the death drive, the paradoxic and silent tendency of the living to the return to the inorganic, the *being left in peace* of Green, has become the bumpy and dynamic *death instinct* or, depending on the authors, the *death drive*.

In the 1970s and 1980s, the concept seems to have taken on renewed vitality among psychoanalysts, not only the French. The European Psychoanalytical Federation's first symposium,[13] in 1984 in Marseillek was, in fact, dedicated to this topic – *is the death drive a necessary metapsychological concept today?* – and an important dialogue took place, in particular between Laplanche, Green, Segal and Widlocher.[14]

The differences between their points of view, as we have seen, are incisive and quite subtle at the same time. Laplanche offers a deeper and more accurate review of Freud's thought than many and, as seen above, at the centre of Laplanche's thinking is, in short, *the inclusion of the death drive in a general frame of sexual drives*: so we have *the sexual drives of life* and *the sexual drives of death*. Only the sexual drive of death corresponds to the unbound aspect, to that deadly and demonic current that, despite starting from the sexual, wriggles free of it, becoming undiluted discharge, a sexual drive in its most radical appearance. Sexuality is everywhere, for him ("la sexualité c'est n'est pas tout, mais c'est partout").

André Green has a more dualistic outlook and identifies it instead as a thrust in itself, contrary and opposite to the sexual drive. Here we are in the empire of *death narcissism*, where sexuality loses its centrality and primacy (1983). Interesting to note how Green and Segal are in agreement, although in different senses (a clinical concept and close to destructive aggression for Segal; a founding metapsychological principle for Green), in considering primary narcissism, "insofar as it is de-objectivising," a true "expression of the death drive," as well as emphasizing its enormous clinical importance (Rabain, 1989, pp. 765–766, translated for this edition). Green does try a synthesis between the age-old question between drive (held to be too solipsistic in the subject and mysteriously anchored to the biological aspect) and subject. But truth be told this was already present in late Freud. Without a doubt, the drive always needs the object, but this does not detract from the fact that, in my opinion, there is also a life drive *a priori*, of the subject itself, irreducibly subjective and ancient, mysterious, that will then find in the object both support and satisfaction as well as a target for discharge and action. The two instances are not therefore antagonists, but they do not necessarily go together. If the intrapsychic cannot survive alone, obviously, there is, and *there must* be a subjective drive heritage, observable from birth in the differences of infants. Perhaps calling this innate has been superceded as it evokes in psychoanalysis the terror of a world without objects. I find that this "terror," born after the accusations against Freud's "biologism" (in inverted commas because I do not share this view), has been excessive in psychoanalysis and has led to a tendency, as seen above, to totally ignore the intrapsychic, its history, the importance of reconstruction and therefore of subjectification, relegating the human being to an obliged member of the relationship, leading, as we shall see when talking about contemporaneity, to the current empire of the object, to that "clinic of confirmation" that has ended up putting in shadow precisely the subject from which psychoanalysis was born (Valdrè, 2015).

In Italy there are relatively few specific studies on this, although the death drive is often mentioned in various works. A special issue of the "Rivista di Psicoanalisi" on aggression in 1971 with papers, among others, by Bellanova, Weiss, Servadio and Gaddini comes to mind. The latter, in particular, feels the need for further investigations in this regard, revalues the psychoanalytical concept of psychic energy (which is also considered, wrongly, obsolete), believing "credible the hypothesis of an *aggressive energy qualitatively different* from the libidinal, present and operative since birth" (Gaddini, 1972, p. 139, my italics, translated for this edition). Thus, even here most authors have dealt with the death drive inside reflections on destructiveness and pathological organizations (Fornari, 1966; Lussana, 1972; more recently De Masi, 2007), although there is no lack of isolated but attentive, metapsychological interpretations, among which I would name Masciangelo's works (1988), the recent interpretations reported in bibliography from Borgogno and Viola (1994), up to the reflections, repeatedly mentioned here, of Francesco Conrotto (2008) and Falci (2005), in response to the debate with Khan in the "Rivista di psicoanalisi."[15]

To conclude this brief and necessarily incomplete overview that makes reference only to the main movements, the United States, where various schools and approaches co-exist, the "positive" American mentality that already Freud had found objectionable (his unenthusiastic comment on "the simple and free ways of the New World" on his first visit there in 1909), does not receive the concept well and struggles to understand it. There the debate is more focused on the relationship between nature and culture, deficit/innateness, that will find expression in the well-known arguments of Kohut/Kernberg. Green interestingly points out that in North American psychoanalysis Kernberg attempted a complex synthesis between aggression, drives and object relations, that we can see in some significant contemporary European contributions. There are also many authoritative voices alone that rehabilitate the role of a sort of primitive violence, necessary to life, among which I would say the most significant is Bergeret's (1994) "fundamental violence."

In post-Freud, in short, as Green comments in his dialogue with Urribarri (2013):

> [. . .] No one wants to listen to anyone talking about the death drive, but everything that is put there to replace it to have a clearer conception sends us back to the death drive. And there are some attempts at reformulations to overcome the reformulation presented by Freud [. . .] But that does not change the problem; the problem is that there is destructiveness *admitted by these authors*, that hinders analytic work.
>
> (pp. 125–126)

For now there is no better theorising that, linking together in a theoretically coherent mosaic, explains death as nothing and death as destructiveness, the death of the self and aggressiveness, death inside life and life inside death, death in its clinical, behavioural and social manifestations. But we cannot afford not to recognise that all this exists and puts at risk both individual and collective life – today just as yesterday, and perhaps today more than ever with contemporary terrorism. The question is inevitable: why is there so much resistance in the face of such a widespread and common concept that is observable in clinical practice, in society, in the phenomena of life in general? In this resistance inside the psychoanalytical world (we have seen how the concept is more accepted in other knowledge areas), I believe the already cited anguish of death, of one's own death (Bonasia, 1988), is important, one that at different levels dwells in all of us, the breaking of the confidence pact with life, the disquieting awareness that death lives inside us, arm in arm with life, that we depend on the delicate play of drive predominances, that "we choose" whether or not to commit suicide. It is not only the "optimistic" Americans but all of us who are horrified deep down at the idea of being bearers of death. Given this premise, the other reluctancies and adversities relate to the underlying theoretical questions that Freud leaves unsaturated: if two types of energy are acknowledged as biological in derivation, according Freudian dualism, or should only one type be recognised that would then find different "fittings"; if the far-from-easy semantic slide is acknowledged that means the passage from a biological concept to a metapsychological one, where perhaps the biological component of the drive is disposed of a little too hastily; if it is a necessary theory fundamentally, and so forth. The questions, the doubts, the issues that the concept raises, as well as the reasons to embrace its validity on the other hand, are numerous on both fronts.

But I would stress that on a more profound level we are still in full harmony with Conrotto when he writes that everything is "in my opinion, *an unknowing attempt to circumvent the shocking Freudian hypothesis according to which there is a* district of the psychical apparatus structurally incapable of building and containing representations and leanings to psychic death" (2008, p. 174, my italics, translated for this edition).

It is not the presence of aggressiveness and the even more blinding and devastating destructiveness that are difficult to recognise as a human instance, but the silent tendency to psychic death, yielding to non-life, to non-thought, that a Japanese haiku from a culture accustomed to death expresses as follows:

> No, I am happy.
> Because I want to die.
> What I crave for is despair.
> I want to go back to nothingness.

At the conclusion of my slight digression, I come to the elaboration that I think today, from a metapsychological profile and thus on a level that should be maintained in order not to confuse us with aggressiveness, is the most interesting, because it attempts to marry, or to bind, the drive theory with the importance of the object (on several occasions Green emphasises that *there is no drive without object*) to integrate the *disturbing hypothesis* of Freudian intuition with the needs of the contemporary clinic. In order to trace a linear path, I am aware that I have limited the choice mainly to the more numerous and organised contributions of French-speaking psychoanalysis.

Contemporary contributions: the reinterpretation of Green, Laplanche and French psychoanalysis

> Pourquoi la pulsion de mort?
>
> (P. Denis, 2002)

The reflections of these authors, in addition to Green and Laplanche, that we can take as reference to the *dualistic* vision and the *monistic*, respectively, of drives, sees a debate within a large group among whom I would name Bernard Penot, Paul Denis, Piera Aulagnier, J. M. Quinodoz, Dominique Scarfone, Le Guen and J. B. Pontalis,[16] whose central points are unanimously agreed on, can thus be summarised:

* Today *Todestrieb* is considered a broad theoretical-clinical concept, which means concurrently: (a) the coercion to repeat; (b) the search for Nirvana, of zero tension and (c) tendencies to destructiveness. Thus, we can find it used equally to describe and explain different phenomena, but they all come under this conceptual umbrella.
* The need to maintain psychoanalysis well rooted to metapsychology, "ultimately, the other name of psychoanalysis" for Assoun (1996).
* Do not confuse and do not overlap the death impulse with aggressiveness: the antagonist of Eros is not *destrudo* – a concept that, in fact, Freud soon abandons

– but *disinvestment*, a silent disinvestment or even a *counterinvestiment* (Cornut, 2002), an *antidrive* (Green, 1995),[17] stressing the reinforcement that the rejection of representation receives. We will return to this last part, that I believe reflects contemporary clinical practice, at the end of the book.

• The Freudian concept of zero tension, the quest for Nirvana, that Green revises as an unbinding, (*dé-liason*), dis-objectualising drive remains alive and well in clinical practice – only think of the field of substance addiction or severe autism – despite the theoretical *impasse* that should not be underestimated.

• So-called psychic health, an ideal on the horizon that is never entirely reached, does not depend on the total exclusion of the death drive – which is impossible – but on the *dynamic equilibrium* of the mix between the different thrusts. It is as if each of us were born with a certain set of drives including both types and, depending on the mirroring, less or more, received from primary care and on the environmental *defaillance*, the balance will lean more towards the one or the other, with wide-ranging oscillations in different moments of life.

• The two drives, life and death, in a dualistic but contemporary vision when the Freudian text is carefully read, rather than oppose each other *coexist*, converge:

• Death as the work of the living, as Freud shows, is an active death, *a living death*; otherwise it would be the opposite of death (Le Guen, 1989, p. 536, my italics, translated for this edition).

• *Beyond the Pleasure Principle* is to be understood according to the term used by Freud, *Jenseits* (on the other side), the other face of pleasure, but *still another pleasure: the pleasure of having no tension*. This concept is very important. It is not the absence of pleasure but of *another* pleasure, free of representation, white. At a clinical level, as can be seen in many cases, it would not necessarily mean the patient consciously or actively searches for death, even if that is the outcome: they seek a sort of Nirvana pleasure without conflict, without tension – the Lacanian *jouissance*, at the heart of every *addiction*. Conrotto talks of the drive's "double game": it leads to death, but subjectively gives pleasure.

• If many believe today that biological entrenchment has been superseded, it is perhaps a "death" that has been taken a little too much for granted. Seen as the weak and confusing area of theorisation, it should be recalled that in the Freudian metapsychological order the "biological," like the "psychological," constitutes an embankment on which the psychoanalyst can anchor psychic reality and thus be able to proceed with further speculation and explanatory models.

We will return to this when speaking of the *disturbing contiguities*, and the two aspects of this re-reading that seem the most stimulating that I would like to put at the centre of reflection. They open a crack that we could define as possibilist-evolutive, even inside the death drive; its contribution to the *subjectivising* function and therefore necessary for development, and a less than total absence of representation that seems to characterise it in some cases.

For the sake of completeness, it should be recalled that, although fairly marginal, there is no lack of *critical* points regarding the existence of the need of an autonomous death drive, even within this same debate:

- The *Todestrieb* complicates and confuses theorisation, so why not let it derive from sexuality (Laplanche)? For French psychoanalysis the basic theoretical crux remains, Is there a single drive or are there two, but assembled differently? Are they substantially different or not?
- According to some, a certain Manichaeism is created, good/evil, good/bad.
- The very drive concept, as fully described in 1915, is weakened.
- What remains clear, as also pointed out by Ribas (2002), Conrotto (2008) and Falci (2005), is the methodological weakness for which the return to the inanimate is not inferred from biological data, but, on the contrary, these are hypothesised at the service of the great conjecture.
- Can the death drive have an object, asks Le Guen (2008). If as regards Eros the answer is easier, it is because Eros invests objects and also in narcissism the libido invests the Id treated like an object. The matter is not so clear for the death drive. One can say that its ultimate purpose is death, the dis-union of what the libido had tied together; its object, so to speak, is the destruction of the individual. And what is the source of the death drive? Life itself?

This same author, in his *Dictionnaire* (2008), after having defined the death drive in line with Freudian conception, adds, however, in apparent contradiction with what has been seen above, that the death drive defines itself for its purpose, that is to say, the return to the inorganic, destroying the bonds of Eros. An essentially speculative and epistemological Freudian need reiterates that it is substantially silent and is sensed in life in its expressions of sadism and masochism. On the Freudian path, Le Guen also specifies three periods of the concept's elaboration in Freud: an initial period in which Freud refuses the idea of an aggressive drive as advanced by Adler in 1909; the central period of the 1920s with the full affirmation of the concept that sees *death inside the individual*; and the greater emphasis, beginning in 1924, on the mix between Eros and the death drive, the impossibility of isolating a pure drive. I believe that this latter aspect is the most fertile and precious legacy of the entire metaphorical construction of the death drive in Freud, with which to measure ourselves today.

Equally controversial is the death drive for Laplanche and Pontalis (1967), who quite rightly believe, however, that the concept is not isolatable but understandable only if inserted into the whole context of Freudian work. They also attempt a differentiation with Kleinian drive dualism – apparently the most faithful to Freud: in Klein the two drives are antagonistic but would work in the same way, while in Freud their aims *and* their functioning are different – although their argument is not very clear. I find useful, however, their highlighting of the absolute *novelty* of the Nirvana concept, that would almost be a "subset" of pleasure, tending to the absence of tension and complementary to pleasure itself tied to direct discharge.

Paradoxically, by introducing the death drive, it is as if with Nirvana Freud has extended the field of human pleasure; pleasure is not limited to the achievement of the object or to excitatory discharge, but also includes the *absence* of all this. Laplanche dedicates an ample study (1970) of the death drive, where he asks: *Pourquoi la pulsion de mort?* What need was there, in brief, to introduce a concept that in his opinion does not clarify but complicates an unnecessary drive dualism? While considering *Beyond the Pleasure Principle* Freud's most fascinating work, in common with modern views, I do not share the work's obscure rootedness in the biological, and I consider it to derive not from the clinical sphere, but rather from the fields of philosophy and mythology. One may only partially agree with this. Freud himself acknowledges "a mythology" in the drive theory, but what cannot be denied is the extreme evidence of the death drive in the clinical experience, where Freud first discovers it, stumbling into it despite himself: patients were not getting better, *psychoanalytic disillusionment* was born. By introducing the theory of seduction and the possible enigmatic message of the object as a source of confusion for the child, Laplanche substantially links the death drive to the sexual drive. Everything, that will then take the road towards death or life, derives from the sexual, it is the *sexual death drive* – terms which seem to be a paradox. The death of the Ego can occur in two ways, either through the invasion of an unbound sexual drive or through the avoidance of all tensions obtained by the narcissistic Nirvana Ego. This second concept is interesting because it seems to coincide with Green's *death*, to which we shall return.

Among the partial detractors of the death drive, I quote for the sake of completeness – and for the curiosity of his thought – Guillaumin (2000) who in *L'invention de la pulsion de mort* postulates that the new drive that appeared "suddenly" in Freudian thought as an invention to explain those impasses little investigated at the time and to which Ferenczi will return, where analyses have stalled or become those so-called endless analyses, due to transference-countertransference collusion, not understood by Freud at the time, who would thus have "brought the death drive into play as a dark force to which to attribute failures and repetitions" (in Doninotti, 2011, p. 64, translated for this edition). Guillaumin, in short, rejects the idea of the existence of a death drive, justifying it only as technical ploy to define situations of analytical stall; it is true that the death drive, in its manifestations of negative therapeutic reactions and repetition compulsion, *contributes* to the impasse in analysis, but it seems simplistic to make it the only cause.

Denis Ribas (1989) wonders about the relationship between the death drive, temporality and *anguish of death*: the two terms are not in fact superimposable. While the concept of death is not represented in the unconscious, the anguish of death can be clearly perceived as a terror of annihilation, fruit of projections of destructive movements of the Ego. For Ribas, the anguish of death is perceived by the human being because it has more to do with the libido which emerges from defusion than with the pure death drive, and I believe that this is acceptable. He gives as examples the agony of the dying and the pain of the elderly. Although understandable, I think these are, however, different instances: the anguish of death, representable and perceptible as a "nameless terror," and the death drive, silent or manifest in the ways seen so far, seem to be different, though clinically close. With emphasis on the clinic of defusion, Ribas fits into the line of thought that I consider to be the most fertile and interesting today, close to Green's dis-objectualising function, to Gaddini's early non-integration, even to Bion's B element (Geissmann, 2001).

Roussillon (2000) as well, among the most important recent authors, speaks of non-differentiation as a function of the death drive and, from *Mourning and Melancholia* of 1915, in the *shadow of the object that falls on the Ego* the first psycho-analytic description of death is found: Death, through the shadow of an object that one cannot let die, turns back on to the Ego and so there is indifferentiation between Ego and Non-Ego, the death of the Ego. If Ribas emphasises the differentiating-separating role of the death drive, to be described in more detail later, for Roussillon the opposite seems to be true: death is where the undifferenti-ated prevails, where differences are killed, the scraps, and then only the repetition of the same has space. Death, for him, would be intrinsic to the drive. It does not require a drive dualism. It is just a "register" of the drive function: "When the drive tends to reproduce the same, when it tends to the identity of perception, to perceptual hallucination, whether it is libido or destructiveness, *the drive is of death*" (in Doninotti, p. 85, my italics). This is very close to Green in an attempt to conjugate drive and object, overcoming the old and now sterile diatribe: the drive needs an object, it *relies* on an object and so therefore, the drive dies if it encounters a deadly object, a *dead mother*.

Probably the source of a certain confusion, but not devoid of suggestion, is Hellerau's position (2000). He alone has hypothesised a form of inherent energy of the death drive in a Freudian sense, to which he gives the name Léthé. Derived from Greek mythology's river of oblivion, Léthé refers clearly to the Nirvana thrust, to the drive oblivion, which is the ultimate goal. The clinically useful aspect of Léthé is how darkly present for Hellerau it is in many patients, even apparently those who are depressed, and how it is a source of unconscious pleasure. Therefore, technically, attempts to flush out this hidden river of oblivion are destined to fail or to cause negative therapeutic reactions, as the patient will put up resistance (as occurs, in fact, for all defences). If on the one hand the Léthé seems to be well integrated into the metapsychological framework, there are critics, such as Green, due to the confusion between oblivion and removal; I believe, however, that the term retains a hint of the mythical Léthé, even in common parlance, the effort of having tried to name the silent drive beyond Nirvana, to describe it like a *river*, something that proceeds, unstoppable, that drags you along towards lethargy and death.

Anne Denis (2006), in a contribution which I quote for the sake of completeness but which does not seem to me to be particularly significant, partly reformulates the Freudian death drive, calling it the death principle, and taking an interest particularly in the side of *murder*, the drive to kill that, for her, is only a part of the death drive, particularly active in relationships and human institutions. This "drive to kill," physically or psychologically, is active in both small and large groups, and is seen in totalitarian situations where the individual is "killed" as far as thought and identity are concerned, for example. The sole remedy for this perversion of the human bond for Denis, like Green, issublimation.

It is thanks to Widlocher's synthesis[18], during the 1986 EPF Congress, that both the points of convergence and divergence between the speakers are highlighted, summarizing, in concrete terms, the points seen above. Among the former are the abandonment of the reference to the biological model and the distinction with primary aggressiveness or envy, and the importance, in modern terms, of the concepts of *binding* and *unbinding*, virtually replacing the old fusion and defusion, which acquire, however, different shades in the various authors. Among the divergences, the return to the inanimate and the inorganic that for Segal is a source of pain is for others the opposite, one of pleasure or at least of absence of pain; the vision of primary narcissism, that the French maintain in a Freudian sense is for Segal entirely an expression of the death drive. Segal is somewhat critical of the vagueness of the term Nirvana. She deems it a tad idealised, offering as an example the strong aggressiveness which holds addicts prisoners, even if apparently they are lulled into a Nirvana state. Further, the terms *investment* and *disinvestment*, to which we shall return, are read slightly differently. Green is the author who gives them the utmost importance, making the disinvestment of every representation coincide with *death narcissism* (1983).

In other words, if the efforts of Freud to anchor himself to the biological, typical of his thinking that sought "scientificity" in psychoanalysis and his era of positivism, are today the most obsolete and least convincing of his *capital intuition* (Falci, 2005, p. 809), what remains not only valid but still in part to be explored is the philosophical, cultural, anthropological scenario to which his work introduces us, questions about the course of life and history, about Evil understood not only as a destructive stubbornness, but also as a *desire*, as an absence of goodness and empathy towards the other, as an obtuse search for non-tension that leads not only to an aggressiveness that is in some way vitalist against the object, but to a banal *seriality* that ignores it, that finishes it off, *just* for simply existing, for being other-than-self. This is, in my opinion, the prevailing figure of Evil from the 1900s onwards. War and destruction have always been seen in the human race. They have even been considered necessary, but only modernity has revealed what Freudian intuition postulated and Hannah Arendt has told so well, in the banality of Evil, nestled in the sleep of reason. Its silence, its seriality.

It should be added that, although most authors and modern psychoanalysis today reject anchorage to the biological part of the drive as its least demonstrable or convincing aspect, there are some who, in post-Freud, have made mention of Freud's intuitions by linking it to neurobiological developments. It is, indeed, Green (2007), who can be considered Freud's greatest heir in the study of the death drive, to call to mind the already mentioned studies of Ameisen (1999) on cell suicide, in which he recognises the disquieting closeness with the latest Freudian drive theory.

Life is but the neutralisation of self-destructing forces – cited by Ameisen – in a perspective that renounces all intentionalitiesIt is with *Beyond the Pleasure Principle* that Freud performs the operation that we have defined, however we may think, as shocking: he inserts psychoanalysis in awkward categories that have never been studied or previously thought of, *the desire of death* and *the death of desire.*

The thoughts of Andrè Green

We propose the hypothesis that the essential aim of life drives is to ensure an *objectualising function*. This does not only mean that its role is to create a relationship with the (internal and external) object but that it shows itself capable of *transforming structures in objects*. In other words [. . .] it can get to the level of an object that does not possess any of the qualities, some properties or attributes of the object, provided that in the psychic work performed it maintains a sole feature: *significant investment* [. . .]. At worst, *it is the investment itself that is objectualised* [. . .]. On the contrary, the aim of the death drive is to provide as far as possible, by means of unbinding, a dis-objectualising function.

(Green, 2010, pp. 201–202, translated for this edition[19])

I think Green, already widely quoted on a number of occasions, needs a short section devoted to him. He alone has provided a deep, extended, complex but not obscure revisitation of the Freudian death drive that has succeeded in its effort to maintain fundamentals while revitalising them in the light of contemporary psychoanalysis.

Although not without some reservations and concerns (for example, as we shall see, as regards the ambiguous bond with sublimation), about the death drive he premises that he is "obliged to recognize the validity of the last drive theory of Freud" (ibid., p. 201), especially in his later works from 2000 onwards.

There are two main issues that Green asks: how the death drive operates in the psychical apparatus and how it relates to the theory of narcissism. It is perhaps, in my opinion, his most brilliant legacy, to have been able to combine drive and narcissism in a fundamental structural framework of *life narcissism* and *death narcissism*. Very useful in clinical practice, a clarifier in theory, narcissism loses every moralising connotation to become neither good nor bad in itself, but different according to the direction it principally finds: towards life or towards death. The triad which sees together, similar and distinct, the *negative* concept, death narcissism and the unbinding or dis-objectualising function, represents the heart of Green's formulation on the death drive. This constellation is so complete that, in my opinion, it answers each question, clinical and theoretical, on the Freudian "shocking hypothesis."

The originality of Green lies above all, I believe, in an attempt not so much as to "clear" the death drive itself, but to make it a *living, contemporary* concept, seen in most patients today, in society and in life: how can the presence of death in our patients' lives be eluded, the deadly narcissism that distinguishes them, the "white," the vacuum of new psychotic forms, the loss of binding with the object or its maintenance as an essential compass to carry on in life? Indirectly, through the concepts of the *objectualising function*, where the bond with the object is kept, and the *dis-objectualising function*, where instead this bond is lost, he attempts a synthesis that is a modern replacement of the old drive/object diatribe that no longer has reason to exist: the drive leans, by its nature, on an object, or even on its representation, and only if this happens can one can speak of investment. Otherwise we are faced with the universe of disinvestment, to which we shall return in conclusion as a characterising feature, or at least one of the possible features, of modernity.

Repetition compulsion, one of the most recurring expressions of the death drive, acquires a particular force. It cannot be reduced to pure drive play, it creates a vacuum in the psychic apparatus, it kills the humanly essential function of temporality, it carries out a "murder of time" (Green 2010, p. 202). Not renouncing the immediate pleasure of the Act, of the *agiren*, repetition compulsion makes a solipsistic circuit: closed, it renounces reality in favour of repetition, clinically, it connects to what Green, in his later work, called disillusion in psychoanalytical work, analytical failures that collapse under the force of compulsion and masochism. The analyst, as we know, finds himself in a serious *impasse*: trying to open breaches, to break the circle of the eternal return means risking a renewal of the trauma from which the compulsion originated, increasing the patient's resistance:

> The secret of the analyst here is in letting himself be destroyed without resistance – as far as one can – or just enough to make the destructive operation useful. A little sadistic libido is mixed with a lot of deadly narcissistic libido [. . .]. It is therefore through displacement of the primitive intrapsychic bond, what is discharged almost automatically so that nothing is preserved nor does it risk being definitively lost, that *a proposal for an inter-subjective bond* (which connects the two psyches) presents itself, demonstrating that the relationship can be objectualised. It is then that the game of representation develops, it enriches, diversifies – *becomes live*, in other words.
>
> (ibid., p. 203, my italics, translated for this edition,
> see endnote 19)

We will see this in two cases in the clinical part of this book, something dead (but obviously *not* completely dead) returns to being alive. Does Green's vision seem less "pessimistic" than Freud's later thoughts? It may be so: transference force can move erotic libido onto other objects, and not all analytical failures are, for him, ascribable to the death drive.

In summary, if the meeting points and agreement with the Freudian death drive are more numerous, in Green, the author of such a profound review, differences of opinion or in any case of perplexity are not lacking: the reworking of terminology to replace the drive, a biological evocation that we have seen is not demonstrable, the more generic "destruction drive," oriented internally (masochism) or externally (destructiveness); the refusal of a Nirvana component, that is to say the teleological tendency to a complete discharge of the drive towards the inorganic; lastly, doubts about the primary character of masochism "that seems to be the result of an outward movement completed that folds in on itself" (Green 2010, p. 204). With respect to the libidinal drive, the death drive would not be in a relation of either supremacy or of irreversibility and, let us say it once more, it depends to a large extent on the *quality of the object relationship*: because the function of the object is to contribute to the bond between the drives, a holding in check by the object can cause that unbinding, that dissolution of the bond from which the death drive originates. In my opinion, the latter is one of the most important aspects that erases any doubt on the so-called solipsism of Freudian theory: it is the object that binds the drives, and if this is lacking or deficient or absent, all that remains for the unbound drives is to roam free, under the banner of death, as an object is missing (or if it is a *dead object* the bond will therefore be unusable).

To save life, in short, it is *the love of the object that becomes the fundamental objective* (Green 2010, p. 205) but, at the basis of all this, in agreement with Freud, he places narcissism as life's safeguard: this is the first form of investment on the Ego that rejects death, that acts as an ally of Eros. Life narcissism. Together with the concepts of binding and unbinding, the dualism life narcissism/death narcissism is Green's more fertile, clinically richer idea, as narcissism is "the cornerstone of the theorisation of the death drive" (ibid., p. 206).

In conclusion to the ample reflection brought to term in *Pourquoi les pulsions de destruction ou de mort?* (Why the destructive or death drives?) *The structure of narcissism*, Green concludes with a loving admiration for Freud's unsurpassed writing skills: "Freud says all this in two sentences . . .".

Disturbing contiguity: the death drive and sublimation

> [. . .] He promises the sky and lets go of earthly love in which life is rooted.
> With its deviation from Eros it has become the apologue of death [. . .].
> (Green, 1993, p. 308, translated for this edition,
> see endnote 19)

It is through the evocative relationship of "similarity" with the so-called lower animals, that Freud exemplifies and closes, in one of the more complicated passages, in my opinion, of *The Ego and the Id* (Freud, 1923), one that I have defined as the disquieting contiguity with one of the most vital transformative processes areas of the sexual drive, sublimation (Valdrè, 2015).

Let us look at this whole passage again:

> If it is true that Fechner's principle of constancy governs life, which thus
> consists of a continuous descent towards death, it is the claims of Eros, of
> the sexual instincts, which, in the form of instinctual needs, hold up the

falling level, and introduce fresh tensions. The Id, guided by the pleasure principle, [. . .] fends off these tensions in various ways. It does so in the first place by complying as swiftly as possible to the demands of the non-desexualized libido – by striving for the satisfaction of the directly sexual trends. But is does so in a far more comprehensive fashion in relation to one particular form of satisfaction in which all component demands converge – by discharge of the sexual substances, which are saturated vehicles, so to speak, of the erotic tensions [. . .].

This accounts for the likeness of the condition that follows complete sexual satisfaction to dying, and for the fact that *death coincides with the act of copulation* in some of the lower animals. These creatures die in the act of reproduction because, *after Eros has been eliminated through the process of satisfaction, the death instinct has a free hand* to accomplish its purposes. Finally, as we have seen, the Ego, by *sublimating some of the libido for itself* and its purposes, assists the id in its work of mastering the tensions.

(Freud, 1923, p. 26, my italics)

The comparison, the questionable "likeness," will certainly appear forced and excessively restricted to pure economic discharges. Nevertheless, I have quoted this passage in its entirety because it possesses, as many Freudian metaphors and comparisons do, even with the biological and animal world, its own suggestive power. What happens to an animal that is less complex than man, but is still inhabited, indeed exclusively dominated, by drives? If the living organism (and not only human) tends naturally to death, pushed by sexual drives to seek fulfilment through orgiastic and procreative discharge, from which animals unlike humans cannot escape, once sexual tension has been discharged and Eros satisfied, the other drive that was bound before, the death drive, at this point remains *free* and defused, and thus the animal that has just been satisfied by love, dies. His destiny is fulfilled: Eros is satisfied, the animal may die. There are many species that we could say love and die and pay the price of Eros's irresistibility with death, their living simply no longer needed.

In humans, endowed with consciousness and subjectivity, everything gets more complicated, everything is refined. Humans, too, are pushed by the pleasure principle to seek fulfilment, humans, too, have no respite, in the form of *desire*, in requests by Eros, but they can satisfy them directly in part, and divert them in part, *transform* them into other destinies. No other living being apart from us can do this and one of these, one of the more *human, par excellence*, is sublimation.[20] In sublimation, mentioned in various points of Freud's work (1897, 1901, 1905, 1908, 1923), but whose main essay on the matter is *Leonardo da Vinci and A Memory of His Childhood* in 1910, the sexual drive is offered a great *opportunity*: to transform itself, to become other, to detach itself from the direct object of pleasure to then *invest in its representation*, thus renouncing the object but keeping the internal representation. A great *opportunity*, then, an excellent option, but also a significant renunciation: drive renunciation, always so difficult, painful and incomplete, fragile but necessary not only to individual life but, as Freud reiterates in the great works of his mature years, to the process of civilisation itself. Thus sublimation and civilisation coincide. But what happens in sublimation? Of the many definitions that appear in his work, in a typical Freudian manner and as occurs with his fundamental theorisations, once introduced, they are not abandoned. For the sake of simplicity we will use this one from 1908:

> The sexual impulse [. . .] places extraordinarily large amounts of force at the disposal of civilized activity, and it does this in virtue of its especially marked characteristic of being able to *displace its aim* without materially diminishing in intensity. This capacity to exchange its originally sexual aim for another one, which is no longer sexual but which is psychically related to the first aim, is called the capacity for sublimation.
>
> (Freud 1908, p. 67, my italics)

Originally a sexual pleasure, it replaces another apparently very different one that does not seem to have anything to do with the sexual, but instead it draws its source from there. Although to a lesser extent, sublimation is also part of those Freudian concepts continually mentioned but not universally accepted (Argentieri, 2005). I am among those who, however, as for the death drive, with no idealisation (as this very chapter demonstrates) welcome it fully inside the intertwining and the continuous variability of drive destinies. For sublimation to occur, that is to say, for a sexual goal to be replaced by another capable of providing a certain pleasure but no longer a sexual one, it is necessary that the (sexual) drives are equipped with a particular *plasticity* as they must in part or in full (see *Leonardo*) be subtracted from removal because they make themselves available to another destiny. The original source, in fact, that will make itself transformable in sublimation has its roots in the partial drives of an infant and in *sexual curiosity*: Leonardo, who Freud takes as an example of pure genius and perfect sublimation, in Freud's retrospective investigation was a sexually curious child who nonetheless moved the desire for pleasure *entirely* to hunger for knowledge. Nothing is stronger than a diverted passion. Sexual pleasure, depending on an individual's ability and disposition, will thus be transformed, replaced by other *destinations*: cultural destinations, mental pleasures, small and large sublimations present in all of us, variable in the course of life and usually more distinct and more necessary with the advance of time. These destinations require, just as the primary object did, a certain idealisation to provide the Ego with a pleasure that is not ephemeral but of lasting sublimations. The process is complex and it does not extend to all individuals in equal measure. It is difficult for many patients and quite delicate in the analytical care required, where it should not be forced or favoured but left to spontaneously emerge. This is always a partial and fragile process because a complete renunciation of direct satisfaction is not possible: shoved out the door, it climbs back in through the window, determined to exact its due just like a tax collector. The scope of sublimation, in individual life and culture, is immense.

From the ability to eschew drives the following ensue: individual growth, the possibility to mourn (of which sublimation is basically the archetype, mourning *par excellence*), subjectivity, transition through the Oedipus stage, the intersection with narcissism and, on a cultural plane, the very survival of civilization.

Even the most skeptical of the drive theory cannot fail to recognise how extraordinary human drive destiny is: from polymorphic, mysterious and restless magma of partial instincts, humans are unique among all living beings in being able to make this drive heritage available to build friendships, create works of art, civilisation and thought, and what Ambrosiano calls "passionate work" (2016). With the passing of the years, in general, as direct satisfaction becomes increasingly rarer and more difficult, sublimation, while not a life-saver or a guarantor of happiness, does, however, allow access to substitutive activities such as cultural ones even indirectly enjoyed, that are capable of giving a certain pleasure, a certain warmth and sense of an existence that is neither empty nor besieged by the forced and overwhelming need of satisfaction. All this, of course, as with every human achievement, is not without a price, nor is it without pain. I would sum up with Green (1993) the greatness and the limits of human sublimation, what it can and cannot give us. He says that sublimation is not a guarantee or a protection, rather it gives the opportunity for a different sort of "jouissance." Sublimation's power lies in its objectualising function, accompanied during life by loved objects that remain faithful as they can disappear only if we abandon them.

Now, if we are facing a process that is so intrinsically vital, indeed so necessary to individual and collective life, why should we call into question the death drive? Why speak of contiguity, if not for the fact that, as we have seen, Derridean *life death have* always cohabited and been accomplices or allies. But is there something more specific in a psychoanalytical sense? In my previous work on sublimation, I assumed that among the possible causes of the decline of interest, already seen in metapsychology in general towards sublimation and its disincentive in contemporaneity, were in part the controversial and unsolved theoretical knots that even sublimation, as well as the death drive, brings with it, and one of them is the relationship with the death drive. I think that we have here, on a purely conceptual level but with ample clinical and social repercussions, one of the more interesting and intriguing aporias of Freudian psychoanalysis, but one that has raised, overall, little curiosity or exploration. Too complex, too agonising? Whatever the reasons, let us try for a reinterpretation here. Given that I quote this possible contiguity for the sake of completeness and because I find it extraordinarily intriguing, in the sublimation process I see an always partial and difficult process, but one that is prevalently vital. Only its excesses – which can express themselves with an excessive tyranny of the Ego ideal in a sort of "illness of ideality" (Chasseguet-Smirgel, 1999), in a mutilating rigorism of the super-Ego or in an excessive renunciation of drives, which I find are rare but ideally possible, especially as regards the tyranny of the Ideal – can form an overlap, a drift of sublimation onto the terrain of the deadly drive. In such cases can we still speak of sublimation or are we in other conceptual and frankly psychopathological areas?

The question and the dilemma that we are discussing here is, however, of a different nature, one that Freud himself mentions, as we shall see, in a passage in *The Ego and the Id*, and arises from the unconscious mechanism that is at the base of each sublimation: desexualisation. In order for the sexual drive to be disposed to change its objective and to invest in objects that are no longer sexual, it must be *desexualised* so it can keep the same intensity of the sexual drive and the same force, but devoid of the sexual component. We now know that whenever desexualisation comes into play in psychic life we are dangerously *à coté*, contiguous and close to the death drive. I believe that no other concept like sublimation, with its range of pleasure and pain, individual and collective, represents so well the profound nature of the mix, the blend and the weave that life and death possess in the depths of human nature.

Freud himself, with apparent and disconcerting ease, declares this contradiction in *The Ego and the Id* in the space of a few pages. First he recognises that:

> The transformation of object–libido into narcissistic libido which thus takes place obviously implies an abandonment of sexual aims, a *desexualization* a kind of sublimation therefore [. . .] which begins by changing sexual-object libido into narcissistic libido, and then, perhaps, goes on to give it another aim.
>
> (Freud 1923, p. 30, my italics)

A complex process, sublimation goes well beyond a simple movement that would make it the defence mechanism that it was initially considered to be. No, sublimation implies the crucial step of desexualisation (one of the disputed points, we have seen, of the concept of sublimation itself, where someone asks what need there would have been to introduce this desexualization). Immediately after, Freud anticipates the crux that interests us:

> We shall later on have to consider whether other instinctual vicissitudes may not also result from this transformation, whether, for instance, it may not bring about a *defusion* of the various instincts that are fused together.
>
> (Freud 1923, p. 30, my italics)

So desexualised, and returned to the Ego, the libido:

> [. . .] may also be described as sublimated energy; for it would still retain the main purpose of Eros, that of *uniting and binding* in so far as it helps towards establishing the unity, or tendency to unity, which is particularly characteristic of the Ego. If thought-processes in the wider sense are to be included among these displacements, then the activity of thinking is also supplied from the sublimation of erotic motive forces.
>
> (Freud 1923, p. 43, my italics)

But, on the following page, we read that:

> The transformation [of erotic libido] into ego-libido of course involves an abandonment of sexual aims, a desexualization. In any case this throws light upon an important function of the ego in its relation to Eros. By thus getting hold of the libido from the object-cathexes, setting itself up as sole love-object, and de-sexualizing or sublimating the libido of the id, *the ego is working in opposition to the purposes of Eros and placing itself at the service of the opposing instinctual impulses.*
>
> (Freud 1923, p. 46, my italics)

And he concludes the chapter with the metaphor of the lower animal, which dies having loved, in harmony with these last few lines. So how can we extract ourselves from this contradiction? Is the path to sublimation really paved over the death drive (Green, 1993)?

If we base our arguments on these last Freudian lines, that completely repudiate what had been said on the previous page, we must recognise that:

> Sublimation-desexualization would be an adverse pulsion to sexuality (. . .) On the one hand sublimation appears a vicissitude of the sexual drive, a purified form which has its place among other possible destinies, but which remains within the patrimony of Eros, and, on the other, sublimation is *the adverse counterpart* of Eros, which, far from serving its aims, sides with those forces which are antagonistic to its purpose. The paradox cannot easily be overcome [. . .].
>
> (Green, 1999, p. 219)

We might ask ourselves if the paradox *should* be overcome or, with Freudian confidence and awareness, if the association of the two faces of that "two-headed eagle" (David, 1998) which inevitably seems, at least on a conceptual level, to be the soul of sublimation, is merely part of the irreducible complexity of the human psychic. Deriddean *life death*, the *cell suicide of* immunology: is it really necessary to resolve this contradiction, or should it not be accepted as such? Humankind strives to live but has in itself death, the unavoidable drive thrust at its shutdown, a bearer of a paradox that the desexualisation needed in order to make the sexual libido available for other objectives, *during this passage*, from the object to the Ego, is at risk of unbinding aggressive drives that once defused, will operate against Eros. Although it is difficult, or perhaps impossible, to express a final opinion, and although the clinic, as well as the devastated lives of many artists (as we shall see) seems to confirm the easy turning of sublimation (from which art originates) into the death drive (suicide, depression, etc.), I am of the opinion that, except in rare cases, with sublimation the eagle's head or, shall we say, the prevailing polarity, is in the land of Eros. Because sublimation, in my opinion, meets, "intersects and blends with the process of *symbolisation*, that is to say with a process of signification that replaces the thrust towards the drive discharge" (Conrotto, 2016,[21] translated for this edition, my italics), it occupies the fertile soil of life. Symbolisation is the basis of thought. It is the game with the reel with which the infant Ernst (Freud, 1920) manages to tolerate the absence of the mother without going crazy, to replace the object with its representation, to *play*.

The lower animal of the Freudian metaphor, instead, is completely prey to the death drive, once detached from Eros, but we small Ernsts possess, when all goes well and each to a different extent, that representative capacity, that *psychic figurability* (Botella, 2001) that is at the basis of development, bereavement, identification and, collectively, civilisation. We will see later how a weakening of this capacity determines the difficulties of the so-called new clinic and the cultural climate of much of contemporary life.

Where sublimation can woo the death drive is especially in the risk that an excess of dependency by the ideal of the Ego (or rather by the Ego ideal, more regressed and omnipotently narcissistic, according to the useful differentiation made by some authors) comes to constitute what is defined as an "illness of ideality" (Chasseguet-Smirgel, 1999). Sublimation is in fact always connected to idealisation and a certain reorganisation of the Ego ideal; as the primary object was idealised, so, too, are the sublimated objectives and substitute objects from which the subject may become, as can be observed in certain artists, dependent, tyrannized, to the point of a real "compulsion to create" (Kavaler-Adler, 1993). I think, however, that more complex factors contribute to the mysterious phenomenon of the relationship between art, creativity, sublimation and destructiveness (Valdrè, 2015). It cannot be denied that it is not difficult to observe artists, or even ordinary people particularly devoted to a passion, become slaves of perfectionist ideals at the expense of important limitations of the Ego or of melancholic import; let us not forget, in fact, that the libido, in the famous and critical *passage*, from the object becomes narcissistic and therefore there is the risk of a lapse into depression. The boundary is fragile and the terrain slippery. If one can become sick with too much sublimation, as Ambrosiano writes (2015), then the same can happen with too little, and I would add: *Above all* with too little.

I believe we are faced with real expressions of the death drive, as intended in the Freudian meaning of disinvestment from objects, only in cases of serious or very serious autism, where any libidinal investment is lacking. But these cases are rarely observable because they are rarely treatable in the analysis room. Even in certain ascetic forms, easily associated with sublimation because in effect the subject renounces objects to invest, for example, in the image of God, I agree with Kristeva (2008), in her vast and fascinating journey into the character of Maria Teresa of Avila, that there is no question of phenomena, such as ecstasy, free, stripped from sensual pleasure. It is not an operation of the intellect, of pure reason, that makes Teresa say, "We are not angels, for we have a body."[22]

The mystic, like many others (see note) in the history of female monasticism, *enjoyed God*. Every bodily deprivation, from demented fasts to self-inflicted pain with exhausting prayers, were for Teresa (whose most intimate thoughts we have the good fortune to know because she wrote down notes throughout her life) a source of immense pleasure but not an abstract purely mental pleasure, such as when we are looking at a work of art or reading a book. No, the pleasure of Teresa and the so-called holy anorexics is a pleasure that fills the body, is a "true lover" (*verdadero Amador*) (ibid.). It is true, of course, that it is a limited-enjoyment. We could say that enjoyment is through investing in deprivation and pain, but from the mystic's own words that the author uses, and from the overwhelming sensuality Bernini imbued her with in his famous statue, we are definitely close to the terrain of Thanatos, but not of the mute drive: it is an *orgiastic* enjoyment that Teresa describes and Bernini's statue embodies so magnificently, a head thrown back in prey to pleasure, a mouth half open . . . is this perhaps the marsh of disinvestment?

A good example to the contrary that corroborates the contiguity between the death drive and sublimation but offers it a transformational outlet, is that of the American essayist Margaret Bullitt-Jonas (who will be dealt with more amply in the next chapter), who became an Episcopal priest in Boston. In her autobiography *Holy Hunger* (1998), she describes with great finesse and intensity her passage from compulsive eater and *food addict* to a path of aware and growing *spirituality* that brought her to a recovery from deadly self-sabotage through the discovery of God. With the subtitle *A Woman's Journey from Food Addiction to Spiritual Fulfillment*, the book describes the journey of a woman from dependence on an object of sensory oral pleasure – food – the most primary, the oldest, the most cunning in the conduits of associated pathologies (in excess or by default), to a genuine, true replacement, and I would say transformation, by a spiritual "object," the most bodiless that exists: God and, parallel to this, her writing and the committed service she still pursues in Overeaters Anonymous where she had sought treatment. We should remember that Freud, in his disarming correspondence with Pastor Pfister, never hid the superiority, the "most comfortable form" (1909) of religion with respect to psychoanalysis:

> In your case they are young persons faced with conflicts of recent date, who are personally drawn towards you and ready for sublimation, and to sublimation in its most comfortable form, namely the religious. (. . .) You are in the fortunate position of being able to lead them to God (. . .). For us this way of disposing of the matter does not exist. (. . .) as the other ways to sublimation which we substitute with religion are too difficult for most patients, our treatment generally results in the seeking out of satisfaction.

(Freud, *Letter to Oskar Pfister*, 1909)

The type of spirituality derived from the group accessed by Bullitt-Jonas is interesting from our point of view because what is offered by Overeaters Anonymous is not a naive or unaware faith, but of a type of spirituality:

[. . .] For people who have known anguish, for people who've daily confronted with the choice *between life* and *death* and discovered, time and time again, how mortally difficult it is to make the choice for life. It begins with the disastrous admission that our lives are out of control. We've tasted hell [. . .].

(Bullitt-Jonas, 2000, p. 133–134)

In different words, the great sculptress Louise Bourgeois (1993) expresses the same idea when she writes:

I am an addictive type of person and the only way to stop the addiction is to become addicted to something else, something less harmful. What the *substitute* is is the body of my work. The sculptures reveal a whole life based on eroticism; *the sexual, or the absence of sex is everything. . . .*

(p. 227–228, my italics)

A work of art, a spirituality towards God for someone who is desperate, with a body destroyed by the self-attack of binge eating disorder, uncontrollable and suicidal, replace the auto-erotic object or its food equivalent with happy, alternative goals that will last a lifetime and will even be vehicles of success in these gifted people.

Successful contiguities can co-exist, therefore, alongside fallacious, dangerous and frail contiguities, as we will see in the lives of some artists chosen as examples in chapter three.

In conclusion, Freud's blatant contradiction that we have seen remains complex, mysterious and unresolved, namely the relationship between the death drive and sublimation; if for some the desexualisation incorporated in sublimation certainly represents a danger, thus making sublimation a less desirable drive destiny, for others, it is still the prevalent call to life through the necessary passage *from the object to its representation and therefore to the symbol* that carries the day.

Also undisputed is the disquieting blend, the interlacing and contiguity between life and death that sublimation expresses so well, an irreducible paradox that we carry within, that can always, at any time, wade the ford and change signs because the fruit of such a complex recast that is sublimation is marked by a characteristic, its fragility. Losing or a crisis can occur when we can no longer tolerate the weight of drive renunciation, and so veer into the defusion of the destructive drives in that

Sublimation attempts to transform internal destructiveness [. . .]. However, the alloy that is formed with the new object (of sublimation) is an unstable and variable alloy. This instability of the new entanglement with the object of sublimation reflects the nature of this new object, which is fragile, and which remains at the mercy of its creator who can always destroy it.

(Séchaud, 2005, p. 1327, translated for this edition)

The subjectivation function:

> Death is very likely the single best invention of life. It is life's change agent. It clears out the old to make way for the new. Right now the new is you, but someday not too long from now, you will gradually become old and be cleared away.
>
> (Steve Jobs)[23]

I think, as I believe many of us do, that Jobs was a sublime artist of modernity. As with all artists, his intuition was illuminating and paves the way of our discussion.

If, as we have seen, life is not given only by the life drive – a positivist ingenuity abandoned completely at the turn of the twentieth century – but by mixing, by the balancing act of the two drives, of death and life, are we not forced to recognise a *positive function* as well, a value, within the same death drive? Why would it exist, when not detached or unmixed, if it did not possess even just a something that *serves* life? That is what Le Guen (1989) calls the "*bon usage de la pulsion de mort*": Todestrieb is certainly a dangerous ingredient, but is there a *good use*, a feature that works not only to keep us in life but to make us grow and evolve? It would seem a paradox (but as we have seen, the *Todestrieb* is an elective ground of paradoxes) but it is perhaps not so and, from an overall perspective, *the accounts balance*: is everything that concerns *Todestrieb* really entirely devoid of, or excluded from *representation*? If so, you could not even conceive of discourses on the death drive, it would not be *sayable* (Scarfone, 2004). How can we talk about something that is entirely unrepresentable if not by at least by admitting what Zaltzman calls *borderline representability?* (1997).

Here, too, the border is thin. It is true, as writes Mangini (2014), that the psychoanalysis that comes about with Freud is a scientific discipline that establishes its epistemological statute on the representable (even if this paradigm has been extended with the "new" pathologies) and that therefore death, because it is unrepresentable to the unconscious, would not have the right to citizenship. But I agree with Scarfone and Zaltzman in identifying instead a representational possibility for the death drive as well, as an object we speak about and, even more specifically, the possibility that the *Todestrieb* falls within representability at the limit, on the borders, at the edges of *beyond* the representation; but not beyond that border.

When Nathalie Zaltzman, a French psychoanalyst of great interest on the contemporary scene[24] and a careful reviser of Freudian work, who always understood psychoanalysis to be a working tool of civilization (Kulturarbeit), speaks of borderline representability, what does she mean? On this concept, she differs in part from the Freudian idea of a death drive that is totally unrepresentable in the psyche; she defines this type of drive as anarchic. Even though its origin lies in the death drive, it represents a sort of vitalist, rebellious current that in extreme individual and historical conditions may even help rescue the human being. Deriving her observations from extreme situations such as wars, genocide and massacres, courageously pondering the little-explored relationship between Kulturarbeit and extreme evil, on the potentials and the impasses of the work of civilisation, on the strength of man in the face of barbarity and on the surprising presence of the human in the inhumane, Zaltzman derived the concept of anarchist impulse (pulsion anarchiste), a sort of byproduct of the death drive, that is a fil rouge running through her entire work. Although one can also define it this way, it would be reductive to give the modern name of "resilience" to this sporadic human capacity to visibly adapt itself, to survive and sometimes even to do so creatively, in the most extreme situations; to conceive the idea of a drive that, even within the Thanatos ambit, somehow binds itself in disarray to Eros, in an anarchic and unpredictable form, to sustain life – this is a completely legitimate idea.

Do not drives, by their very nature, possess deep down a certain degree of *indeterminacy* and *unpredictability* (Mangini, 2014, p. 71, translated for this edition)?

On the separating and therefore vital function of the death drive Pasche (2000) and Ribas (2006) write, in particular the latter when he focuses on connections between the death drive and mourning: we could neither think nor love without the ability to invest but then also to *divest* the object, we could not start the processes of mourning that allow us new investments, we could not sublimate. In short, un-mixing is the basis of every psychic transformation, including evolutionary ones. It is not the existence of the processes of *déliaison* that are necessarily negative but, depending on their degree and prevalence, they can acquire positive or destructive functions. These two sophisticated authors also note how the usual translation of the term mix can sometimes be confusing, giving the idea of an amalgam of drives because, in fact, the so-called mix would not give rise to a single drive, but to different degrees of the two drives. The French description of *intrication et désintrication pulsionnelle* seems, in fact, to be more specific and relevant.

The infinite number of outlets, the unexpected pathways of life, even in extreme situations, not only historical but in the personal psychic world, would not exist if the drive equilibrium were ordered and predictable.

> The network of human relationships inside the Lagers was not simple, it could not be reduced to the two blocs of victims and persecutors. [. . .] The world in which one was precipitated was terrible, yes, but also *indecipherable*: it did not conform to any model, the enemy was all around but also *inside* the "we" lost its limits, the contenders were not two, one could not discern a single frontier. . . .
>
> (Levi, 1986, p. 37, 38)

While maintaining the integrity and indeed in respect to the original Freudian discourse, I find these contributions extremely interesting: specific, if sporadic, they open onto scenarios that are very stimulating for contemporary psychoanalysis. Without going so far as a Holocaust scenario, the unrepresentable, or at least the poor capacity of representation, is today a pervasive characteristic of many patients.

If psychoanalysis wants to survive, it must come to terms with the statute, perhaps not envisaged by Freud, of the frailty of the capacity of representation in the human mind. Holocaust worlds, personal and private lagers, exist and regulate the psychic life of many people. The "anarchist impulse" would thus be a further possible *destiny* of the death drive. Alongside the Nirvana form, lifeless and silent, it would be a sort of rebellious sister, disorderly in its vitalism, which tries desperately to *repeat to elaborate*, overturning the deadly face of coercion to repeat. The anarchic impulse is in contrast to the idea of the representational silence of a drive. It is a strong asserting thrust that wants to be represented. Indeed, it is the *representation of breaking, the borderline-representation*. In the borderline experiences analysed by Zaltzman, the anarchist impulse is presented not as an abstract idea, but as a concrete declination of how this destiny of the death drive can protect life, too, thus with significant clinical and social impact. While not venturing into all of this author's work, in the borderline situations that she describes, as reported by those who have lived them and survived, such as Primo Levi, what happens would be a "taking possession of the physical and mental life of a human being" and that, in order to resist, the subject mobilises extreme drive forces, of death, yes, but paradoxically protective, because only those who possess them can face such mortal challenges.

> I call this version, a more individualistic and libertarian version of the death drive, the *pulsion anarchiste*.
>
> (Zaltzman, 1997, p. 139, translated for this edition)

It is, moreover, quite a common experience that sometimes, when we strive to overcome obstacles, when we engage in libidinal "struggles" to obtain something, we can, in certain cases, kickstart, re-libidinise the drives, thus removing us from dangerous renunciation or deadly slides. I remember the case of a patient who, after being left by her husband, was cast into deep depression. Her involvement, although not pleasant, in the ensuing legal action to defend her rights proved to be an unexpected vitalizing awakening, neither hostile nor persecutory, that kickstarted, so to speak, the idle engine of her mournful libidinal world.

I would not judge Zaltzman's reflections in the same way as "reparative" instances (otherwise everything is death drive); no, they maintain the whole tragic forcefulness of the human dialectic between life and death, they admit the existence of an evil at human limits, but they have the advantage of increasing the complexity of our scenario, it seems to me, to make relevant, believe it or not, all the modernity of the death drive.

Connected to these reflections is therefore the conception, the hypothesis, of a function that we can define not only as one of survival but more purely as *subjectivation* of the death drive. Here is an embarrassing question: can the *silent* drive contribute to subjectivation, to the development of the self, in more human terms, understood not as mere biological life, but as the construction of identity and a specific psychic reality?

Far from considering the death drive as the main aspect to which subjectivation is entrusted, we can recognise, however, that it will *contribute* towards this. I believe that investigating, or at least mentioning, this aspect aids a more concrete understanding of what we mean when we also speak of the *vitality* of the death drive, although paradoxical (and we shall return to this when we discuss artists), as not merely a theoretical or speculative concept, but, as our immunologist put it, something that lies *at the heart of life*. In what way?

The work that we have defined as *unbinding* has not only aspects of disorganization and potential destruction, but also of subjectivation. Here I must clarify that the partially positive and vital acceptance of the term unbinding refers *not to the unbinding of a death drive that develops into disinvestment*, but to an unbinding that, out of the potentially deadly fusion with the primary object, the mother, leads *to investment in the father, the "third," the outside world*. In fact, the term unbinding is not free from possible ambiguity and confusion, so it should be specified that the spirit with which I use it obviously does not coincide with the deadly un-mixing (that could be expressed, for example, through sadism), the opposite of *unbinding to bind to new investments*. This is what Jobs means in his speech to the students: do not be afraid, that is how we grow, this is how we evolve.

Although there is extensive literature in psychoanalysis regarding the function of the Father and the "third" that I will not detail here, and even if it would seem to be counter-intuitive, it is usually not connected to the contribution of the death drive. How could a subject be born without a quota of the unbinding function, the deadly fusion, that prevents the child from having too much of a bond with the primary object? We would be in the territory of Lacanian *jouissance*. The reciprocal is also necessary, so the mother must be capable of a certain unbinding to allow the child to gradually detach himself from her and grow, to invest in a third (the father), *to mourn, sublimate, allow transference in her care* . . . Every possibility of future drive investment and all subsequent identifications derive from this capacity to unbind and thus the unbinding function passes through the Oedipus stage and all human development. If nowadays the cry goes up that the paternal function is alarmingly in crisis, both symbolically and practically speaking, this helps to explain the spread of pathologies of poor representational capacity (narcissistic and borderline spectrums, for example) and the difficulty of sublimating and making creative investments that a large number of young people and adolescents have, for example, as we will see in subsequent chapters.

Just as the universe is held together by the centripetal forces and centrifuges, in Le Guen's (1989) delightful metaphor, human development needs a *bond* of centripetal forces which invest in the object, but if this investment were total and exclusive the subject would collapse in the object and would die. The counter-posing centrifugal force of the unbinding, of disinvestment (Le Guen, 1989; Scarfone, 2004), is therefore necessary.

Other authors use different language, principal among them Winnicott (1965), and speak of "non-integration" (a concept similar to unbinding) to configure a psychic situation in which there is not an attack on the bond, but a state of *disorder of experience* which is periodically returned to, to then re-emerge on the subjectivist path. A far from linear path, never defined and never to be taken for granted, is how we can imagine subjectivism (which constitutes, finally, the end of life), like a bumpy journey along a road studded with tunnels through which one enters and exits to get back on track, dark passages but necessary as well to the journey overall. In short, there is no other way of proceeding if not in a zigzag fashion, by synthesis and dissolution, integration and non-integration, binding and unbinding – personally I prefer these last two terms as I feel they give the best picture of what we are proposing, namely an unceasing detaching and putting together. In some stages of life unbinding will prevail, detachments will be necessary and new investments, too, while in other phases the opposite will be the case; it is not the succession of phases that are a concern but rather stagnation, fixation or an excess of bonding or an excess of unbonding which are the origins of pathologies of the opposite sign.

Among the modalities with which the death drive puts itself at the service of the Ego, the role of *narcissism*, amply examined by Green (2010), should not be overlooked: "The life drive by means of narcissism arises in defense of the Ego, preventing it from destroying itself" (Vecchio, 2016, p. 296, translated for this edition). Narcissism, contributing to the expulsion of the bad and hatred of self would thus be the "first winner" (ibid.) in the conflict between the two drives in favour of life, even though it is a delicate and fragile balance with the ever-present possibility of a counter-offensive by the death drive that wants to countermand the imbalance introduced by the life drive. Green's in-depth study, reprised in the review of Sisto Vecchio, retraces the words of Freud, when he writes in *Beyond the Pleasure Principle*:

> But how can the sadistic instinct, whose aim it is to injure the object, be derived from Eros, the preserver of life? Is it not plausible to suppose that this sadism is in fact a death instinct which, under the influence of the narcissistic libido, has been forced away from the ego and has consequently only emerged in relation to the object?
>
> (1920, p. 54)

It is in this rather convoluted passage that Green traces the decisive role of narcissism in stemming the destructive thrust of sadism that, as an expression of the defusion of the death drive, would be intent on destroying the Ego. It is, however, a common observation, if we leave the terrain of psychoanalytic theory and imagine that, without a sufficient narcissistic structure, that "minimum necessary narcissism" Bolognini (2008) talks of and whose importance tends to be underestimated, as narcissism in psychoanalysis has been subjected to both semantic confusion and a bad name (accused of making a desert of the object world), life is not possible. Attacks on the self that we will see, the pervasiveness of self-destruction in all its forms, is in my opinion, very closely related to fragile narcissistic attitudes that perhaps today are more widespread or more unmasked and evident. Narcissism, then, like the scaffolding of a building, from an early stage of psychic life would prevent the Ego's collapse. Depending on the resistance and the oscillations, even physiological ones, of this scaffolding, depending on how much, with what depth the death drive is able to seep in like silent water that sometimes soaks the foundations of buildings, the Ego will or will not hold fast. In the interesting reconstruction that Green makes, narcissism is the cement that holds together the life drive with the survival of the self and of the object – for Green an attempt to always have synthesis between the intrapsychic and the objectual is important. With this first form of the Ego's investment, which is narcissism, death is rejected, and love of the object with its transformations will become the objective. A *remainder*, however, will always be left. We are born with an excess: everything that cannot be, for constitutional or environmental reasons, outwardly directed like aggressiveness, will twist against the Ego like original masochism, as will be described in greater detail later. Narcissism, then, that a part of psychoanalytical thought has tended to conceive as deadly due to the absence of investments, instead assumes a vital significance or, at the very least like the death drive, it has two faces, *life* and *death*: death, when it navigates in the area of Nirvana disinvestments; life when it contributes to the Ego's defence, to its protection and thus lays the foundations of subjectivation.

Thus the role that Freud gets narcissism to play is that of "an army against the assaults of death instincts" (ibid, p. 29).

We have already mentioned coercion to repeat, that I will discuss in the following chapters and that in my opinion is one of the most frequent guises donned by the death drive; we tend to unconsciously repeat precisely those traumatic and painful forms that marked our childhoods, and that we often undergo analysis in order to repair. The hard core of each analysis, then, and a tragic source of individual unhappiness, even the coercion to repeat, can be seen in a manner that is not so uniform, but is also susceptible to different destinies. M'Uzan (1969) distinguishes a "classic type," a true expression of *Todestrieb*, of a different shape and *collaborative* in its own way, it contains a certain desire for change, for a certain capacity to evolve: the first he calls repetition of the identical and the second repetition of the same. The differentiation is subtle and interesting, although it is likely that in most cases both attempts of repetition are present, one more stagnant and the other more elaborative. One blindly and obtusely repeats without elaboration; the other (in some ways not far from the anarchistic drive) fights to be able to do so.

We conclude this brief and necessarily incomplete theoretical review in the light of its less obvious or less apparent disputes and points of view, and also in full sight of the cracks that Freudian thought has fruitfully, I believe, left open, retracing the paradoxes, the border territories and the intimate vital function, subjectification, present also in the death drive for the preservation of life, as well as the fundamental role of narcissism's cementing protection. It would seem that far from "holing up" in an airless niche of theoretical speculation, *Todestrieb* can be seen in the light of all its modernity and of the powerful impact that it has on clinical practice, life, history, culture and, last but not least, psychoanalytic technique.

My reflections cannot be exhaustive but they are, however, an expression of my own personal journey. They place emphasis on the one hand on the recovery of metapsychology (or whatever you want to call it!) while considering it, as does Freud, *our mythology*, a necessary bulwark to our speculation, and on the other hand on the grandiose Freudian attempt to ask searching philosophical questions about humankind, about the existence of Evil and *not* of aggressiveness (concepts that we will never tire of distinguishing), about the effort to live, about ethics. A concept that was born in 1920 but that also dwells in the conflicting nodes of the contemporary world and will dwell there forever, and that inevitably calls us as psychoanalysts into question. Thus revisited, I believe that the theorisation of *Beyond the Pleasure Principle* deserves to be recovered both in cultural and psychoanalytic debate and, in my opinion, may be enriched by the contribution of the three Lacanian registers – the symbolic, the imaginary, the real – outside psychoanalytic-school dogmas. I will return in closing by speaking of contemporaneity but there is no doubt that, today, culture and psychoanalysis are threatened in the symbolic register.

Without entering into the complex Lacanian universe, it suffices here to mention that for Lacan the reality of human beings is constituted by these three intertwined levels. To illustrate them Žižek (2006) compares them to a game of chess. The symbolic represents *the rules*, those guarantors, those fixed points without which no game can be played; the imaginary level corresponds "to the way different pieces are shaped and characterized [. . .] and it is easy to envisage a game with the same rules, but with a different imaginary" (ibid, p. 8); it is ultimately the real, the entire set of circumstances that affect the game, such as the nature of the players or intrusions and unforeseen events that could disrupt the game.

With a slightly audacious metaphorical leap, I think today we can read and keep alive metapsychology (Freudian "mythology") if we consider it to be our guarantee, both psychoanalytic and social, of possessing the *rules of the game*, those that Riolo (2015) called *invariant*, fixed points you can count on even if they should, in the course of movements and fashions, change name.

The weakening of the symbolic is due, as we shall see, to a lot of contemporary clinic practice that embraces the *états-limites* or limit states, the universe of drug addiction and *addiction* in general, on both the phenomenally destructive side (the death wish) and on the Nirvana side (the death of desire). The composite range of modern drug addiction (which ranges from substance abuse, to gambling, to cosmetic treatments, to the use of the other *as a substance* . . .) lies, in my opinion, precisely "in a place that is *beyond the pleasure*, where all tensions are set at zero and Thanatos is master [. . .] an intolerable experience of joy so dangerously close to the anguish of non-existence [. . .] between excessive joy and annulment of all" (Cimino, 2011, p. 105, translated for this edition). A similar concept, once again studied by Cimino (1989), is expressed by Fachinelli as *the ecstatic mind* (in part seen in the case of Teresa of Avila), an essentially Nirvana mental state contiguous to the territory of the death drive.

The "positive," constructive versions of the death drive such as the subject-ification factor has also been seen and it does not disprove, in my opinion, the bitter Freudian system that sees a *beyond* present within a person, but enriches it with a new dimension: a positive solicitation that obliges us to detach ourselves from the primary object and from the fantasy of the One, fusion without thought or enjoyment, the painful *discarding* that allows us to access the symbolic and civilization. We have assumed, in conclusion, that even the death drive is not a unitary monolith but that it lends itself to *different destinies*. It is with this idea that I would like to leave the theoretical part, with this unfurling fertile seed. Which destinies? The deadly Nirvana that desires only the silence of the Ego and the drowsiness of every conscience; destructive attacks on the self or on the other; coercion to repeat, masochism and negative therapeutic reactions, but *also*, alongside all this, a rebellious anarchistic drive, coercion that presses for elaboration, repetition of the same and not of the identical. The recovery of interest is therefore personally placed both around the metapsychological concept itself, the "cornerstone," but it does not end there and so extends and glimpses possible *transformative* link-ups, the always extraordinary possibility that the mind has to elaborate anguish and trauma through the path of subjectification and transforming, as far as possible, the demons of the self-destruction in representation. Thus life cannot be reduced to a "swampy timeless sod" (Falci, 2005, translated for this edition), but may also contain in its most tormenting currents small cracks of representability that will allow us on the one hand, clinically, margins of intervention and in society a source of hope for survival. I agree with the words of Khan (2005):

> If, after Freud, I give to this radical confusion the theoretical name of death drive [. . .] then disputes around the acceptance or refusal around the death drive have *rarely questioned its universal anthropological value*. It is from the point of view of clinical practice and technique that its operativeness has most often been put into question. An operativeness that has followed in the footsteps of overall effectiveness, ignoring that, far beyond the new pathologies that we face, of it goes the same cultural dismemberment.

> (p. 419, my italics, translated for this edition)

Notes

1. Published in *Rivista di Psicoanalisi*, 2012, 3: 605–626. The original article has been amplified and expanded for this book.
2. An early twentieth century figure, Tessa was a reserved person who wrote poetry in the Lombard dialect. The collection of his poems, including this verse, is thanks to Pier Paolo Pasolini.
3. The frequent use of terms in French in this work and in the book in general is linked to the fact that it was mainly French, or French-speaking, psychoanalysis that kept alive the debate on Freudian metapsychological themes, including the death drive. As we will see, metapsychology and the set of drives were abandoned by successive more relational orientations.
4. His first biographer, Wittels, gives a certain importance to this event in 1924, but it may be overestimated in that it occurs a few months after the release of the book.

5. It should be remembered that initially even Freud was seduced by a nationalism that called all Austrians to the honour of the Great War, so much so that two of his sons enlisted as volunteers. His enthusiasm was short-lived and soon Freud saw that what had seemed a swift resolution was transformed into carnage. But I believe that, on a personal level, it was precisely that initial, idealistic support that led Freud to realise just how gregarious people are, as well as how a person who individually is reasonable may easily be attracted by the magnet of the masses or of a group, to the extent of losing any self-criticism. This formed the basis for all future psychoanalytical work on groupality and its basic unconscious assumptions.

6. Epistolario Freud-Salomé, in *The Late Sigmund Freud*, Dufresne, T., p. 20 Cambridge: Cambridge University Press, 1983.

7. From *Conditions of Nervous Anxiety and their Treatment, Vol. 18*, Stekel, W., London: Routledge (1923).

8. See Valdré, (2015).

9. I quote, for the sake of simplicity, only the principal authors.

10. For more detail, see also Recalcati's extensive literature, in particular *il vuoto e il resto. Il problema del reale in Jacques Lacan*Milan, CUEM, 2011 and *Jacques Lacan. Desiderio, godimento, soggettivazione*, Milan, Cortina, 2012.

11. The suggestive parallel between Kleinian and Lacanian thought is proposed by more than one psychoanalyst, including Conrotto, Laplanche, Green, Le Guen, all insisting on the *difference between the death drive and aggressiveness*.

12. From sources of Jones (cited in Borgogno and Viola, 1994).

13. The European Psychoanalytical Federation.

14. Interventions at the symposium were partly summarised by Rabain in a special issue of the "Revue" in 1989.

15. As already mentioned, the 2016 National Congress of the Italian Society of Psychoanalysis, "The logics of pleasure, the ambiguity of pain," indirectly touched on the theme of the death drive, as it underlies the dynamics of life/death, pleasure/pain.

16. Interventions discussed in Congrès des psychanalystes de langue française 2002 and collected in different numbers of the Revue (see References).

17. In the dialogue with Green in *Roman Seminars*, 1995.

18. Green, Ikonen, Laplanche, Rechardt, Segal, Widlöcher, Yorke, *La pulsion de mort*, PUF: Paris, 1986.

19. From the full Afterword of Andre Green's book *Illusioni e Disillusioni del lavoro psicoanalitico* that does not appear in the edited English edition.

20. I dedicated an earlier book to this topic, *On Sublimation: A Path to the Destiny of Desire, Theory and Treatment*. Reference, therefore, should be made to this text for a more complete analysis of the concept from all points of view.

21. F. Conrotto, *Does the death drive really have anything to do with sublimation?*, a paper given at the 2016 Italian SPI National Congress, Rome, May 2016 (cf. *supra* note 6).

22. Maria Teresa of Avila, Chapter XXII, 14, The *Annals of the Saint's Life*, in The *Life of Saint Teresa of Avila by Herself*, translated from Spanish by David Lewis, 2006. Before this essay-novel dedicated solely to Teresa, a similar hypothesis was put forward by R. M. Bell, *Holy Anorexia*, University of Chicago Press, 1985.

23. Steve Jobs, extract from a speech to the Stanford University Class of 2005, after being diagnosed with pancreatic cancer.

24. A Russian Jew who lived in Paris, Zaltzman was an original and important member of the contemporary psychoanalytical scene and, with Piera Aulagnier, a part of the Quatrième Groupe, a very active psychoanalytic organisation in France.

References

Ambrosiano, L. (2015). Sulla sublimazione: un percorso del destino del desiderio nella teoria e nella cura, *Rivista di Psicoanalisi*, 3: 803–814.

Ambrosiano, L. (2016). *Sublimazione e lavoro: passione, limite, nuove economie*, paper given at XVIII SPI Congress, Rome, May 2016.

Argentieri, S. (2005). Sublimazione: un concetto teoricamente scomodo e clinicamente ambiguo, *Psicoanalisi*, 1, 40–45.

Assoun, P.L. (1996). *Littérature et psychanalyse: Freud et la création littéraire*. Ellipses: Paris.

Aulagnier, P. (1979). *Les Destins du plaisir*. PUF: Paris.

Bell, R.M. (1985). *Holy Anorexia*. University of Chicago Press: Chicago.

Bergeret, J. (1994). *La violence et la vie*. Editions Payot et Rivages: Paris.

Bion, W.R. 1(965). *Transformations: Change from Learning to Growth*. Heinemann: London.

Bokanowski, T. (1989). Le concept de pulsion de mort, *Revue Francaise de psychanalyse*, 53: 504–536.

Bonasia, E. (1988). Pulsione di morte o terrore di morte? Una ricerca sul problema della morte in psicoanalisi, *Rivista di Psicoanalisi*, 34: 273–315.

Borgogno, F. and Viola, M. (1994). Pulsione di morte, *Rivista di Psicoanalisi*, 40: 459–483.

Botella, C. and Botella, S. (2001). *La figurabilité psychique*. Delachaux et Niestlé: Paris.

Bourgeois, L., Bernadac, M.L. and Obrist, H.U. (1998). *Destruction of the father, reconstruction of the father; writing and interviews, 1923–1997*. Violette Editions: London.

Bullitt-Jonas, M. (1998). *Holy Hunger*. Vintage Books: New York.

Chasseguet-Smirgel, J. (1999). *La maladie d'idéalité. Essay psychanalytique sur l'idéal du moi.* L'Harmattan: Paris.

Cimino, C. (2011). Estasi e perturbante. Nei dintorni di Thanatos. *Aut-Aut*, 252: 103–111.

Conrotto, F. (2008). Tra il sapere e la cura. Franco Angeli: Milan.

Conrotto, F. (2012). Pulsionalità tra azione e simbolizzazione, in *Metamorfosi della pulsione* (Eds. Munari F. and Mangini E.). Franco Angeli: Milan.

Conrotto, F. (2016). *Does the death drive really have anything to do with sublimation?*, paper given at XVIII SPI Congress, Rome, May 2016.

Couvreur, C. (1989). Une équation a deux inconnues, Revue Francaise de psychanalyse, 53: 643–660.

Cornut, J. (2002). *Le contre-investissement, butée contre la désintrication*, in www.spp.asso.fr/textes/contre-investissement-comme-butee-contre-la-desintrication-jean-cournut.

De M'Uzan, M. (1969). Le même et l'identique, *Revue Française de Psychanalyse*, 34: 441–453.

Denis, A. (2006). Principe de mort, destruction du sens, contresens, *Le vois nouvelles de la thérapie psychanalytique. Le dedans et le déhors* (Ed. Green A.). PUF: Paris.

Di Chiara, G. (2009). L'inconscio: denuncia di scomparsa, eppur rimuove . . ., *Rivista di Psicoanalisi*, 55: 343–358.

Doninotti, E. (2011). *Psicoanalisi della distruttività. La pulsione di morte*. Domenighini Editore: Padua, Italy.

Dufresne, T. (1983). *The Late Sigmund Freud*. Cambridge University Press: Cambridge.

Falci, A. (2005). Declinazioni del destino, *Rivista di Psicoanalisi*, 51: 799–822.

Feldman, M. (2000). Some views on the manifestations of the death instincts in clinical work, *The International Journal of Psycho-Analysis*, 81: 53–65.

Freud, S. (1895). *Project for a Scientific Psychology*. S.E., *1*. Hogarth: London.

Freud S. (1908). *'Civilized' Sexual Morality and Modern Nervous Illness, S.E., 9.* Hogarth: London.

Freud, S. (1911). *Formulations on the Two Principles of Mental Functioning. S.E., 12.* Hogarth: London.

Freud, S. (1915). *Thoughts For The Times On War And Death. S.E., 14.* Hogarth: London.

Freud, S. (1915). *Instincts and their Vicissitudes. S.E., 14.* Hogarth: London.

Freud, S. (1920). *Beyond the Pleasure Principle. S.E., 18.* Hogarth: London.

Freud, S. (1921). *Group Psychology and the Analysis of the Ego. S.E., 18.* Hogarth: London.

Freud, S. (1923). *The Ego and the Id. S.E., 19.* Hogarth: London.

Freud, S. (1924). The Economic Problem of Masochism. *S.E., 19.* Hogarth: London.

Freud, S. (1930). *Civilization and Its Discontents. S.E., 21.* Hogarth: London.

Freud, S. (1938). *An Outline of Psychoanalysis. S.E., 23.* Hogarth: London.

Freud, S. (1963). *Psychoanalysis and Faith: The Letters of Sigmund Freud and Oscar Pfister.* Hogarth: London.

Giaconia, G. (2005). *Adolescenza e etica.* Borla: Rome.

Galimberti, F. (2000). *Wilfred R. Bion.* Mondadori: Milan.

Green, A. (1983). *Narcissisme de vie, narcissisme de mort.* Les Editions de Minuit: Paris.

Green, A. (1990). *La folie privée. Psychanalyse deccas limites.* Gallimard: Paris.

Green, A. (1993). *Le travail du négatif.* Les Editions de Minuit: Paris.

Green, A. (2010). *Illusion et désillusion du travail psychanalytique.* Odile Jacob: Paris.

Hinshelwood, R. (1989). *Dictionary of Kleinian thoughts.* Free Association Books: New York.

Kavaler-Adler, S. (1993). *The Compulsion to Create: A Psychoanalytic Study of Women Artists.* Routledge: London.

Khan, L. (2005). Destino del destino. *Rivista di Psicoanalisi*, 51(2): 413–432.

Lacan, J. (1956). The Seminar on 'The Purloined Letter', *Écrits, Yale French Studies*, 48: 39–72 (1973).

Laplanche, J. (1970). *Vie et mort en psychoanalyse.* Flammarion: Paris.

Laplanche, J. and Pontalis J.B. (1967). *Vocabulaire de la psychanalyse.* PUF: Paris.

Le Guen, C. (1989). Du bon usage de la pulsion de mort, *Revue française de psychanalyse*, 53: 535–554.

Levi, P. (1986). *The Drowned and the Saved* (First Vintage International Edition, 1989).

Mangini, E. (2014). Pulsione e rimozione nella tela di Penelope, in *Metamorfosi della pulsione.* Franco Angeli: Milan.

Pasche, F. (2000). *Le passé recompose: Pensée, mythes, praxis.* PUF: Paris.

Petrella, F. (2005). I disagi della psicoanalisi nella post-modernità, *Psiche*, 2: 30–45.

Pontalis, J.B. (1988). *Perdre de vue.* Gallimard: Paris.

Rabain, J.-F. (1989). Compte rendu du colloque sur la pulsion de mort, *Revue Française de Psychanalyse*, 53: 767–780.

Resta, C. (2016). Freud e la guerra: pulsioni di morte, *La filosofia e la Grande Guerra* (Ed. Amato P.). Mimesis: Milan.

Ribas, D. (1989). Pulsion de mort et temps, *Revue Française de Psychanalyse*, 2: 987–1004.

Ribas, D. (2006). Destructivité et désintrications pulsionelle, in *Collection Pluriels de la Psyché* (Ed. Cupa D.). EDK: Paris.

Riolo, F. (2015). Eidolopioesi. *Psiche*, 2: 147–150.

Roussillon, R. (2000). Paradoxes et pluralité de la pulsion de mort, l'identité de pérception, in *L'Invention de la pulsion de mort* (Ed. Guillaumin J.). Dunot: Paris.

Sandler, J. and Freud, A. (1985). *The analysis of defence.* International Universities Press: New York.

Scarfone, D. (2004). *Les Pulsions.* PUF: Paris

Schmidt-Hellerau, C. (2000). *Pulsion de vie, pulsion de mort. Libido et Léthé.* Delachaux et Niestlé: Paris.

Sega, H. (1993). On the clinical usefulness of the concept of death instinct, *The International Journal of Psycho-Analysis*, 74: 55–61.

Spielrein, S. (1912). Destruction as a cause of coming into being, *Journal of Analytical Psychology*, 39: 155–186 (1994).

Stekel, W. (1907). *Conditions of Nervous Anxiety and Their Treatment.* Routledge: London (1923).

Urribarri, F. (2013). An interview with Andre Green: on a psychoanalytic journey from 1960 to 2011, in *The Greening of Psychoanalysis: Andre Green's New Paradigm in Contemporary Theory and Practice* (Eds. Kohon G. and Perelberg R.). Karnac: London.

Valdrè, R. (2015). *On sublimation, a path to the destiny of desire, theory and treatment*. Karnac: London

Vecchio, S. (2016). Pourquoi la pulsion de déstruction ou de mort? *Psiche*, 1: 295–301.

Winnicott, D. (1939). Aggression, in *The Collected Works of D.W. Winnicott, Volume 2* (Eds. Caldwell L and H. Taylor Robinson). Oxford University Press: Oxford (2016).

Winnicott, D. (1965). *Maturational Processes and the Facilitating Environment: Studies in the Theory of Emotional Development*. London: Hogarth Press.

Zaltzman, N. (1997). La pulsione anarchiste. In *De le guérison psychanalitique* (Ed. Zaltzman N.). Paris: PUF.

Žižek, S. (2006). *How to Read Lacan*. Granta Books: London.

2

IN THE CLINIC

The search for Nirvana: Nando

"Don't let me think, please!"

As well as an Oblomovian anti-hero, in our first sessions Nando sends a simple message to me, "Do whatever you want, but don't let me think, please!" It is a contemporary and sincere statement exhibiting ambiguity between extreme passivity (do whatever you want) and extreme opposition (*don't* let me think). From the first and difficult sessions I find Nando "nice" in countertransference. He does not wear a mask of stupid activities, dull enterprises or fake conformities.

As a consequence of a long past of dependence on various substances (alcohol, cocaine, psychedelic mushrooms and so on) and today of a massive use of cannabis, Nando seems to have become immunised against every lie. Quite simply, Nando *doesn't feel like* doing anything, even lying is hard for him. Furthermore, as a consequence of many meetings with therapists, psychiatrists and community recoveries to which his mother sent him in vain and to which he went passively, he feels discouraged that I can help and understand him. Although he is free of the heaviest and most destructive addictions, he does not understand what to do with his life, which appeared to be suspended in a sort of limbo in which he lost every chance to graduate (he abandoned university, of course) and every sort of job, no matter if important or not. He dreams of becoming a licensed producer of cannabis. Unfortunately, he cannot realise it: he would have to live in places like California but does not want to ("I lost my opportunity, now the market is too saturated . . . I should have tried before . . . and I have too many problems by now . . ."). His mother still has some hope: she is aware of the benefits of her analysis, sends him to me. She is frantic. This is probably his *last chance*: by now, Nando is 30 years old, he is free of the most destructive dependencies but he does not do anything in his life. The question is: what to do with him?

I know that the chances of success are slim. He appears unable to represent and dream; sedated and in oblivion due to the many joints he smokes, and impulsive and aggressive when their effect wears off or when certain frustrations stimulate him too much; without any plans, just a vague idea of escaping somewhere (he thinks of activities that could make him rich without working or of going to live in countries where he could produce cannabis legally). His thought is concrete, his way of speech is punctuated by pauses that do not signal reflection but rather "mental holes," white and empty areas without any thought. This is Nirvana. With Nando I was fortunate in being able to conduct a complete analysis and I think that, more than any other patient I've had in many years who showed a tendency towards zero tension due to drugs or other substances, Nando is a paradigm of what Freud meant when he proposed the concept of the death drive. It is important to stress that "don't let me think!" is Nando's maxim, like an Oblomov character, as described by Pontalis (1988), was he a melancholic, possessed, anguished and wrecked by the lost object? It would not appear so, as he does not bear the tormented and suspicious traits of the melancholic. On the contrary, Pontalis asserts, he seems cheerful and his condition can be called apathy or indifference with lying down the best position for maintaining it with inactivity as a basic principle . . . perhaps the only form of hate living in this sweet, sensitive man is a *hate of time* (Pontalis, 1993, p. 43)

I face a paradox: how can I analyse someone who explicitly asks *not to think*? There is the other side of the death drive: aggression. Although in the previous chapter I focus on the distinction between death drive in its pure form and aggression, it is the mix between the two occurring in Nando that led me to agree to help him. There is an extraordinary energy in him for feeling so much hate (for example, against his parents), so much rage against the most minimal obstacles and such a desperate need to be loved. He was engaged once, but the engagement ended two years before our analysis. He has many friends, some very important, some former drug addicts and some not. I think that Nando can have affective relationships and be loved and "tolerated" in spite of his passiveness and his excessively aggressive behaviours.

As usually happens to me in situations in which it is the analyst's counter-transference that does most of the work for most of the time, it is what I feel in the first sessions that compels me to agree to start the analysis, that makes me accept his conditions: "I will start the analysis, but I do not intend to take psycho-pharmacological drugs, they make me feel very bad, I cannot quit smoking, it makes me feel aggressive and I cannot sleep . . . at least not for now."

It is clear that the death drive is present in Nando, but it appears less pronounced than during his adolescence, which he describes as characterised by apathy and alcoholic oblivion. This means that other drives are trying to emerge in him. In fact, why would Nando accept coming to my consulting room four times a week to carry out something on himself that he does not fully understand but perhaps, in a deep area of his mind, must see as a chance? My acceptance of his "conditions" (and I want to stress that I accepted them as something necessary at the technical level), my lack of surprise and judgment, my sincere interest in his life and mind, which he considers "void and wasted," must have led Nando to trust me. Now, he lives abroad with his girlfriend and works part-time in real estate. Here I will refer only to those aspects of his analysis (that lasted five years) relevant to our topic, that is, the death drive and its destinies.

In his first year of analysis Nando cannot dream and freely associate, he can only switch between aggression and oblivion. Sometimes I realise he arrives in the consulting room completely stoned, but I prefer not to verbalise it. These are the "Nirvana sessions." He is completely immersed in his Léthé (Schmidt-Hellerau, 2001), he sails this river of forgetfulness that he knows very well. He does not care about anything, has no memories. I feel that on a technical level it would be an error to offer interpretations in these sessions: it would even be impossible. How can we represent something unrepresentable? Moreover, I feel that it would be an error to destroy such a strong defence mechanism at this point that would risk losing and exposing Nando too much. In this phase I don't want interruptions or negative therapeutic effects. I choose to listen to him and make my associations without verbalising them, I am able to think, I don't feel blocked. Similarly, to the Oblomovian anti-hero, but with a higher degree of internal aggression, in these moments Nando is in a mental state difficult to describe in words. The main feature of these moments is the absence of *words* or language or a symbolic structure. I quickly realise that *Nando does not feel anything*. He is not angry in these "Nirvana sessions," has neither friends nor enemies nor the pain consequent to an impossible desire nor the struggle for the lack of an unreachable object. He can sleep well, without dreams, nightmares or demons: he has no tension. He has spent many years in the mental states that now characterise his analysis and his life.

> What I lost was the sense of *the rhythm of time*, its silence, and its waits. (. . .) It is easy to have an aim in life and fully enjoy it: remove it. We have very few aims and desires.
>
> (Nove, 2010, p. 32, my italics, translated for this edition)[1]

Time. Pontalis' *Oblomov* and the reports of those who had lived for many years in these artificial paradises focus on the role of time: time disappears. These mental states allow elimination of the painful dimension of time, that is, that time reminds us of our commitments, responsibilities and, above all, our transience, It is rather mysterious but, apart from the odd occasion when he gets the time wrong, even when he is in these mental states, Nando *always* comes to our sessions. In these sessions he brings what Nove calls the enjoyment, the *jouissance*, of not having any aim. I think of another young patient I met many years ago who lost himself in a similar fog: I realise that the death drive is so strong, seductive, hypnotic and pleasant that it leads many people, someone clever like Nando or Nove, to choose the nothing instead of the pain or the avoidance of any investment.

In countertransference, I experience interchangeable moments in which I am fully aware and alert (To what? To Nando's nothing, of course, a nothing that I can listen to in the moments in which I don't lose focus) and moments in which my mind wanders. So, too, there are rare moments in which I feel sleepy. In a certain sense, I find these sessions less difficult than the sessions in which Nando is hostile and furious. What I find difficult in these sessions is that they are uncommon and the only *moments for staying together in a shared area of Nirvana.* I do not feel infected. I wait. I only make brief comments because I feel that at the moment Nando cannot tolerate longer or more cutting comments. When he argues that it is "useless to come to the sessions, it is the way I am, completely empty . . . ," I simply reply that it is ok, that he brings me himself the way he is and that I appreciate his effort to remember and to come to our sessions. I add that for us, his "emptiness" is a "fullness" that we will give a meaning to when he gradually is able to do without.

> Patient (Nando): I am a child, I am at primary school. I have a backpack on my shoulders, a big backpack, not for children. . . .

Here comes the first dream. Nando reports it "to make me happy." He does not provide any association except that when he was a child at primary school he was happy and his parents had not yet separated (a very difficult separation for his parents and a painful time for Nando as an adolescent) and he was very good at school, perhaps one of the best pupils in his class.

> Analyst (Rossella): Perhaps you desire to feel good, I mean, to be as that child before "everything happened" (I quote him back to himself) . . . but you carry a heavy burden, a very heavy burden. . . .

There is *desire*: the engine of life restarts with difficulty. Nando was not so deprived that he never experienced contact with a good object; rather, he experienced and lost it and, as the child showing antisocial tendencies (Winnicott, 1984), he never found comfort for this loss. However, there is some hope. I do not want to insist with the word *hope* because I know that for such patients it can feel like a persecution if often mentioned. As the veteran Italian film director Mario Monicelli points out, *hope is a trap*. I know I must not imagine progress or have expectations that Nando might deem illusions. I know that when the Nirvana phase finishes I will have to face the death drive, which will soon come around in its noisy, annoying and considerable forms, such as repetition compulsion and negative therapeutic reaction.

> (. . .) and (I) begin to hope, like so many times before, that my heart explodes, that my brain erupts, and that the death dance can resolve, for once and finally, in death.

(Clegg, 2012, pp. 99, 100)[2]

Here it is necessary to refer to theory. How does Freud discover the death drive, which is mute by its nature, and if the din of life comes from Eros?

Although *Beyond the Pleasure Principle* appears as a theoretical work, it is from clinical practice that Freud starts his reflections. Quite surprisingly, clinical practice allows Freud to focus on apparently incomprehensible phenomena falsifying the idea that our lives are based on the pleasure principle. If so, it would follow that people aim to recover and feel good. But things are different and for Freud this is a perturbing discovery. The idea that the pleasure principle is the guarantor of mental life is problematic: patients do not get better, they seem to be possessed by a "demonic force" leading them to seek pain, to regress, to eliminate the wellbeing they reached through analysis. They start to repeat childhood or recent traumatic experiences and lose coping strategies they previously used to try and deal with them and are paradoxically the reason for starting analysis in the first place. Because the death drive does not appear in its pure or noisy form, Freud postulates its existence on the basis of four specific phenomena: (1) the dreams of traumatised people, as described in the first chapter, in particular those affected by *war neuroses*, who, instead of forgetting, continue to dream of their traumatic experiences; (2) *repetition compulsion;* (3) *negative therapeutic reaction* and (4) on a more theoretical level, the observation of *the Fort/Da game* he accidentally observed in his grandchild Ernst. In this game, the child was able to tolerate the absence of his mother by interiorising her and *transforming something passive into something active.*

The death drive in all its forms is apparent in Nando, sometimes mixed with Eros. In the first part of his analysis, as well as in most of his adolescence and early adulthood, Nando mainly seeks Nirvana, the oblivion, the sleep, the retirement, the quiet after the disinvestment. He is moved by the maxim "*Don't let me think, please!*" as an imperative need, in order "(. . .) to restore an earlier state of things" (Freud, 1920, p. 36). Mangini (2014) is right when he argues that these states play a fundamental role in the process of subjectivisation and "are also signals, as well as *silence*, of *necessary breaks* essential for an adequate mental functioning" (p. 73, translated for this edition). Nando's silent breaks are not all alike: sometimes it is as if he has fallen into the mires of Nirvana and no one is able to pull him out, and other breaks are certainly those "necessary" ones that are essential for psychic working out. These breaks are more mature and constructive than the apparent verbose saturations in some patients who seem able to freely associate but that actually pose hindrances to any genuine access to themselves. These saturations are also hindrances for the analyst, who is deceived by all this associative capacity but is actually excluded from the patient's internal world.

When Nirvana starts to disappear, Nando ups his aggression. This is the most difficult part of the analysis. Mostly his parents, and sometimes some people from the external world, are the targets of his limitless hate and uninterrupted anger, guilty of every act and deserving reprimand. Nando argues that his parents are guilty of having broken up badly and at an inopportune moment for him; he defines his mother as "crazy" and his father as "severe and unaffective," unable to have found a job for him, thus reporting an omnipotent fantasy eliminating every responsibility. In fact, he fantasises that *his parents*, and not he, must *make amends* for what they stole from him. His hate extends to his city and Italy in general that, despite having some realistic features, are representations of the mother, Mother Earth: all must make amends. The content of the few dreams – always brief, without associations, and served up without showing any importance or representational intention – he reports in this central part of the analysis is persecutory: Nando is chased, robbed, molested. I confront the most discouraging phase for every psychoanalyst: after many sessions and periods that seem to lead to new representations or more symbolic forms of expression, to novel perspectives on his internal world, here comes the negative therapeutic reaction. Nando does not come to some sessions, often completely *forgets* what emerged in the previous sessions, falls back into auto-aggressive and hetero-aggressive behaviour or into substance use "as before." As Freud proposes in *Beyond the Pleasure Principle* (1920), the expulsion of what is bad and hateful outside the self is necessary in order to save the self and attests the violent arrival of Eros, that is, those life drives to which narcissism must refer for protecting life. In fact, it is worth noting that in the interplay between fusion and defusion the reflection of Eros and Thanatos intersects with the theory of narcissism, which Freud discusses in 1915:

> Through narcissism, the life drive defends the Ego and blocks its destruction.
> (Vecchio, 2016, p. 296)

The transition from the peaceful Nirvana, without conflicts and waits, without hate and love, to a state that can be called *mors tua vita mea* characterised by hate for the objects, by negative therapeutic reactions, by repetition compulsion is a necessary passage. In Nando's case, the *mors tua vita mea* comes from potentially conflicting situations, especially with his mother. I agree with Green (2011) that negative therapeutic reactions can be nothing but a phase of the analysis and must not be mistaken for failures. These reactions must be attentively assessed and considered because they reveal a reversal from pleasure to displeasure, which works in the field of the death drive.

In this phase Nando acquires a new energy that to his great satisfaction allows him to go regularly to the gym – along with analysis, the gym will be his "grid," as he calls it, necessary for pulling himself together and "relieving," but also for shaping a better Ego Ideal through body care – and to travel and meet people not only for smoking joints but also for hiking, fishing and doing sports. Those passions and activities blocked during the long years of oblivion are reactivated. In the sessions, he shows a histrionic form of verbal aggression that is seldom directed towards me: he considers me as an object to preserve or at worst to indirectly attack through negative therapeutic reactions. He says that he would rock the world, he is angry with the drivers in the streets, causes trouble to his friends, etc. However, after some days or weeks, Nando changes his mind, shows remorse and sadness for these expressions and for having ended a friendship, removed a person or offended a relative. Sometimes he tries to fix the damage done.

After passing through Nirvana, aggression and compulsion, to oversimplify an immensely challenging analysis, Nando starts the crucial phase of the first *investments*. Brief dreams introduce this phase.

> Patient (Nando): I was going to buy a ticket (. . .) perhaps for a flight (. . .) maybe.

These investments can be found in the almost recurring dream of "being with a girl (. . .) an undefined girl (. . .) I don't know what we were doing, how I would like (. . .) I'm tired of being around men all the time" and in parallel those everyday decisions and choices that for many years had been almost impossible. It is as if Nando is regaining his potentialities represented in the dream of the child with a backpack on his shoulders. Now the backpack is lighter than before because it can be shared with me. This means that Nando can try to go beyond that "white" protection of disinvestment, as Green suggests. This part of the analysis is thorny and characterised by fear. In fact, when we do not have protection anymore and we do not risk abandonment or betrayal, we can return to life and decide to return to our passions but we must face many fears: would we be abandoned or deceived again? Could we trust *ourselves* and others? Now Nando is aware that, when he will invest in something, he will have to be responsive, on time and able to account for himself. To abandon what Joseph (1982) calls *the addiction to near-death*, that is, that drug addiction able to catch so many young people, must be tremendously difficult. I believe no defence is so powerful as disinvestment – for Nando this appears in the form of Nirvana and thus of *near-death*; in other cases it can be different, for example, it can have autistic features – for keeping us safe against potential disillusions and possible abandonment of the object.

As Joseph (1982, p. 449) says, "(. . .) just to die, although attractive, would be no good. There is a felt need to be aware of and to attend to one's destruction." Nando as an adolescent was simply attending to his self-destruction (and making his parents attend through blaming them). It is plausible that, as a typical adolescent and as occurs always in analysis in similar cases, Nando faced death everyday in order to blame his parents and to keep them in suspense and also in order to feel alive and to have that identity he did not have. The risk illusorily led Nando to believe that he had control. He perversely felt himself to be the centre of a world from which he was excluded and abandoned and to *be noticed* by an imaginary audience, with his relatives in the front row that must continually focus on him. His "personal fairy tale" (Francesconi and Zanetti, 2009) took him outside reality and autistically protected him through the action of the mute drive of his personal Nirvana.

I completely agree with those who argue that the true autism (and not the mere presence of some autistic nuclei) is the most extreme form of disinvestment. Of course, this was not the case for Nando. In fact, I would not have experienced him as "nice" in the first countertransference if he had been completely disinvested from the world of objects. I explain this countertransference as a consequence of a projective identification able to accept that vital part hidden but not absent in him. In other words, Nando did not depend on the near-death and did not show a full disinvestment at all.

Nando was an aggressive and dynamic child and an extremely intelligent and passionate boy with a frail narcissistic structure of personality. In a difficult phase such as pre-adolescence, this structure had exposed him to a painful fear of being abandoned and an expectation of being compensated for this abandonment. He protests against his objects through a massive use of drugs and anti-social behaviour. Thus, he is able to keep his objects continually alert and to avenge himself for their lack of attention to him. The price he pays for this is the complete suspension of life development and the refuge in that peace that drugs can offer.

On a technical level, I think that in this analysis it is crucial to tolerate and *respect* the near-death path – this is paradoxical given that Nando regularly comes to the sessions – he proposes to me: *don't let me think!* For a certain (necessary) time I do not let him think, at least not too much: I do it for him. With these patients the analyst must do the most work especially in the long first phases. The analyst must do it through a careful use of countertransference, reveries, those dreams she is able to dream in the patient's place and to work through in her mind. Because Nando considers me as the only object able to tolerate him and to give a meaning to his nonsense, he infrequently attacks me and, when he does, he is always in touch with me. For example, every time he does not want to come to a session, he sends several text messages in order to *test* that I am still at his disposal: Nando knows that he can always come back to me and that I will never accuse or judge him. When Nando starts to make his first investments (travel, part-time work, girlfriends), I support them in the analysis but without showing *too many* expectations towards them: if Nando had felt these excessive expectations, he would have soon relapsed into negative reactions and compulsions. These expectations are certainly connected to those his parents had of him. Although problematic and broken, his family was wealthy and educated and he was the only one in his family who did not finish university. Expectation is probably his major threat: in his past he did not meet many expectations either towards his primary objects or himself. Now he is able to feel me as an analyst as someone able to accept him whatever he is going to do, to give a relatively unconditional "love," although he is aware that fully unconditional love does not exist. Rather, when the investments start to become more concrete and substantial, I support them either through the interpretation of the above-mentioned brief dreams or through more explicative than interpretative interventions. (As an aside, in Nando's analysis I find it difficult to provide interpretations, as if they were something to satisfy my narcissism and not his needs.) For example, about *his* desire *to buy a ticket, to fly* high, I argue that the ticket has a price to be paid and that the flight could be cancelled, the airplane crash, the trip a disappointment. I am lucky: Nando always accepts the use of metaphors and we even use them every time a discourse, a word, an interpretation seems to be forced into an impasse.

After another important phase of mourning, Nando gives up the California dream of his adolescence. Following a satisfactory, happy and constructive vacation, the purchase of a plane ticket to an Asian country leads him to finish analysis. In fact, in that country he meets a "less complicated girl than those living here, a girl who does not know my past," sees a possibility of working in real estate with an Italian he met there, of accessing his passions such as sports and the outdoors, and of having difficulty in buying hashish ("this could really help me . . . there I smoke less, you know, I don't feel like smoking very much and above all I must be always smart and alert"). The fact that Nando has some passions he did not create during analysis but ones that were already present in him, is his safety net: there exist in him old and childish investments that the fear of living cancelled but did not obliterate. After returning from the holiday, he plans to move there but with an open ticket, in case he feels like coming back.

I am perfectly aware that this conclusion can appear as nothing but the umpteenth escape, another paradise far away from an inadequate Mother Earth. I do not deny that it is partially an escape. Nonetheless, I think that this is Nando's only alternative to psychic or even physical death. He comes to visit me twice, 3 months and then 6 months after moving, just to renew his visa.

About the country in which he now lives, he says:

> Patient (Nando): They have a different concept of life and death from us . . . especially for the old people living in rural areas, like my girlfriend's parents, it is a whole, how I can say, you are born, you live, you die, *living and dying are fused together*, and they do not kick up a fuss when someone is born or dies. I do not want to say that I agree with them . . . I thought back to my analysis when I was there, I actually think about it very often, I miss it but there it does not exist at all, and I know I can write to you whenever I want . . . well I don't precisely know why I thought of my analysis there . . . I think that those simple people *had understood something we are not able to understand*.

Forget yourself. ————

(Henry Miller)[3]

Masochism and attaches on the Self: Jade

> (. . .) Her eyes are, as required, deep blue, gray,
> dark, merry, full of pointless tears.
> She sleeps with him as if she's first in line or the only one on
> Earth.
> She'll bear him four children, no children, one.
> Naive, but gives the best advice.
> Weak, but takes on anything.
> (. . .) Can't figure out this bolt and builds a bridge.
> Young, young as ever, still looking young.

(. . .) Where's she running, isn't she exhausted.
Not a bit, a little, to death, it doesn't matter.
She must love him, or she's just plain stubborn. (. . .)

(W. Szymborska, *Portrait of a Woman*, 1976/1998, p. 161)

I don't want to propose some simplistic connections and to risk proposing a psychoanalytic discourse on gender. I am aware that masochism and femininity are two words open to simplification. Nonetheless, if I look at my professional and personal experience, I can say the attraction for the Nirvana of drugs is more common in men, whereas the so-called masochistic problems, the struggles, the most painful annihilations of the narcissistic structure, the mental submissions in women. After this necessary premise, I want to present a summary of the analysis of Jade, a patient who presents all the various expressions of this side of the death drive. As with Nando, I do not make generalisations, especially on gender – and I stress that it is always a person who suffers, male or female. Thus I will focus on those features relevant for my arguments only. Nonetheless, more than the case of Nando, that of Jade offers many ideas and suggestions that deserve to be explored. I will not deal with the issue of hysteria and the multiple hysterical identifications the patient provided, the repeated and surprising varieties of enactments in which she presented all the deeply split parts of her self that were slowly integrated. What clearly appears from the start of Jade's long and complex analysis is the relevance of her macroscopic repetition compulsions (her choice of men, two partners with narcissistic, abusive and disturbed personalities), her repetitive list of physical self-harm – obviously much of which was due to a conversion mechanism – for which she visits many physicians and subjects herself to painful and useless surgeries, her indefinite search for harmful or at least difficult experiences.

"Where's she running? Isn't she exhausted?"

Where are you running, Jade? Aren't you exhausted? Would you take a rest from your grief on this couch?

She is a pretty 45-year-old woman. She brings her struggle of life to me. Her look does not reveal any struggle: she is elegant, smart, controlled in gesture and speech, a little shy. Nevertheless, I immediately feel the *running* described by the great poetess, the constant running of a woman who, as I can see throughout analysis, persists in her efforts to reach the frustrating (and thus elusive by its nature) object, but clings to it, does not let it go, continues to consume it even when the food coming from the object becomes a poison. Differently from Nando, Jade is a *dreaming* patient and, with the report of her first dream, she sends me the message that I will encounter many difficulties:

Patient (Jade): A difficult client came to the bank. She is very arrogant, she is very difficult to deal with . . .

She has been working at a bank for many years. She is a recognised expert in financial investment and she knows that the client in the dream thinks she is always right and tests everyone's patience. As we can see, her unconscious cooperated with me from the outset: it helps me to become aware that the educated, gentle and compliant woman coming to me in order to *invest her personal resources and emotions* in the analysis bank is not Jade in all her entirety. There is also another woman, who wants to do as she pleases. She is trying to separate from her husband. Her long, highly detailed, sometimes obsessively repeated reports about him and their life together occupy all her mental field and our analytic field for a long time.

Her husband M. is an "idol" for her. She adores him in an almost surprising way for a clever and elegant woman as she is. She describes M. as fascinating, seductive and excellent in drawing. She likes drawing, too, but does not reach the professional levels of M., who organises exhibitions abroad. However, for M. drawing is only a hobby because he is not able to earn much money from it. It is Jade who earns money with her job at the bank and supports M. financially. M. humiliates her for many years: he demands sexual practices she does not like at all and sometimes finds unpleasant or painful; he mistreats her in public, especially with those friends linked to the artistic circles because "I had never been ok enough for him: too fat, too thin, too solitary, too well- or too badly-dressed;" he does not take care of her when she is ill; he does not want a son or daughter, he fears being overshadowed by a child. Very briefly, a long road of carelessness, some beautiful moments, the allure of following him to the art exhibitions where she could show her own drawings, often appreciated by the viewing public. In parallel with this difficult relationship, Jade has "another life," a life in which she silently destroys her body, in which she has a long sequence of "somatisations. (. . .) Most physicians tell me I am ok, but sometimes one of them finds something and wants to operate. My friend P. is a physician and cannot bear any more of my visits. And then I often fall down or slip . . ." She remembers a long period with a broken arm and M. does not take care of her in any way. She also suffers from itches, anal fissures, migraines and she now realises that all these things can have a psychological origin: "It is as if I wanted all this suffering, in a certain sense . . . I don't know, perhaps I want to draw attention to myself . . . but I really feel poorly."

Before marrying M., when she was young and worked in another city, she had an even worse relationship with S., a pervert quite similar to her husband: "At the time, he had more success than M., it was as if he had hypnotised me, I moved in with him but it did not last very long, at a certain point I ran away. Women liked him a lot, as much as they liked M., he entered a room and wanted to be noticed, to be flirted with. In private he was violent, obscene, he wanted to do obscene things . . . now I realise that he was disturbed but at the time of our relationship I indulged him, I thought I was wrong if I did not find pleasure with him and give pleasure to him, if I was disgusted by what he demanded of me . . . I believe I would have died if I had remained with him." Her first steady boyfriend had been problematic and abusive, too. Perhaps he had been an alcoholic as well, she confides.

Jade is perfectly aware of her *deadly* repetition of the *identical* (de M'Uzan, 1977) but she asks herself why she did not realise it before and had to risk psychic or even physical death before seeking help.

The primary motivation for analysis is to separate from M. She looks like a sort of Emma Bovary who brought down her idol and thus, as Flaubert writes, the idol's gilding sticks to her fingers. I am surprised, and I make her notice this, that in these critical situations she is *always able to save herself*: she wants to save herself from those frustrating circumscribed situations she describes to me, from the sadistic S. whom she fled with the help of a friend, from her husband M. who ambivalently attracts her. The repetition of the identical seems to mix in with the repetition of the same, as usually happens: both these types of repetition compulsion, one deadly and the other able to elaborate, as distinguished above, can be found in this complex woman. She replies to me that she has never realised this but that it is true: "Every time I'm in a tight corner, I'm able to save myself. I certainly do not accept all the cosmetic surgery they suggest." When suffering reaches a certain limit or, from another perspective, when the amount of unconscious pleasure and secondary gain is diminished in her overall instinctual balance, Jade saves herself. At that point, she is resolute and firm, she does not change her mind. In other words, the death drive cannot go all the way: at a certain point, for reasons that were mysterious and now are clear thanks to the immense help of analysis – Jade will define analysis as a lifesaver – the link with Eros seems to be stronger, narcissism is able to protect her abused Ego or, according to another perspective, there is an integration of the different split aspects of her self.

There is nothing mysterious about her relationships with S. and M.: both trace back to a primary object, the mother, a distant, hypercritical and "always ill" mother, to whom, it is worth noting, the father gives all his attention. On one hand, Jade identifies with this mother, especially when she is ill and seeks doctors; on the other, she continues to seek love objects that repeat her mother's distance, hypercriticism and indifference.

Is Jade unlucky because she meets only this type of man? No. In the first two years of her analysis Jade meets a completely different man: he is sympathetic, welcoming. She tries to date him, but she underestimates him, she seems to be annoyed by him. This is a typical modality I find in some of my female patients: they suffer with an abusive object but, when they find a different kind of object, they underestimate and humiliate it. They are unable to accept something good.

> Patient (Jade): I realise I treat him like M. treated me . . . it's incredible! I don't know why . . . there is nothing about him that I can accept, how he dresses, how he eats, how he speaks . . . but he loves me . . .

Now masochistic Jade is becoming sadistic. This is an example of how the death drive can easily overturn. So, too, the dependence is overturned: E., the new and good fiancé, is a sort of puppet in her hands. However, it is worth noting that:

> Patient (Jade): You know, I do not enjoy it . . . I feel guilty. It is true, it is as if, with a "normal man," *I* wanted to dress in my mother's clothes, in S.'s, in M.'s . . . but the difference is that they all enjoyed it, in their eyes I always saw a perverted pleasure, especially in M.'s. But that is not the case with me: it is the contrary. The fact is that *I can't do without* criticising him in that moment, but soon after I regret it, I feel like a *bad person* . . .

In fact, Jade decides to start analysis. A part of her wants to be able to accept the good or, to use a typical metaphor of our relationship, to get the small stomach of a concentration camp survivor – concentration camps haunt her first dreams – used to tiny quantities of good and not poisoned food. For her, it is crucial to understand the difference between the way she behaves with E. and the way M. and S. behave with her in order to not feel guilty: M. and S. enjoy humiliating her, for them it is the kind of *joy of attending a massacre* Nietzsche describes for both a crowd or an individual, whereas she feels guilty, ungrateful, crazy. Thus, she does not understand and asks for some help from an analyst. It is important to stress that a hypercritical component and thus very strong Super-Egoical aspects reside in her and work against her, another feature I find in many female patients. Jade is not open to pleasure: she likes drawing but she thinks she has no talent and feels herself to be lesser than M.; she does not enjoy sex, she engaged in it only to not humiliate the partner; she seldom takes some rest; she exerts strong control over the quantities of food she eats. She is the first object of the disease of reaching something ideal, if not of sadism. In this sense, her aggressive drives are free to go against herself and welcoming and accommodating objects such as E.

The analytic relationship is the only place in which she can talk about her "obscenities" without being judged. She is grateful for it. The question is, how is all this (self-inflicted, projected, searched) *evil* in Jade's life displayed in the analytic relationship?

> We have been struck by the fact that the forgotten and repressed experiences of childhood are reproduced during the work of analysis in dreams and reactions, particularly in those occurring in the transference, although their revival runs counter to the interest of the pleasure principle.
>
> (Freud, 1933, p. 105)

Even after having discovered the death inside life, Freud is surprised. It is the same for me. Until the end of analysis Jade has recurring traumatic dreams: at the beginning they are the only dreams appearing in her unconscious theatre; later they are infrequent, perhaps to stress not only the return of her traumas, but also to show how her mind keeps and will always keep these traumas in memory.

Patient (Jade): I'm in my father's home, where I grew up, in my room . . . oh my God, it's a painful place . . . but I'm happy to find P. (her new partner, he is completely different and "new" compared to her previous ones) and my beloved dog, Mary. I see that Mary has a big hole inside, she bleeds . . .

This is one of the dreams Jade reports near the end of analysis. She is now both able to associate herself with the returned trauma of a childhood spent in a house where suffering was the only form of existence and to share the dream with her new partner, P., a man she meets during analysis, who, "completely new" for her, is neither abusive nor sadistic nor neglecting, a man who is able to love her and to be loved by her, a man she does not humiliate or underestimate. Indeed, at the end of analysis Jade is able to recognise when she is moved by that internal destructive drive that leads her to humiliate him. In this dream she identifies with Mary and she can clearly see the big hole, the internal wound.

Patient (Jade): I know I have this wound. I will have it forever. But I must not and I cannot act in any way . . .

I make her notice that it is true, the old lives with the new. I point to a detail to which she seems to not attribute much relevance – perhaps this is because she does not value herself or, more than underestimating herself, she *does not see or consider herself – she is able to see the hole and take care of herself*. She is impressed by this detail: yes, I am. *I am*: it seems weird to say it! This is "the gold of subjectivity" (Semi, 2011): for every one of us subjectivity is the outcome of a difficult journey, but for some patients it is much more, it is a treasure they discover after a very long hunt. In my mind, I make an association with another patient, D., a woman involved in masochistic dynamics with her objectual choices, characterised by a tendency to hurt herself and with very low self-esteem. When she is able to feel that *she was herself*, that is, she is an aware subject, able to make difficult acts and choices but in a completely different way than before, she shouts out in a session: "I am! It's me!"

She becomes subject and object of her actions, of her life. It is an emotionally strong experience.

The same holds for Jade. The first dreams she reports are pure repetitions of a trauma (sometimes as deadly *repetition compulsion*, sometimes as an attempt at working through) in which she is *raped*, as she was as a child, *violated, humiliated, deprived*, taking the different forms that the processes of screening and compromise-formation give to the dreams. But, although they do not lose their traumatic aspects, the subsequent dreams have novel features, not only for the presence of P. as a new object but also for the presence of a new capacity to look *inside herself*. Further, they seem able to offer an integration of the split parts of her self and thus can be viewed as a sign of a recovered capacity of giving cohesion to her personality ("When I look in the mirror, I can see myself").

The death drive occurs in all its forms in both her analysis and life. In fact, after some sessions in which she is in strong touch with herself, Jade has surprising negative therapeutic reactions, which are typical also in D. These are repetition compulsions of behaviours that can be defined as "non-protection," that is, in which she seems to do everything to expose herself to something painful. A good example for explaining this perverted mechanism is the following dream she reports in the second year of analysis:

> Patient (Jade): . . . I'm going out . . . I notice I have left the book open
> . . .

The book is associated with the personal agenda with telephone numbers and addresses and should have been left *closed*. For Jade and me the *open book* becomes a useful metaphor through which she learns to recognise those situations in which, with the great but devious intelligence of a woman hurting herself, she exposes herself to the sadistic and humiliating attacks of the object (for example, trying to meet her ex-husband and proposing their old dynamics again) or of some parts of herself. I think that this aspect is the most harmful and also the most difficult to be observed both in my countertransference and in her life outside the analysis room. The dream of the *open book* becomes a recurring metaphor during the rest of the analysis and plays a crucial role in reducing her negative therapeutic reactions.

Now I want to refer to theory. In 1920 Freud discovered that every analysis shows negative therapeutic reactions. This is not a simple clinical fact; rather, it is the expression in the clinical work and thus in the transference of the theoretical relevance of the death drive. In other words, it is one of the ways through which the analyst can be in touch with the death drive.

As Green (2011) points out, the analyst must not assume that only harmful experiences tend to repeat themselves: the positive and pleasant ones do, too. The analyst must focus on instinctual fusion and thus on repetition. Furthermore, the analyst must not confuse analytic "failure" with negative therapeutic reactions, which represent a specific aspect, sometimes something circumscribed, in general occurring after prolific analytic work. In this sense, these reactions appear as an inversion of the therapeutic process.

> Negativity thus seems to be the product of an inverted orientation. It is as if the aims had been reversed, giving priority to an orientation independent of the pleasure principle, or even contrary to it, following the paths traced by unpleasure. This paradoxical trajectory develops under the sway of prevalent masochism.
>
> (Green, 2010/2011, p. 46)

Masochism is certainly one of the main features of Jade's first life, as she calls it. It can be found in both her social and affective relationships and in her perception of herself and her body. In comparison with D., who was aware of her low self-esteem, Jade does not seem aware of how much she underestimates herself. It is clear that she does not have a high opinion of herself, but it is also clear that in some areas of her life, for example her job, she is appreciated, appreciates herself and is able to assert her rights. The point is that Jade *does not feel herself*, does not feel her own presence.

With regard to (primary) masochism, it is important to take a look at theory again. I agree with Green (1986) that masochism allow us to see the close connections between sexuality and the death drive, but is also one of the most controversial of Freud's notions. The central idea of Freud is that the death drive *is primarily directed towards our internal world* and can be directed towards the external world only *a posteriori*. Some aspects of Jade's case are similar to a case of a patient of de M'Uzan (quoted in Green, 1986) for whom the search for suffering permitted not only the avoidance of anxiety as well as the experience of pain as a direct means of pleasure. This is the main idea I have about Jade and other patients: "(. . .) In many cases, the indifference (of the object) leads the Ego to lose interest both in itself and in the object. For me, this is a clear expression of the death drive and cannot be compared to aggression or primary masochism in any way" (Green, 1986, p. 267). A deep split in her mind permits her to tolerate the damage coming from her childhood, where sexual abuse was the tip of the iceberg. The effects of the mechanism of splitting can be seen in the fact that Jade *does not feel* the pain of this damage even if she has a clear memory of it. She is dissociated.

> Patient (Jade): Now I realise that what I report to you are enormous and difficult things . . . but I don't feel them now, I didn't feel them before, it is as if another woman had experienced them. I was a good girl . . . when X (a family friend) raped me I did not say anything . . . my mum was always ill, my dad . . . I don't know . . . my brothers had their problems. No one saw me and perhaps I learned to not do it either.

We need time, persistence and patience if we are not to give up when faced with negative therapeutic reactions and apparent "relapses," in understanding that Mary's wounds are Jade's wounds. It is a complex symbolic action in which in her dream she condenses not only the act of "looking inside or looking at the wound without running away" (for example, in the symptom or in the re-enactment of the abuse), but also the act of *loving herself*. This is because Jade actually loves her dog. It may be the only living being she loves without any ambivalence: Mary was present in her darkest and most difficult moments. It could seem trivial but, if I had to find a title for a book about women like Jade, D. and many others, I would simply suggest *Hurting Yourself*. Their cases lack what Bolognini (2008) calls "necessary Oedipal narcissism:" a girl not sufficiently invested in paternal love (although he was not physically absent, Jade's father always demanded that she be perfect, a high performer) finds it in love objects in adulthood. In the case of Jade, who seems to have also lacked the support of her mother, I can even say that such a support is substituted by an active trauma. This leads Jade to search for men who confirm that *she could not be seen* (at best), that she must be *perfect and a high performer* (especially in sexual activities, but not only), that she is *worthless*.

This is typical in the complex construction of the female identity (and sexuality) (Freud, 1931). Being a woman implies all these difficulties. A further paradox further complicates repetition compulsion: a *damaged subject* will not only repeat, *she will actively look for negative qualities in the other* (Bollas, 1993). As with D., Jade excels in finding men with these qualities ("It is clear from the beginning") and for a long time, until P., is fascinated by them. This fascination cannot be limited to the seductive qualities of the objects – ladies' men who are handsome, elegant, cold – but is rooted in a deeper attraction for the destructive aspects of the self. Thus, every time she discovers the positive qualities of caring or simply gentlemen, Jade excels in underestimating them in the same way she was underestimated by previous men. Similarly to those first men, she even becomes abusive, sadistic and bored. What Eigen (2001) calls *damaged bonds* are active and ready to destroy life in various and subtle modalities, for example, escapes from and devaluation of good objects or potentially transformative situations, active searches for repetition compulsion ("I really wanted to marry M. . . . I was truly convinced!") or passive eroticised waiting (*the open book*) exposing her to the repetition of past situations. Jade becomes aware of this quite soon, but she needs much time and repetition both in transference and life before she can find a true balance and finish analysis.

Women such as Jade always have in mind an oft-repeated *refrain*, a sad but sacred subtext that can be compared to almost imperceptible background music in a certain environment. Later I will consider Knapp's work. For now I mention that the main focus of her writing is eating disorders and addiction in general, what can be called the modern "*hurting yourself*," the contemporary feminine death drive.

> I can have success, but not material comfort. I can be independent and strong, but only if I cling to a piece of childhood dependency. I can seek the recognition and satisfaction that eluded my mother, but I must pay for it.
>
> (Knapp, 2003, p. 77)

Through the splitting, which saved Jade's life when she was a child but which taxes her mind today, she can achieve partial success and be strong and independent. *Where's she running*, the poetess asks. Jade never rests; her first stop is the analysis couch. I do not deal with sexuality so much because it would require another discussion. Although *sexuality*, in both mental and physical terms, invades the analytic field, especially in the first sessions, as it invades her affective relationships, it does not bring Jade any pleasure. Her love is desperately unrequited. It is an active and partially conscious search for a sacrifice: "Whilst masochism in the pervert remembers excitation from the real (. . .), the hysteric's masochism is the transformation of body excitation from its carnal logic to an erotic undoing, from the pulsions moving towards its orgasm to the *waves of despair* created by the self's abstention from sexual life with the other" (Bollas, 2000, p. 28, my italics).

As with food, with sex Jade always swings from asceticism to excess. Perhaps abstinence and promiscuity are always present in her life and are always characterised by *dis-pleasure*: indifference, submission or symptomatic pain (vaginismus). I would like to focus on the *waves of despair*: I do not want to focus on whether there was an unconscious pleasure in Jade's eroticised pain – I do not have a precise answer on this question. Rather, I am more interested in dealing with Jade's despair, which can be defined as split and detached from her self and which allows her to start to feel her emotions. Looking at the hole inside Mary leads her to accept her weaknesses and needs and thus to renounce the image of the strong woman who is perpetually running.

At the beginning of analysis, I am countertransferally impressed by the insistence of her sexual sadomasochistic scripts and patterns. I am impressed by the fact that she reports all the oppressions and humiliations with apathy and indifference, describing in detail how she had to dress, which sexual positions she had to assume, etc. This countertransferal emotion is crucial: on the one hand, Jade puts her dissociation (her dangerous difficulty to see herself that makes her risk her life with her first fiancé) inside me and, on the other hand, she wants to *surprise me*, to hit me in a desperate attempt to be noticed by me. The only way for the good child Jade to be noticed instead of her ill mother is for her not to become a rebel but *to use her body and show an illness*. Thus, Jade shows not only many physical symptoms – I consider these effects of a conversion mechanism, because they are all translatable in a shared symbolic language – but also her *sexual body*, here intended in the terms of *psychosexual development* in Freud's framework. Although I consider Jade's various changing and histrionic physical symptoms to be hysterical conversion reactions, that is, *ways of telling something that words cannot tell*, I want to refer to a rather different theoretical framework, the one proposed by the French school that considers the death drive as an active instance in psychosomatic disorders (Fine, 1989). In these disorders, no matter if mortal or treatable, the death drive is postulated both as a causal factor and source of psychical destabilisation. In general, the patient disinvests her disease, experiences it as something other from her. This factor is clearly evident in Jade. It confirms how difficult, if not impossible, it is to mark clear clinical separations: the death drive also plays a role in hysteria. In Fine's model, the psychical disorganisation can stop, fix or advance, and have different expressions in different individuals and even in different phases of an individual's life and analysis. This disorganisation seems to be due to an internal object that is unable to contain the different parts of the individual's self. Thus, because of this inability, the individual's conflicting parts are split and free to evacuate in the individual's organs or other parts of her body, causing psychosomatic pathologies or serious hypochondria. These pathologies and hypochondria can be interpreted as defences from the fear of returning to early confusional states. In this sense, these defences must be clinically treated with caution. In the individual with a psychosomatic disease, different movement in progress and regress, life and death, development and anti-development, coexist and are in tension. The understanding of all these contrasting movements and of their disorganised or not "sequences" is crucial in the therapy for psychosomatic disease.

As I just said, Jade needs some time to understand that she can be seen and *remembered* and thus discards in both life and analysis the use of the eroticised theatre for hurting herself and for calling my attention in transference and the love object's attention in life. Only with P., in spite of her difficulties in finding a shared pleasure, is Jade able to renounce masochism. She is surprised that "he likes the ordinary and 'normal' things, he is not interested in weird things . . . he understands when I can't take it anymore. He understands that I'm not against him, it's only my problem . . ."

The quality of the analytic listening must not be taken for granted. In the first year of analysis she dreams:

> Patient (Jade): I lost my earring, the one with the pearl, it was my mother's earring . . .

The *pearl* of the analytic listening, that is, the fact that the analyst is able to keep her in mind ("I'm always surprised that you remember everything about me . . .") in contrast to her mother, is what will permit Jade to identify herself and to become able to listen to herself.

I'm aware that the death drive will not disappear from this clever, elegant, forever running woman. However, I'm also aware that now this drive is mixed with other life drives and thus she will not leave *open the book*, will not draw upon her disease or her masochistic scripts in order to be listened to by others and *herself*. Now the mirror reflects a whole image of her, certainly not a perfect one, but at least a sufficiently *integrated* one that is ready to deal with her Ego ideal.

> I was so dazzled from his appearance that I confused him with my father's assassin. I confused him with that big shadow of protection and safety. But that shadow is not my father. I did not come for searching for God. Here I did not search for anything. In fact, I did not find anything. God was not there, you were not there. I do not have genitals anymore, they tore them off, but (. . .) you were not there and thus there is nothing any more.
>
> (Bachmann, 1988, p. 148, translated for this edition)

The death drive and transgenerational transmission

At a first glance, the issue of the death drive and the issue of transgenerational transmission are distinct. Nonetheless, they are strictly intertwined. In fact, drives, as well as affections, traumas and memories, live inside of the individual but, when they are agglutinated nuclei (Bleger, 2013) – that is, deep, ancient and experienced as *impossible to work through* by an individual – they are unconsciously transmitted through generations.

The classical studies by Kaës, Faimberg, Enriquez, and Baranes (1993) first identified this phenomenon, which was examined in depth later (Bohleber, 2007; Herzog, 2008; Kogan, 2015). Recent studies on transgenerational transmission reevaluated Bleger's 1967 studies on agglutinated nuclei. The analytic work with patients who were sons or grandsons of Holocaust survivors or victims of other massacres clearly showed the presence of *non-worked through traumatic areas*, strongly repressed and denied by relatives, parents and grandparents who the patients could have never met or known. Such areas were represented in masked forms in the dreams of these patients or hidden behind their symptoms. It is as if the laws of mental life would confirm the old saying "the sins of the fathers shall be visited upon the sons." It is important to stress that Freud (1913) foresaw that psychic inheritance guarantees continuity between generations and that the general task of the new generation is to go beyond what "was unfinished at an unconscious level" by the old generations. Freud's discovery is extremely relevant: it is not the simple process of children identifying with their parents (or with some aspects of the Super-Ego of the parents): it is something more, deep, ancient, mysterious, inaccessible.

Working-through and representation are the pillars of a healthy mental life. They are not optional. If the individual's mind is unable to perform this important work, subsequent generations will have to do it in his place. It is

> (. . .) a phenomenon that can be described as *something urgent* or as a sort of necessity to transmit led by a mandatory mental imperative (. . .) It is the necessity to transmit what cannot be hosted by the individual herself. (. . .) It is an unconscious transmission characterized by negativity because this transmission is not based on what it lacks, but on what had not happened, that is, on the absence of representation and memorization (. . .). They are objects that cannot be transformed and thus will remain *encysted, dead, inert*.
>
> (Kaës et al., 1993, pp. 23, 29, my italics,
> translated for this edition)

There is a "colonisation of the past" (Bohleber, 2007, p. 333). This colonisation is not directly observable. The past was not worked through and thus it became unknown and split in the ancestors. It is transmitted to the successors as an expression of the death drive, in forms of mute agglutinations, in the details of a symptom or dream. It is plausible that most of us do not realise it and we become aware only when we seek analysis for symptoms and suffering we do not understand or connect to something transgenerational. The Israeli psychoanalyst Kogan (2015) reports that Holocaust survivors and sometimes their offspring – the latter seem to assume that the Holocaust is now the *archetypical* symbol of unrepresentable collective trauma – present "psychic holes" in their minds, mute and dead areas that cannot be accessed through symbolism and that can be reconstructed only through long and difficult analysis. It is clear that the parents' denial negatively affects the children's processes of symbolism and thus their ability to live and transform. The children's personalities appear injured, concretised and defective.

Now one may wonder why I offered this premise on the mysterious and ancient phenomenon of transgenerational transmission. In fact, we are not dealing with the Holocaust or other genocides and their survivors. However, I think that this argument can be applied to the individual, to the history of someone's family and ancestors, to their personal dramas. The mechanism seems to be quite similar: if the parents deny or do not work through their history, the children will have deadly consequences and effects. As I will show later, contemporary psychotherapy's lack of representation and symbolism can foster this and thus the tacit transmission of the pain suffered, no matter if inflicted or denied, by the parents and their children.

Jade's mother was mentally disturbed all her life. Her illness was something unknown to Jade, something she could not talk about. Her mother was presumably psychotic. Jade reports that "she always stayed in bed, I rarely met her, my father provided for everything. Now I'm sure she had a serious mental illness . . . and now I understand her suffering and that her malice and cruelty were due to her illness." She does not say very much about her maternal grandparents, but she has a vague memory that her mother had a "really unhappy" childhood. Jade has a mentally disturbed cousin. All these vague and fragmentary elements paint a picture of a family that simultaneously dealt with and denied mental illness. Neglect and silence are typical when negating massacres in history and trauma in families. Jade's sister died of cancer when she was young and her brother was a very active man with many mental difficulties.

Can we hypothesise that Jade transfers in her hysteric speaking body the *unworked through* mourning of her mother? Is it the cause of her masochistic attacks on her self? That is plausible. I believe that her physical symptoms permit Jade to be alive and offer her the chance to attempt a symbolic translation. Otherwise, her destiny would be that of her mother, "a sick person in a bed."

I think that every patient or mentally suffering patient has always something relevant to discover in terms of their family history or their history across generations. In this sense, if it were possible to deal with this history, to symbolise it and to give it meaning, we would discover that certain agglutinated nuclei, certain embodied and dead features, are at the basis of many tacit things and of many psychopathologies ready to be transmitted. This is a very difficult and hard aspect that I want to classify as an archetypical repetition compulsion that excludes and involves the individual at the same time. It is a paradox: the individual must repeat something unknown and far from himself, something in which he is simultaneously involved and excluded.

The family of Nando's mother had a very conflicting and complex history: hostilities, reprisals, ancient and unsolved hatreds. Nando's maternal grandfather was a rich industrialist who excluded his daughter (and as a consequence Nando) from managing the family company in favour of his son, Nando's uncle. Typical of a patriarchal culture, Nando's mother was excluded from the activities of the company, perhaps the most significant aspect of her family: the message was that managing the company was not women's work. Thus, Nando was born under the sign of exclusion. It is plausible to suppose that, according to the reality principle and to his personality traits, Nando would not have been interested in the family business. But here the reality principle does not matter: in Nando's phantasies and experiences, the painful (and, of course, Oedipal) ghost of being excluded from the family wealth – although in reality he was well-off – will never abandon him. This ghost assumes concrete form in Nando's aggressive behaviour against his family and in his refusal to work or to accept jobs he deems inferior "to what could have been." Perhaps, it is this ghost that contributed to him choosing addiction as a refuge, as a means of forgetting, a response to something experienced as an injustice. I think that the most difficult aspect of this situation was not addiction *per se* but, rather, the idealisation of something elsewhere, of something he never had as the only place to be. This exposed Nando to the risk of destroying every real and good object in his life. What he never had oppressed him. Although difficult to reconstruct, we can hypothesise that his mother had a similar history because she was "the excluded sister." The difference between them is that her mother expressed her resentment in a depressive form, while Nando did so in an aggressive form. Hatred and rage as negative emotions led Nando to a masked and continuous attempt to kill the vital parts of his mind through drug addiction. As I said above, these parts came from good aspects of both his family and himself. They prevented his physical death and total disintegration and led him to analysis.

I believe that "colonisation of the past" will never leave us. It is a chain that makes us innocent prisoners. If we are lucky, the best we can do is to work through these parts of ourselves. The most we can hope for is that the symptoms give us a *chance* to understand them or that the "psychic hole" is not so big as to constitute complete psychological illiteracy.

Because we live in a world marked by the Other, even the death drive (and, perhaps, above all the death drive), a drive irreducible to the subject but also non-representable, is precisely the drive most specifically predisposed to transgenerational transmission due to its untranslatability and impossibility to be directly represented.

I believe that dream analysis is the main tool for accessing these dead areas, as shown in the studies of the above-mentioned authors. In fact, the silent agglutinated nucleus of our predecessors' death drive can never be accessed directly and consciously: it was expelled and encysted because it could not be thought or decoded in any way. Memory can cure and makes us human. It is hard to say what the fate of this in all of us will be. I can hypothesise a spectrum going from light and simple situations to heavy family trauma and collective drama involving entire populations which discover repressed memories.

Forgetfulness means disaster. Memory redemption.

(A. Knoop–Graf)[4]

Women's bodies: a new breeding ground for the death drive?

My view of my body was certainly distorted. [. . .] This was the infinite hunger for love and recognition, the hunger for sex and satisfaction and beauty, the hunger to be seen and known and fed, the hunger to take and take [. . .]. I was ruler of my own corporal continent, the Queen of Anhedonia.

No fat, no fleshy protrusions.
No blood, no seeping.
No needs.
[. . .]

(Knapp, 2003, p. 84)

It would be a more than legitimate question to ask whether the female body is actually a new terrain for the death drive. After all, this phenomenon can be traced back at least to the Middle Ages thanks to the writings of women such as Saint Teresa of Ávila and other anorexic saints, women well-read and able to write in a language generally precluded from and uncommon for the majority of women of that time. In their writings it is evident that the female body was the *theatre* not only of hysteric conversions but also of more peculiar expressions of what Freud would later call the death drive. Thus, it follows that this phenomenon is anything but new.

Nonetheless, cases such as Saint Teresa's comprise elite and small specific groups from which we have precious testimonies. The issue of testimony is the core of this chapter. I do not intend to revisit eating disorders and their well-known and well-documented in literature dynamics, evolutions and genetic, psychoanalytical and socio-cultural hypotheses; nor do I intend to identify with a gender (the female one) or an era (the contemporary one), the mysterious immensity of the theme we are exploring.

Rather, I intend to continue with the words and *testimonies* of some contemporary female writers and essayists who advance hypotheses that are similar, both psychoanalytically and socioculturally, to those we can make by reading Saint Teresa's diary and that are borne of *their personal experiences* of potentially mortal addictions: that of alcohol (but not only) for Caroline Knapp (1996) and of food for Margaret Bullitt-Jonas (1998). I find biographies and memoirs invaluable and I have always enjoyed reading them. Nove and Clegg illustrate that *this is not a feminine phenomenon*, rather one that finds in the feminine a different, transversal and specific expression. The two men can help us to understand the Nirvana desire, the "dance of death" and the need to be numb to the point of being unable to think, leading to substance abuse a step away from death. Both had the chance to overcome their addictions and tell their stories. In the same vein, I chose Knapp and Bullitt-Jonas for the precise and disarming sincerity in which they describe their addictions and the *desire* that drove their self-destruction. Only those who have survived certain extreme experiences are truly able to describe them and do so better than any specialist aiming to formulate hypotheses from such testimonies. After all, did psychoanalysis not emerge from the accounts of Freud's patients? The choice of Knapp and Bullitt-Jonas was not easy because North American literature on this topic is very rich, well informed and full of thought-provoking ideas. What led me to choose these two authors was the fact that I found them *fearlessly honest*[5]: they put into words the hell of the addiction they suffered for almost their entire lives and, especially in the case of Knapp, they hypothesised about the body and addiction. These hypotheses have a universal character, as they go beyond the single individual's experience.

Another recent memoir that I found very sincere is Violetta Bellocchio's *Il corpo non dimentica* (The body does not forget) (2014), in which she details how seven years of alcoholism affected, as her title signals, her *body*.

So what is the basic assumption, the bedrock hypothesis of these intense, painful and extremely personal narratives? That the female body, with all its appetites and desires, is the battleground of a diabolic and lethal battle to destroy these very appetites and desires.

There are some ingredients whose mixture results in a dangerous and lethal cocktail: first, the perverse, subtle and typically Western idea that a woman must remain eternally young, beautiful, slim, sensual and desiring; second, a peculiar childhood characterised by certain recurring features that I will discuss later; third, and above all, a peculiar instinctual and emotional disposition typical of a depressive, empathic, receptive and highly intelligent personality. Not only is the body a mirror of the world (Chasseguet-Smirgel, 2005) for both men and women, or a theatre of female perversion (Kaplan, 1991),[6] but, according to Knapp, the combination of contemporary values, specific family dynamics and intimate inner worlds predisposed in this way, make the female body the place in which every desire dies and every appetite is destroyed. This can occur in various forms observable in clinical practice: anorexia, bulimia, alcoholism, compulsive shopping and an obsession with plastic surgery that leads to disfigurement.

Although not a psychoanalyst herself, Knapp is an expert in psychoanalysis – her father was psychiatrist Peter H. Knapp, who did groundbreaking research into psychosomatic medicine – as are the other authors we will meet in this book. She goes into analysis and in *Appetites* (Knapp, 2003) she refers sometimes to the theories of Freud and Lacan. "Desire," said the French analyst Jacques Lacan, "has *indestructible* permanence. Desire is *inextinguishable*" (Knapp, 2003, p. 165, my italics). The need (the hunger) can be easily satisfied, but the demand, the desire, that completely human struggle that does not settle for mere survival, can persist once the need is satisfied. The issue of the complexity between desire, need, and demand starts at the beginning of life, in the relationships with the mother and her breast. Such a relationship certifies the connection between love and food: it works as an ancient imprinting in all those devastating *food addictions* that damage women, whose development is generally more complex than that of men. An unsatisfactory mother, as the cold, sober and silent mother represented in Knapp's memories, can satisfy the need, the hunger, but not the desire: this desire, this appetite persecutes Knapp her whole life. It does not matter if she alternates food deprivation with binge eating and drinking: it is the same. Knapp connects the issue to the pure death instinct as formulated by Freud. This instinct exists in all of us. It is the desire

> (. . .) to recapture that early state of narcotized bliss, a place devoid of the tension between wanting and being, a condition of complete calm and release. Some of us do get back there from time to time – it's where we go when we're lost in music or rhythm or work or sex, or when we do drugs or drink alcohol (. . .) but *as a more permanent state it is lost*, its memory folded into the soul (. . .) it's no more than an echo, a whispering ache, that inarticulable sensation that something – *something* – *is missing*.
>
> (p. 166, my italics)

The strength of these words is testament to the fact that adequately understanding and working through an experience lived in both one's body and mind, allows us to access something that can appear difficult even to the most skilled psychoanalysts. Knapp is the spokesperson for millions of women who express the death drive in its most pernicious form, the death of desire.

A woman refers to her body more than a man or at least in different modalities.

The hysterical female body allowed Freud to invent psychoanalysis: the great intuition of the *talking cure* from which our discipline derives comes directly from the need to *translate in a verbal language* this body language. I do not want to examine this topic in depth, but it is on the female body that many media controversies are based today, that aesthetic canons are developed, that disciplines and diagnostic categories (for example, eating behaviour disorders) are invented, that symbols and messages typical of every era are built.

I wrote about Jade, a typical contemporary woman calling to my mind many women, some my patients, some not, under the same *sign* or code: before the mind can represent it, the body is the field in which a battle is fought: it is a war between the acceptance of desire, appetites and life and the strong denial of them. The many Jades I meet are all good girls, strongly invested on the cognitive and intellectual side by their parents, pretty, elegant, educated. As Knapp points out, they represent the most educated niches of their generation and *milieu* but at the same time they have isolated, dark and split areas. In these areas, as young girls, they hide food or secretly vomit; as young adults, they hide alcohol, spend a lot of money on plastic surgery, go from sexual abstinence to promiscuity. The symptomatic expressions of these difficulties does not matter. I want to stress that I do not consider these *memoirs* as clinical cases. Further, I want to avoid the biographical approach to psychopathology because it can diminish the relevance of psychoanalytic thinking on the mysterious and disturbing human: a human who, as we have seen, contains death inside life, tacitly muted in the Nirvana drive or in destructive and symptomatic masochism.

My Jades experience it all: calculating calories as a ritual; going to meet plastic surgeons without any *real and valid* reason because they are thin and attractive; spending alone long afternoons in boutiques and long evenings drinking "three Negronis," as a patient told me; discovering the magic of vomiting; having compulsive sex; committing petty theft in a shopping mall – and the list goes on.

"It is a miracle that I'm alive!" Jade says. I agree, it is a miracle to be alive, to be here to tell, to write books, to dream at night, to sublimate during analytic sessions, to share experiences in a group. For this reason I appreciate very much the value of these biographies. A narrative of life experiences is not only a self-cure, but a shared gift to every reader. "(. . .) It is a bit like producing a dream, appealing to multiple sources, current and past, responding to not always convergent intentions, presupposing the permanence and insistence of a desire coming from afar" (Pontalis, 1993, p. 255, translated for this edition).

> In my world – a place that unquestionably still exists, that's inhabited with varying degrees of intensity by *all too many women* – appetites had a nearly opposite meaning, the body experienced as *dangerous and disturbing and wrong, its hungers* split off from each other (. . .). Appetite is about eating, certainly, and that's a piece of it that defines life for many women, a piece I, too, know well, but it's also about a much broader *constellation* of hungers and longings and needs. It is about the deeper wish – often experienced with particular intensity and in particularly painful ways by women, *to partake of the world, to feel a sense of abundance and possibility about life, to experience pleasure.*
>
> (Knapp, 2003, pp. 1, 2, my italics)

Knapp is a strict anorexic during university in Boston, eating the same things everyday: a sesame bagel for breakfast, a yogurt for lunch and an apple with a small piece of cheese for dinner. She starves her body and mind (*starved myself*) with enormous dedication and the feeling of triumph typical of these mental states. She is proud to pass by food shops and to avoid them: no weakness, no need, no desire. The strictness with food does not disappear but it lessens. She does not remember how and when her slow descent into alcoholism starts. It is something that characterises her university years and first years of a brilliant career as a journalist. She never stops working, she never gives up, she never gets drunk with other people. On the contrary, she is an example for many female colleagues and students. Meanwhile, she has a destructive relationship with Julian and then a tender love story with Michael. At the end of the day she dresses up in her *liquid armor* (Knapp, 1996), a balm for her mind, similar to the hashish that Nando uses to stop every emotion. This is the Nirvana side of the death drive in Knapp, whereas the sadomasochistic relationship and the anorexia is the open and visible side. This open and visible side is generally against the person herself and also against others. This distinction is relevant at the theoretical and clinical level when we deal with it in the consulting room and in transference, but it is not in the complexity of everyday life, in which everything is mixed up, sexual promiscuity with sexual repulsion, starving and exercise addiction with the "liquid armor" of alcohol or binge eating. I do not think that observable behaviour is crucial in these situations: rather, it is the hunger (or Lacan's *demand* or desire) underlying it. The hunger is denied, unsaid, something making us feel guilty. The appetites and libido drives that contemporary life stimulates and demands (we must feel pleasure in everything) are subtly prevented, especially in women. For many young women, this ambiguity translates into an impossible access to simple sources of pleasure. Life is reduced to a long struggle to not starve or die or binge or drink or commit suicide. It is a difficult road that sometimes leads to a rehabilitation centre, sometimes to our consulting rooms, sometimes to a self-help group, as happens to Knapp.

In fact, as with Clegg (2012) and Bullitt-Jonas (1998), Alcoholics Anonymous meetings permit Knapp to stop her destructive behaviour and recover. A secular and intelligent woman, she is aware that a bad dependence substitutes a good one, the dependence on the group, its service activities and the kind of *spirituality* – a concept near but slightly different from that of *insight* in psychoanalysis – that is at the core of 12 Step programs. People help each other, are always at one another's disposal, emerge from isolation; as Clegg writes, describing a day when he is on the verge of relapse, looking for his old drug dealer and accidentally meets a member of his self-help group, only the presence of another human being prevents him from taking drugs. If he had not happened upon Asa, the friend who went through the same hell, he would have rung his dealer's doorbell and lost himself in the usual ritual, his "dance of death." In fact, the ritual of the deadly dance is always and essentially solitary. The person dances alone with the death drive, often in a split and *dark* dimension that runs parallel to a successful life (Knapp calls people such as herself as *active alcoholics*) or in a compulsive and solitary binge: "but later, after everyone had left, I'd steal back into the kitchen, kneel by the refrigerator light, surrender in full. (. . .) *This* is bad – this solitary binge; this needy, demanding, hungry body; this flesh – becomes *I am bad*" (Knapp, 2003, p. 117, my italics).

> I require wine, only when I am alone. (. . .) To get rid of myself, to send myself away.
>
> (Boswell, 2008, pp. 699, 700, my italics)

In my mind I see a montage of patients all asking whether they are bad and whether it is their fault. There is debilitating distress at the beginning in the analysis room: I am not well, I do not like myself. With great frequency we trace childhood events that are not of outright abandonment or immense trauma, but rather in which, like Jade, the child had not been *seen* or experienced as having been seen by her caregivers: the child had not felt herself to be a privileged, exclusive, appreciated object of maternal gaze. Knapp describes her mother as extremely contained, silent, incredibly capable of reacting gracefully to life's events,

a woman who said nothing when she discovered her daughter's anorexia, even as her daughter's body was reduced to a skeleton, a woman with whom it was impossible to get angry and who seemed unable to feel or give any pleasure. In a beautiful passage we read:

> Some of the saddest women I know (. . .) are the ones whose relationships with their mothers felt somehow compromised or distant or tinged with resentment, who grew up with the feeling that their mothers didn't really like them. I am one of these, although my own mother would have been horrified to hear me say that (. . .).
>
> (Knapp, 2003, p. 169)

Bullitt-Jonas remembers how when she was a child a friend asked her why her mother was always so serious and she was unable to give an answer because she did not notice her mother's depression because she was distracted by her father's alcoholism. By using very similar words to Knapp's, Bullitt-Jonas writes: "I became expert in the art of avoidance. I knew how to be a superintellect, able to rationalise (. . .) When as a child I would secretly slip a piece of bread into my pocket after lunch (. . .). Certainly I was not hungry for food. Perhaps it was human contact that I missed" (2000, pp. 11, 12).

There are plenty of similar reports, so many as to seem overlapping: inside educated families, wealthy, in many ways loving, the intelligent girl is not seen, is not nourished by the mother's desiring look. This is not because she is a bad mother but because she is depressed, a "dead mother" (Green, 2001) with whom the girl will identify herself. This is because,

> (. . .) the child is marked by the desiring look of the mother (. . .) in the moment in which the light of the Other's look goes away and turns off. For the child this is a loss. But, to provide a scaffold, the mother's look must be based on desire (. . .). The daughter takes what she needs from the mother's look in order to construct her femininity. Thus, she needs this look as a support for identification (. . .). *The more the mother's look is absent, the more the daughter will require the mother's presence.*
>
> (Zalcberg, 2010/2014, pp. 157–160, my italics, translated for this edition)

This absence/presence becomes hunger for food, substances, sex, objects. What name your poison takes doesn't matter.

> (*"food, sex, shopping: Name your poison,"* Knapp, 2003, p. 10)

Where are the fathers? Knapp's esteemed psychiatrist father, Bullitt-Jonas' literature professor father, Jade's rigid corporate executive father: what about the fathers? Some of them were very present in the child's life, perfect objects for identification and ideal instances to be satisfied because the child is, in fact, intelligent, the best equipped in the family, *the fairest of all*. The father's narcissistic investment falls on her: the girl soon understands that she cannot escape it and, indeed, in the future her great intelligence will be a great resource, but also something like a destiny she did not choose: her success will *console* her mother (the dead mother) and father from their depression. Successful men, the fathers of our two authors were both alcoholics, the "active" kind who do not necessarily openly ruin their lives or lose their jobs or get into trouble. No, it is in secret that the father dances his dance of death. The child is so disinvested from the mother's desiring look or at least scarcely invested in that "necessary Oedipal narcissism" (Bolognini, 1994), an important component in the development of future feminine depression.

If the construction of identity is complex for every human being, for the female child it is much more so. She is asked to disinvest from the mother, the first love object, and to invest in the father. This is particularly difficult. As Freud discovers in his last studies on femininity, the bedrock of the girl's attachment is always her mother and will be never completely substituted by the investment in her father. Furthermore, as Chasseguet–Smirgel (1985) accurately observes, the mother will always love more the male child (who has a penis and thus is a different love object) than the female one (who is similar to her). The female child must turn to the father as a new love object. But this father, *this stranger* in Kristeva's words, has his own shortcomings and appears later in the child's life than the mother, that is, after travails with the first object. Although the construction of identity is difficult for everyone, it is more linear, less tortuous, for the male child than for the female one because for him the first object is the parent of the opposite sex. In the Freudian and Lacanian sense, from the beginning the female child is marked by a *lack* and she must immediately confront the fact that something is missing – the penis that the male child has instead and that is strongly invested by the mother. Thus, she conceives of the penis as a symbol of freedom and autonomy that causes an unconscious envy in her. During her development, this envy can lead to different outcomes, from a sort of claim of masculinity to submission or depression.

Thus, lack is the most painful feminine psychic experience. Not only were Knapp's sad women, herself included, involved in the typical complex female development, but they were desperately hungry for primary objects that had not seen, invested, sufficiently desired and fed them.

There are many complex psychic, ancient, biographical and cultural reasons why women, more than men, are particularly vulnerable to attacks of the anti-vital drive in various symptomatic ways. Knapp writes of the body as a voice and Bullitt-Jonas replies that it is a voice of self-sabotage. The two authors did not know each other.

The lives of the women I consider here are quite similar but end in different ways. Knapp, who gives us such acute, personal and painful pages, including in her ironic column in the Boston Phoenix, does not survive her suffering. At 42 she dies of cancer before seeing *Appetites* published. She "heals," to use a tragically simplistic term, from her compulsions by joining Alcoholics Anonymous. But in the end the death drive fulfils its destiny. Knapp was aware that, although their symptomatic expressions were silenced, the struggle with appetites and its massacre on her body would never end:

> I'm still prone to periods of isolation, still more fearful of the world out there and more averse to pleasure and risk than I'd like to be; I still direct more energy toward controlling and minimizing appetites than toward indulging them; I am one of the least spontaneous people I know. (. . .) I no longer fear sliding back into the anorexic prison, but I am somewhat stunned, and a little rueful, at how arduous it all is, how long it can take a woman to achieve a degree of balance around appetites (. . .).
>
> (Knapp, 2003, p. 190)

Despite her happiness at having reached a hard-fought balance, death won the game very early.

As we saw in the previous chapter on sublimation, Bullitt-Jonas survives. Her appetites are sublimated in spiritual fulfilment, in a prolific search for God, an approachable God "living on Earth" who can be known through the famous 12 steps of Alcoholics Anonymous. What I call a "sublimative conclusion" and I deem as something deeper than a clinical "healing" from binge eating, has a completely different psychic quality from the renunciation of desire that as a girl Bullitt-Jonas thought she had to do to "(. . .) become as saintly as my mother" (2000, p. 54). Now, a vast range of activities and pleasures authentically substitute her vain struggle for control and the cycle of starving and binging. Today, she is an Episcopalian priest, writer and active member of recovery groups.

We have seen how the analytic relationship – that can be seen as a form of sublimation in respect to direct control of the object – and analysis allow Jade to reach an understanding of the outcomes of her compulsions and masochism. She is well aware that "this work will never end . . . I'm not like that anymore but *I'll always be like that.*" Further, it is worth noting that she was very good at drawing although the pleasure that she could have derived from this activity was obscured by her feeling inferior to her ex-husband and by the tyranny of her ego ideal demanding perfection.

In our conclusion we will return to the role of contemporaneity in more general terms but here I want to focus on the specific issues we have dealt with in this chapter. That is, in light of the examples of memoirs I chose, what is the relevance of contemporaneity and of the models it seems to impose on women? I do not want to consider much of the literature that considers eating disorders and their consequences on the body as a minimal expression of feminine contemporary suffering, something similar to what happened with hysteria many years ago. The topic of *appetites* includes *all* the forms through which women inhibit, suppress or poison their access to pleasure and desire. Food is, of course, one of these forms, perhaps the most widespread for its easy access, availability and presence in everyday life, but not the only one. Sociocultural hypotheses provide some answers but, analogous to the opposite extreme of exclusively psychological, intra-psychic or family-dynamics hypotheses, I do not believe that they respond to a complex universe that draws upon the individual, the family and Culture. Knapp hypothesises a scenario that I share and I discuss in some of my previous works (Valdrè, 2017, 2015): the freedom trap. Knapp refers to Kaplan (1991) when she argues:

> Women have infinite choices, (. . .) and this is very frightening. It means you're stuck with who you are. No one is going to tell you who to marry, or what career to pursue, or how to cut your hair, and so you're thrown back onto yourself.
>
> (2003, p. 45)

Of course, the paradox of freedom applies to men and women, and it can be perceived as equally seductive and distressing by both as *people*. However, for women the thousands of options that contemporaneity and emancipation have unleashed collide with an equally powerful subtext message: you can do what you want, all the doors are open, but you *must* be thin, seductive, active, young: full of appetites, but unable to satisfy them. Women are forced to build two parallel worlds, so well described by these authors: a world in which they are "daytime" women, active, controlled and *successful* and a world in which they are "nighttime" women, isolated in rituals and compulsions, whatever the privileged object.

> We had more opportunities and freedoms at our disposal than any other group of women atany other time in modern history; we could do anything, be anything (. . .). And yet by the age of twenty-one, I'd found myself whittled down to skeletal form, my whole being oriented toward the denial of appetite. And at forty-two, my current age, I can still find myself lingering at the periphery of desire. (. . .)
>
> (Knapp, 2003, p. 19)

Dostoevsky understood early on that freedom is so terrible that human beings try to escape it in every way they can. Something similar but expressed in updated terms and applied to intimate relationships can be found in Kristeva and Sollers:

> One mustn't idealise freedom. Freedom can be lethal, too.
>
> (2015, p. 14)

Are these nostalgic references? Temptations to return to the past? Of course not. I am personally of the mind that for women and human beings in general this is the best time in which to be alive. Nonetheless, everything is more complex than before. Too many options confuse and excite. Many messages are contradictory and impossible, like the bodies of top models about whom newspapers uselessly discuss *whether or not to ban from advertising*, aware on the one hand that the majority of women cannot meet these standards if not at the cost of starving (emptying oneself) and, on the other hand, that they promote a consumerism according to which these bodies are attractive and desirable *goals* in virtue of their unattainability. In her column, under the cover of her alter ego Alice K., Knapp fought with the weapon of irony against every kind of insistence, model, *things to do* or *how to be.* Alice is a young woman with a good position and a very full day: she compulsively reads women's magazines to find examples of who to emulate and searches for the perfect boyfriend, the perfect shoes. Every purchase, once made, leaves her dissatisfied and disappointed. Of course, she does not like her body or her ability to organise a dinner or a party. The void torments her, in particular the one that takes place Sundays: she fears the idea of an entire day without plans or work. She creates a name for it, *leisurephobia* (Knapp, 1994).

The freedom I am talking about is the terrifying Sunday of all the Alice Ks. to which Knapp dedicates her column, in which she writes about herself with great spirit and acumen.

There is always *a something better, a somewhere else, an "if I were/if I had"* oppressing the young woman. Certainly contemporaneity did not create the *gap*, the irreducible waste of every human existence between desire and object, but it amplifies it. The young woman focuses on a difficult process of subjectivisation and offers her young body and her desires as symbol and chosen signifier of every era.

As I said, I am deliberately excluding from this discussion many psychoanalytic interpretations in order to emphasise the experiences in the memoirs presented. However, I want to quote the psychoanalytic interpretation of Chasseguet-Smirgel (2005) that apparently (but only apparently, in my opinion) proposes an alternative position limited to anorexia. According to this interpretation, eating disorder behaviours – I use this expression for simplicity but I do not like it at all – in women are not about the denial of desire but *the desire of autarchy.* Desire rules this behaviour but it is *autarchic,* it tends to autonomy and independence from the mother. And what an extreme form of independence it is, with the woman grasping at the illusion that she is able to survive without a crumb of nourishment, literal and figurative, from external sources. Autonomy to the extreme, a lack of hysteria, a war that the mind wages against the body: for Chasseguet-Smirgel so-called eating disorders belong with narcissistic personality disorders. Of course, also according to Chasseguet-Smirgel, the origin of these disorders is obviously always ancient, always linked to that absence of calming and fulfilling experiences in the relationship with the primary object. This gives autoeroticism a violent character, as if to hurl the accusation: "Because you failed to soothe me, to nourish me, I'll take care of it myself, I'll give myself pleasure, I'll starve myself, I'll stuff myself and, above all else, I will never again depend on you or on anything outside myself." The feeling of triumph of anorexics and bulimics, at least in the early stages, comes from this unconscious fantasy that Knapp describes so well: the maxim "I do not depend on anyone. I do by myself!" is the freedom from want *par excellence!* The "victory of the mind over the body" has, of course, nothing

to do with authentic sublimation; we are, indeed, in the area of the narcissistic trophy and the denial of needs, without any transformation into symbolism. At the behavioural level, it can correspond to the intense academic and intellectual activity that some anorexic adolescents manage, for the first time, to maintain, a sort of frenzy of perfection that inevitably stops when the body becomes weak. The object – the *real object*, of course; this is why I find the definition of "eating disorders" reductive – is not food but the body itself, the body confused with that of the mother. It is the sexualised body, whose feminine differences and traits are denied: it is pathology, it is the search for "pure domination." I agree with Chasseguet-Smirgel's interpretation and I think that it has a common point with the experiences reported by the female memoirists presented in this chapter: it is *the desire of not having needs or desires*. In the ancient fantasy that can never be satisfied, linked to self-eroticism through the pleasure of having control by denying food, it is always the body, the young woman's body, that is the battlefield for separating from the mother. For Chasseguet-Smirgel the autoerotic fantasy at the base of this is of the anal phase of development, derived from analytical material that reports direct or indirect anal masturbation, such as putting the fingers in the orifice or angrily squeezing pimples, and of food hidden under the bed, in the fridge, in the broom closet or in other places in order to satisfy their compulsion – extensions of the body, a body that feeds itself autonomously from its own faeces. This independence is, of course, a tragic pseudo-independence, which, as mentioned, constitutes a specific difficulty in feminine emancipation: for Chasseguet-Smirgel the daughter's rebellion, against the mother who imprisoned her inside a female body, takes the form of a so-called eating disorder.

This is more or less how the authors I considered in this chapter describe, with technical words, what they have lived in their own skin. Another possible interpretation (Moroni, 2005) compares anorexia to a sort of primitive religion, in which food is heir to the primitive totem, a totem identified with the mother. Dependence is overturned: the anorexic becomes the totem to venerate, the divinity. This interpretation, which I quote for its anthropological interest but with which I do not agree, has nothing in common with the asceticism of the anorexic saints whereby the anorexic is the object of her own veneration.

I would like to close with a piece of another memoir, the painful and tormented autobiography of the American author and essayist Judith Moore, *Fat Girl: A True Story* (2005). Concluding this brief reflection which, perhaps not very scientifically, I've chosen to base only on biographies of women who lived and died in this hell, I invite the reader to read about the pain of the fat girl, the best at school, the smartest in the class, but also the one who is and will never be like the other girls:

> I hate myself. I have almost always hated myself. I have good reasons for hating myself, but it's not for bad things I've done. I do not hate myself for betrayals, for going behind the back of someone who trusted me. I hate myself because I am not beautiful. I hate myself because I am fat.
>
> (Moore, 2005, p. 7)

Notes

1. This is a quote from Aldo Nove's autobiographical novel in which he considers his life from childhood to adulthood. After many years of self-destructive behaviour and drug addiction, Nove is now a writer and a poet.
2. Bill Clegg is an American literary agent. He wrote this second memoir after getting sober from crack cocaine and alcohol.
3. Retrieved from goodreads.com/quotes/962-develop-an-interest-in-life-as-you-see-it-the
4. From the speech Anneliese Knoop-Graf, sister of Willi Graf, a German Catholic member of the White Rose anti-Nazi group, gave in Rimini in 2005, "*Dimenticanza è sciagura, mentre memoria è riscatto*" From meetingrimini.org/detail.asp?c=1&p=6&id=3203&key=3
5. The Boston Globe on *Holy Hunger*.
6. Kaplan's classic 1991 book *Female Perversions: The Temptations of Emma Bovary* was made into a 1996 film directed by Susan Streitfeld and starring Tilda Swinton.

References

Bachmann, I. (1988). *Il Caso Franza*. Milan: Adelphi. (Original work published 1978).

Bellocchio, V. (2014). *Il Corpo Non Dimentica*. Milan: Mondadori.

Bleger, J. (2013). *Symbiosis and Ambiguity: A Psychoanalytic Study* (Eds. J. Churcher and L. Bleger). London: Routledge. (Original work published 1967).

Bohleber, W. (2007). Remembrance, trauma and collective memory: The battle for memory in psychoanalysis. *The International Journal of Psychoanalysis*, 88: 329–352.

Bollas, C. (1993). *Being a Character: Psychoanalysis and Self Experience*. London: Routledge.

Bollas, C. (2000). *Hysteria*. Routledge: London.

Bolognini, S. (1994). Transference: Erotised, erotic, loving, affectionate. *The International Journal of Psychoanalysis*, 75: 73–86.

Bolognini, S. (2008). *Nuove riflessioni sul narcisismo*. Paper presented at the Centro Psico-analitico of Milan.

Boswell, J. (2008). *The Life of Samuel Johnson*. D. Womersley (Ed.). London: Penguin. (Original work published 1791).

Bullitt-Jonas, M. (2000). *Holy Hunger: A Woman's Journey from Food Addiction to Spiritual Fulfillment*. New York: Vintage Books.

Chasseguet-Smirgel, J. (1985). *Creativity and Perversion*. London: Free Association Books.

Chasseguet-Smirgel, J. (2005). *The Body as Mirror of the World* (Trans. S. Leighton). London: Free Association Books. (Original work published 2003).

Clegg, B. (2012). *Ninety Days: A Memoir of Recovery*. New York: Little, Brown and Company.

de M'Uzan, M. (1977). *De l'art à la mort*. Paris: Gallimard.

Eigen, M. (2001). *Damaged Bonds*. London: Karnac.

Fine, A. (1989). La pulsion de mort au regard de la maladie somatique. *Revue Française de Psychanalyse*, LIII, 2: 721–735.

Francesconi, M., and Zanetti, M.A. (2009). *Adolescenti: cultura del rischio ed etica dei limiti*. Milan: Franco Angeli.

Freud, S. (1913). *Totem and Taboo*. S.E., *13* (pp. 1–161). London: Hogarth. (Original work published 1912).

Freud, S. (1920). *Beyond the Pleasure Principle. S.E., 18* (pp. 7–64). London: Hogarth.

Freud, S. (1931). *Female Sexuality, S.E., 21* (pp. 223–243). London: Hogarth.

Freud, S. (1933). *New Introductory Lectures on Psycho-Analysis, S.E. 22* (pp. 7–182). London: Hogarth. (Original work published 1932).

Green, A. (1986). *On Private Madness*. London: Hogarth.

Green, A. (2001). *Life Narcissism Death Narcissism* (Trans. A. Weller). London: Free Association Books. (Original work published 1983).

Green, A. (2011). *Illusions and Disillusions of Psychoanalytic Work* (Trans. A. Weller). London: Karnac. (Original work published 2010).

Herzog, J.M. (2008). Los Degradados: Out, down, dead: Transmitted and inflicted trauma as encountered in the analysis of a 6-year-old girl. *The International Journal of Psychoanalysis*, 86: 291–310.

Joseph, B. (1982). Addiction to near-death. *The International Journal of Psychoanalysis*, 63: 449–456.

Kaës, R., Faimberg, H., Enriquez, M., and Baranes, J.-J. (1993). *Transmission de la vie psychique entre générations*. Paris: Dunod.

Kaplan, L.J. (1991). *Female Perversions: The Temptations of Emma Bovary*. New York: Doubleday and Co.

Knapp, C. (1994). *Alice K's Guide to Life. One Woman's Quest for Survival, Sanity, and the Perfect New Shoes*. London: Quartet Books.

Knapp, C. (1996). *Drinking: A Love Story*. New York: Dell Publishing.

Knapp, C. (2003). *Appetites*. New York: Counterpoint.

Kogan, I. (2015). From psychic holes to psychic representations. *International Forum of Psychoanalysis*, 24: 63–76.

Kristeva, J., and Sollers, P. (2015). *Marriage as a Fine Art* (Trans. L.S. Fox). New York: Columbia University Press.

Mangini, E. (2014). Pulsione e rimozione nella tela di Penelope. In F. Munari and E. Mangini (Eds.), *Metamorfosi della pulsione* (pp. 54–79). Milan: Franco Angeli.

Moore, J. (2005). *Fat Girl: A True Story*. New York: Plume.

Moroni, P.G. (2005). *L'anoressia come sistema religioso primitivo. L'adolescente anoressica piccola dea totemica*. In Giaconia, G. (Ed.), *Adolescenza ed etica* (p. 110). Rome: Borla.

Nove, A. (2010). *La vita oscena*. Turin: Einaudi.

Pontalis, J.-B. (1993). *Perdere di vista*. Rome: Borla. (Original work published 1988).

Schmidt-Hellerau, C. (2001). *Life Drive & Death Drive, Libido & Lethe: A Formalized Consistent Model of Psychoanalytic Drive and Structure Theory*. New York: Other Press. (Original work published 1995).

Semi, A.A. (2011). *Il metodo delle libere associazioni*. Milan: Cortina.

Szymborska, W. (1998). Portrait of a Woman. In *Poems, New and Collected, 1957–1997* (Trans. S. Baranczak and C. Cavanagh). Orlando: Harcourt, Inc. (Original work published 1976).

Valdrè, R. (2015). *On Sublimation. A Path to the Destiny of Desire, Theory, and Treatment* (Trans. F. Capostagno and C. Williamson). London: Karnac.

Valdrè, R. (2017). *Psychoanalytic Perspectives on Women and Power in Contemporary Fiction. Malice, the Victim and the Couple* (Trans. F. Capostagno and K. Haralambous). London: Routledge. (Original work published 2014).

Vecchio, S. (2016). Review of *Pourquoi les pulsions de déstruction ou de mort* by *A. Green Psiche*, 1: 295–301.

Winnicott, D.W. (1984). *Deprivation and Delinquency*. London: Tavistock.

Zalcberg, M. (2014). *Cosa pretende una figlia dalla propria madre? La relazione tra madre e figlia da Freud a Lacan*. Milan: Mimesis. (Original work published 2010).

3

IN ART

Repetition compulsion in Blue Jasmine: Woody Allen

> But now I am quite alone in the world.
> My life is empty and I feel lost.
>
> (Ibsen, A Doll's House, p. 90)

Jasmine is alone in the world, her soul as empty as Ibsen's Nora because she has lost all her objects in the magnificent finale and, with them, herself. She ends her oneiric rambling around the city on a park bench, alone, looking like a homeless woman wearing Chanel, with everybody giving her dirty looks. "Now they're all a jumble" are Jasmine's last, empty words.

Allen's masterpiece is a female tragedy that can be assessed from many different and not necessarily contradictory points of view and angles: Jasmine as a hysterical personality because of her continuous conversion disorders and panic attacks; as an "as if" personality (Deutsch, 1942), imprisoned behind a mask, in fiction that is also self-deception and that haunts her all her life, an obvious case of Winnicott's (1960) False Self; someone lacking subjectivity and identity as evidenced by her futile change of name; more simply the umpteenth female character, one of the most moving narratives, in my opinion, of a contemporary woman. All of this is true and more: *Blue Jasmine* is a typical Woody Allen film, simultaneously simple and complex, a sad tale and a psychoanalytic narrative of a personal crisis. For my purpose, I chose to deal with this aspect: Jasmine's crisis is a *foretold* crisis.

It is clear from the first scenes that things won't end well but not because Jasmine is born under a bad sign or faces catastrophic events. Although such events certainly occur in her life, Jasmine has a second and perhaps unexpected *chance* of rescuing herself but she unconsciously throws it away. Her fate seems to be sealed: she is a woman who sabotages and damages herself.

What is commonly called destiny represents in psychoanalysis the most tragic presentation of repetition compulsion. The death drive dominates Jasmine. It is worth noting that the philosophical meaning of the concept of destiny is slightly different from the psychoanalytic one. In fact, philosophy distinguishes fate from destiny. One, fate, cannot be modified, while the other, destiny, can partially be modified and managed. Even common language makes this distinction. I believe instead that, when it assumes the figure of tragic inevitability, it feeds on repetition compulsion, against which the individual is helpless, as is the case with Jasmine.

So what is Jasmine's story that takes her from the upper-class in Manhattan to a park bench in San Francisco, mumbling alone in the grip of madness? What has Jasmine *repeated* so as to avoid making more vital and healthy choices in life?

The film begins with Jasmine (portrayed by the splendid Cate Blanchett) breathlessly arriving in San Francisco, where her sister lives. She is visibly suffering, talkative and panic-stricken, wearing a Chanel dress and a pearl necklace that she never takes off, even when they are inappropriate. She hides herself behind a shield of words. She speaks about herself with any stranger in a torrent of evacuative words, revealing the typical lack of contact with her self and the other: when she gets off the plane, Jasmine's speech is an *empty speech* (Lacan, 1977), not articulated around desire but purely narcissistic, deprived of the dialectic of recognition, flattened in the dimension in which the other is only a narcissistic mirror reflecting only the self, a receptacle for evacuations even before projections. Jasmine does not so much speak as rapidly fire streams of words, empty words so as *not to feel herself.* For the same reason, she gobbles up Xanax. The opening scenes are similar to the first dreams reported in analysis: they contain *everything*. These scenes make us think that, although Jasmine is facing an acute crisis at the moment, she always uses this same modality to be in the world: avoidance, hiding, self-deception.

Jasmine arrives at the apartment of her sister Ginger, who works as a store clerk and has two lively small children and a difficult relationship with a man. Ginger does not ask anything more of life. More than an arrival, Ginger's apartment is for Jasmine a landing place, a life jacket thrown to a shipwreck survivor, a last chance. Adopted as children, the two sisters never particularly loved each other. Jasmine always kept away from Ginger and felt ashamed of her. She was their mother's narcissistically favourite child, the *special one*, destined to something different, to a high level of instruction, a coveted social class, a proper marriage. The focus of my interest here is not Allen's criticism of the financial bubble and contemporary capitalism that destroyed many fortunes. The backdrop of the speculative folly of Wall Street is, as in many of Allen's films, a historical-cultural framework in which to place human comedy. Because people are not exempt from the values of the *Kultur* in which they live, in the burst bubble of modern high finance so many illusions and personal tragedies have unfolded, especially in the United States.

Although the film does not make explicit the fact Jasmine was *the special daughter*, it is clear that this is her status: she signs a "narcissistic contract" (Aulagnier, 2001) that accords her an apparently privileged position from which the simple-minded Ginger is exempt. For Jasmine maternal love is that *look* we discussed in the previous chapter regarding Jade and the bodies of women: a narcissistic love.

In my opinion, narcissistic love is the most common form of love in both the couple relationship and the parent–child relationship. What does this love ask and what does it say? It says: I will love you only if you represent and realise me; if you fill my narcissistic emptiness or the lack of meaning I feel; if you will always be under my control; if you do not disappoint me. It is not unconditional love (I will love you no matter how you are), rather it is a love that depends on the more or less unconscious realisation of the subject's expectations. It is plausible that Jasmine did not receive any proper investment or recognition: she "has a minor role" in her mother's play (Lisciotto, 2016, p. 15). The drama of Jasmine's identity is efficaciously revealed in the choice of her name: *Blue Jasmine* comes from the romantic 1934 song *Blue Moon* by Rodgers and Hart that she had heard the first time she met her future husband. Here comes the magic! The poor and insecure Janet, a desperate character in search of an author, is kissed by a prince and becomes Jasmine. The drama of identity and her shame about the past, about her sister, the poverty, the "bad-blood fantasies" (Levinzon, 1999, 2004) are all transformed into unconscious fantasies in her, an adopted child. The deep, irrational but firm idea of *not being ok* is the indelible unconscious mark of incapacity that undermines the narcissistic balance forever, but secretly.

> The barb in the arrow of childhood's suffering is this: its intense loneliness, its intense ignorance.
>
> (Schreiner, 1998, p. 9)

The film alternates between current-day Jasmine, a woman in crisis forced to seek help from the sister she fled, ashamed for having witnessed a mutual past to be erased, and flashbacks of Jasmine, flitting about between Park Avenue and her Long Island mansion, surrounded by friends as elegant as she is, a successful money manager husband and an adolescent step-son at an Ivy League school. The prince seemed to have really chosen her: fairy tales do come true.

Allen's cinema is a cinema of details: a look, a small change in voice or a stifled gesture *narrate* a character's entire biography and subjective world, similarly to the minor details in a dream. Even in that golden universe, was Jasmine happy? Was Jasmine herself (or a possible self)? Or did she play a role? Or did she really not understand or see anything? The main trait of this woman, as her nephews tell her, is *looking the other way*. Her husband cheated millions of investors, became rich thanks to a financial bubble and betrayed her with almost all her friends (who knew about his financial activities) until he left her for a younger woman. Jasmine's universe is made of paper, of deception and self-deception. Did she really not intuit what was going on or did she prefer to look the other way? If a little denial is necessary to tolerate life, it must be minimal because living in constant denial, in a lie, in poisoning every truth and all knowledge, in Bion's –K, condemns the subject to psychical death. I think that the particular type of "fiction" in Jasmine may correspond to what Britton (1999) poetically describes as "the other room" when he writes about the hysterical personality. The other room is the mental place that we commonly call our imagination, a space for the imagination from which visions, daydreams and hallucinations – that Jasmine has – may originate. It comes into existence developmentally when the primary object is believed to continue existing in its perceptual absence. Jasmine is invisible in the life she lives: between the parties and chatting with her fake friends, no one really sees her and *she* does not really see herself. If we all need a little room in the complex apartment of our mind, if a certain amount of illusion/imagination/daydreaming helps us to survive, living *only* in that room leads directly to the pathetic unhappy ending of the film: a crazy woman in Chanel mumbling on a park bench.

Ginger, on the other hand, lived and lives in the real word. Being the "least favourite" of her parents helped her to avoid the perverted charm of the other room. Her roughness reminded Jasmine (or, more accurately, Janet/Jasmine) of the drama of her origins: now, after her husband's arrest, the economic collapse that forced her to sell her assets, abandoned and ostracised by the smart set that had inhabited her emptiness, Jasmine faces the worst humiliation of all – asking her sister for help. The relationship between the two women, the forced confrontation with reality (searching for work, accepting Ginger's friends and small apartment), constitute the thematic pearl, the heart of the film. Nonetheless, I will deal with another aspect of the film.

Why did I point to repetition compulsion and thus to the death drive? Painfully, Jasmine decides to get back on track, to become that autonomous woman she has never been. She decides to resume the university studies she abandoned as part of the dream of delegating everything to her marriage. She decides to meet new people. Life offers her a second chance. At a small party she meets a man who could become her new prince. He seems to be a real person, authentic, a charming and ambitious diplomat who wants to enter politics. They start an uncertain relationship that seems to have all the prospects of repairing her past, giving it dignity, love and hope and the life of luxury life to which she feels she is destined. He gives her a ring, he asks her to marry him, he imagines her to be a suitable wife for a future politician. He does not seem perverse, indeed, he appears to be capable of loving and respecting her. But with whom has he fallen in love? It is clear from their first meeting at the party that it will be another *debacle*. Jasmine destroys this second chance and repeats the same script, the lie. Had she been honest with the new man about herself, it is almost certain that he would have loved and understood her just the same. But Jasmine does not have it in her to be loved as she really is, without any fiction: she lives with the unconscious maxim that she can be loved and love only by masking true self. For many women the *masquerade* is the dress of repetition compulsion.

> That is how desirable women are, my boy: a little superficial, a little absent minded, inclined to nebulous ideas.
>
> (Reza, 2002, p. 12)

Automatically and unreflectively, she immediately presents herself to the man with a false self: an interior designer (her professional dream), widow of a rich physician, an elegant and sophisticated middle-aged woman who is trying to start a new life in the best sense of the word. He believes her. Jasmine has always been expert in deception and self-deception.

But the latest fairy tale is destined not to last. A chance meeting on the street with Ginger's ex-husband, who lost all his savings because of Jasmine's ex-husband, unmasks her. From desirable future wife, Jasmine is now in everyone's eyes, a vulgar liar, a scammer. Jasmine falls to pieces:

> In the compulsion to repeat (. . .) it is as though, in trying to stop time, we were committing a murder of time.
>
> (Green, 2005, p. 184)

For the other, it is difficult, if not impossible, to know and understand the internal reason of this deceptive structure. For Jasmine, telling the truth represents a double risk: being refused (I will love you only if you are spotless, if you do not have "bad blood"), projecting onto the other the feelings that she is trying out; and the more specifically inter-psychic risk of being the one who cannot stand the truth. The truth, for Jasmine, would be a new experience. The fear of being refused by the other certainly exists in these situations but I think it is a sort of alibi. In fact, when the self has learned to lie and lives only in the other room, perhaps it goes beyond lies and reaches a hallucinatory world full of illusions.

The only moments of truth – lasting just a few seconds and able to surprise both Jasmine, the other characters and the audience – are brief sequences (the magic of cinema paints the unconscious!) in which Jasmine gets drunk, loses her inhibitions and *changes her voice and face and tells the truth*. Like a hole in the ground or a crack in the wall, the truth of the unconscious cannot be entirely suppressed: it appears suddenly when Jasmine cedes the control with which she usually governs all her psychic processes. Unfortunately, this truth does not find any integration in Jasmine's Ego. It is something that appears as a flash in the dark, something split, outside of consciousness and due to the effects of alcohol, something that is considered even more insane by those who hear it. We cannot exclude (in theoretical terms given the inextricable intertwining of life and death) that even the compulsion to repeat, while it reproduces painful situations, does not contain a trace of libidinal satisfaction, unconsciously, in every compulsion. Only the pleasure principle can account for this satisfaction. I hypothesise that for Jasmine there is no trace of a rediscovered pleasure. Rather, there is pleasure coming from *the absence of change*: Jasmine is so frail that she feels pleasure when she does not have to deal with change.

There are many films, mostly dramas, in which characters are trapped in deadly repetition compulsion. *Blue Jasmine* is peculiar. Jasmine is similar to many wealthy but not necessarily well-read women from the upper class. As usual, Allen is able to exquisitely flesh out this character without facile psychology, heavy morals or a complete biography to explain everything. He offers a sort of mosaic composed of details, sensations, small dialogues or monologues, a human tragedy with its own poetry. I want to stress again that Jasmine is not a clinical case: she is a woman who, for many ancient and complex reasons, is trapped in the worst tragedy, the most tragic paradox for a human being. A poetic word for the compulsion to repeat is destiny.

Could Jasmine have acted differently? Could Jasmine have broken the bargain with the devil? Could she have avoided the repetition of the identical and *transformed herself* by accessing her self and revealing her truth to the new object? Perhaps Jasmine made a timid attempt to *repeat to work through* (for example, when she tried to find a job or return to university). As we have seen in Jade's case, the strength of old mechanisms prevails. In repetition compulsion, we do not actually repeat old trauma, rather, *we repeat the ways in which we unconsciously dealt with the trauma*. In this sense, Jasmine illusorily appeals to a false self in order to present herself to the world.

When she meets the new man, Jasmine is at fault because she clearly sabotages herself. She cannot blame her cheater ex-husband or bad luck. Was it the spectre of possibly losing the object that maintains her compulsion to lie? Yes, it was: Jasmine is the kind of person for whom the loss of the object is the same as the irremediable loss of the subject (Racalbuto, 2004).

Freud expresses a similar concept, though apparently a more generic one, when he writes about the "repetition of the same fatality:"

What psychoanalysis reveals in the transference phenomena of neurotics can also be observed in the lives of some normal people. The impression they give is of being pursued by a malignant fate or possessed by some 'daemonic' power; but psychoanalysis has always taken the view that their fate is for the most part arranged by themselves and determined by early infantile influences. (. . .) Thus we have come across people all of whose human relationships have the same outcome: such as the benefactor who is abandoned in anger after a time by each of his protégés, however much they may otherwise differ from one another, and who thus seems doomed to taste all the bitterness of ingratitude, or the man whose friendships all end in betrayal by his friend (. . .) or, again, the lover each of whose love affairs with a woman passes through the same phases and reaches the same conclusion. This *"perpetual recurrence of the same thing"* causes us no astonishment when it relates to active behaviour on the part of the person concerned and when we can discern in him an essential character-trait which always remains the same and which is compelled to find expression in a repetition of the same experiences. We are much more impressed by cases where the subject appears to have a passive experience, over which he has no influence, but in which he meets with a *repetition of the same fatality*. (Freud, 1920, pp. 21, 22, my italics)

Then Freud argues that the most touching and poetic description of this mechanism can be found in Tasso's *Jerusalem Delivered*, precisely when its hero, Tancred, unwittingly kills the beloved Clorinda in battle while she is hidden beneath the armour of an enemy knight. The mystery around the concept of destiny/repetition compulsion as an expression of the breakthrough of the repressed and its secondary unconscious gain (if it exists) is far from being resolved, in my opinion. Is there a relationship, Freud asks, between repetition compulsion and the pleasure principle? It is clear that experiences relived with repetition compulsion are painful and draw on ancient trauma. But within masochism Freud also sees that this type of displeasure *does not contradict* a peculiar (masochistic) pleasure: he refers to it as "unpleasure for one system and simultaneously satisfaction for the other" (Freud, 1920, p. 20). At the same time, however, the mystery deepens because repetition compulsion "(. . .) recalls from the past experiences which include no possibility of pleasure, and which can never, even long ago, have brought satisfaction even to instinctual impulses which have since been repressed" (1920, p. 20).

Now, how is it possible to assess Jasmine in this complex twist of pleasure and displeasure, repressed memories and present life? The way in which Jasmine acts with the new man who could represent a change in her life is a clear example of wicked repetition of the identical: I see that you could be my salvation but I cannot be saved, *I'm destined to be abandoned*, and I myself create the conditions for this. How? I do it through deception and a false self: it is a disguise that seduces myself and the other and I know (because a part of me knows) that I will be unmasked. When it happens, you will abandon and despise me. It is a Pyrrhic victory. I will still be the child seeking her parents: when I find them, I will be loved by them, and thus I will have to perform, to live up to expectations that now are only projections onto the other, because it is unthinkable for me to be accepted for myself.

It is difficult to imagine that a certain amount of repressed (and thus unconscious) masochistic pleasure is at work in Jasmine's phantasmatic interweaving and leads her to failure; if not, the only "pleasure" to avoid is the displeasure of change. Remember that for Freud pleasure is a constant in most of his first reflections. But this pleasure can occur only *negatively*: it is nothing but absence of displeasure. Perhaps for Jasmine the idea of returning to be Janet could represent a non-representable pain: Janet is the rejected part of her self, the part masked by the song in which her illusion was formed. Returning to be Janet would be a catastrophic breakdown or a psychotic fragmentation, that is, something extremely painful. Perhaps psychoanalysis has always underestimated the trauma that the subject experiences when she renounces to her Ego ideal, in the most regressive and narcissistic ideal of Ego.

Perhaps the sum of cumulative trauma (Khan, 1963) attracts Jasmine to misfortune: "(. . .) as soon as a favourable perspective opens up, pessimism gains the upper hand again. In fact, the subject, who, for a moment, had hoped for a happier life, cannot allow him to envisage it and retreats to the unconscious pleasures of his masochism" (Green, 2011, p. 56). I am more inclined to see in Jasmine not so much the secondary gains of masochism as the constitutional (I mean the term in the absolute evocative sense) impossibility of renouncing the idealised image of oneself, the ancient command made by her mother – be an elegant lady of the upper class – relegating Ginger to the refuted aspects of a poor, sloppy and weak self.

The moving finale seems to show a sweet madness that makes us think not of masochistic pleasure but of the powerful collapse of Jasmine's illusion/hallucination of self. It is as if a Twin Tower suddenly collapsed to the ground. But Jasmine must have perceived Truth, the truth about herself, as even more catastrophic.

I want to propose now a very free association as *Blue Jasmine* brought to mind *Black Swan*, Thomas Mann's (1990) last and little-known short story. The main character is Rosalie, a 50-year-old woman, unable to accept menopause, as attested by the permanent end of her menstruation. For Rosalie menopause means the loss of her femininity, youth and fertility. One day she bleeds and becomes very happy: she has regained her femininity! When she discovers that the loss of blood was due to uterine cancer, Rosalie prefers to continue to believe that her menstruation has returned, in spite of her daughter's initial attempts to make her face the truth. At the end, the daughter tacitly accepts this lie and gifts this last illusion to her mother, who can die peacefully.

> If you take the life-lie from an ordinary man then you take away his happiness as well.
>
> (Ibsen, *The Wild Duck*, p. 98)

Eliot asks how much reality humankind can tolerate.
Mann's Rosalie, Ibsen's Nora, Eliot's poetry . . . perhaps writers and poets can understand Jasmine much better than psychoanalysts.

There is another important commonality between Rosalie and Jasmine: nostalgia. It is something that can be sensed in the first scenes of the film. But what kind of nostalgia is it? At a first glance Jasmine feels nostalgia for everything she lost: wealth, power, luxury, friendship, marriage. She does not resign herself to this. At a deeper level, it becomes clear where this nostalgia comes from: it is nostalgia for *what she never had*. This is the strong form of nostalgia and a paradox of human tragedy. A child who has never known love will feel more grief for it than a child who has known and then lost love; someone who has never known fullness will feel hungrier than someone who has been satiated and then no more. Nostalgia for what has been lost can offer solace and relies on those memories that, although moving and potentially persecutory, refer to a something and not to a nothing. On the contrary, nostalgia for what has never been possessed is not for a loss that must be worked through but for one that is beyond remedy.

Thus, Jasmine is a complex character. Beyond the repetition compulsion that leads her to self-damage, there are many other unconscious mechanisms at the basis of her behaviour. We are in the area of narcissistic deficiency: Jasmine's self-esteem comes *only* from external objects, from flattery, proximity and love from others, no matter if it is deceptive. It is very plausible that Jasmine had been aware of the many betrayals of her ex-husband but preferred *to look the other way*: a fake love is better than no love at all. The Prince awakens the Princess with a kiss:

⟶ *Loss of possibility*

many fairy tales contain a deep intuition about (in this case, female) narcissism: it is you who values me, awakens me from the deadly sleep of my nothingness, of my non-existence. It is the other who gives Jasmine a sense of existence. It is not only the force of repetition compulsion but also the weakness of narcissism that leads Jasmine to entrust the other, the new man, and to once again put her legitimacy as a person in the other: if he chooses me, I must be as I *imagine* he wants me.

I think that this illusory and projective structure comes from many narcissistic deficiencies that in turn cause many marital and couple problems. In these cases, as I mentioned above, if subjectivity is entirely deficient and dependent only on the kiss of the Prince, the loss of the object (unconsciously recalled for the paradox of compulsion) corresponds to the loss of the subject that will lead to a madness like the one at the end of the film.

Someone could object that even Ginger, the sister, grows up in the same unfavourable conditions. An adopted child, she, too, has "bad origins fantasies." But, although Ginger may appear unluckier than Jasmine ("Mommy liked me less than you") she does not suffer the pathological narcissistic investment that makes Janet become Jasmine. Ginger is able to deal with the difficulties of life and become herself. No dreams of glory, no Chanel dresses, no destiny in a fairy tale. She works in a supermarket and her first marriage is ruined because her husband is swindled by Jasmine's ex-husband. She has a new relationship with an uncouth and jealous[1] man who nonetheless really loves her. She is *the inferior child* in everything, in beauty, in intelligence, in style but now she is able to live in the real world and to accept it, to tolerate the ambivalence and thus to re-evaluate her man without demanding that he be perfect. She is able to accept the good and the bad; she accepts that he can be tender and irascible, but he guarantees her affection without moodiness. The paradox is that being less loved and desired by her mother's gaze was Ginger's salvation – and Jasmine's ruin. Loved, yes, but let us remember, loved as a narcissistic object, not as a person in her own right. Loved as Jasmine, not as Janet.

We can also glimpse an attempt, albeit an immature and chaotic one, of what we have seen theoretically as elaborative repetition compulsion, marked not only by a deadly component but also by a rebellious attempt to change the situation and avoid the return of the repressed. Armed with the best of intentions, in the middle of the film Jasmine tries to settle in San Francisco to look for a job for the first time in her life and, above all, to return to her studies. The passage is important. It could have constituted, more than meeting any other prince, a real break from the death drive disguised as repetition compulsion. She could have recovered, for example, through the studies she abandoned too soon to chase the false self, the good, creative and personal parts of the old Janet who we intuit to have existed: her authentic taste for beauty, design and art. But, those who are drawn to the splendid expectation that the other will magically resolve all their anxieties find it impossible to deal with subjectivity. Repetition compulsion finds fertile ground in a weak Ego, abdicated to the other and further weakened by the false self. The symptoms speak in place of this damaged Ego: panic attacks and, above all, anxiety disorders. Jasmine is the typical contemporary female patient. How many women enter our consulting rooms driven by the transversally most common symptom of our era, the so-called panic attack? I agree with those who see the *basic mechanism* and not the symptomatic expressions as a demarcation between the pathologies determined by Freud's foreclosure or repudiation (Freud, 1894) and the pathologies determined by repression (Conrotto, 2012; Valdrè, 2014). This traces back to the origins of psychoanalysis, precisely when Freud stopped focusing on actual neuroses (among which we can classify today's panic attack). I believe that this reference is more useful and promising than that to the borderline or narcissistic personality disorders that have become umbrella categories. With rejection, unlike projection or repression, everything is evacuated, expelled and lost, both the idea itself and its representation: the subject is empty and her world is inhabited by illusionary realities (Riolo, 2005). This is the *empty life* lamented by Ibsen.

Referring to *A Doll's House* (1999 [1979]) here is no coincidence. Ibsen's genius draws early on in the character of Nora that archetype of femininity we find in Jasmine, transversal to every age: the woman who lives for the kiss of the other, existing only for recognition by the other, an eternal child and doll whose world suddenly collapses. Nora (despite the many versions that Ibsen had to create to make her acceptable – it was, after all, 1879!) manages to emerge from the illusion and chooses to leave, even abandoning her children, and goes to find herself, to "(. . .) think things over for myself and try to understand them" (Ibsen, 1999, p. 113); the contemporary Jasmine can't do it. If in Nora Ibsen aims to represent the forerunner of rising feminism, *Blue Jasmine* is, in Allen's best tradition, a purely psychological work, pure narrative poetry. Jasmine, like many other Woody Allen characters, succumbs to life and her own illusions, is confused by the too many options that modernity paradoxically offers her (as we saw in Caroline Knapp), is seduced by the dream of success and is tragically unaware of not being talented – and so she bets all her cards on love and ambition. Nora and Jasmine are archetypal characters acting in a contemporary world, which makes them eternal and always enjoyable even after many years. The financial bubble and New York's upper class in *Blue Jasmine* are fundamental not only for describing Jasmine's personality but also for providing a social and cultural context which affected millions of people, especially in the United States, where the phenomenon originated, but also throughout the Western world. We are all seduced by Jasmine's dream: achieving our goals without effort and without paying our dues. If millions of people all over the world were cheated and many of them were less naïve than Jasmine, the desire for wealth and possessions and the passage from need to desire and from desire to uselessness that consumer society continuously promotes, all must come from very deep unconscious needs in every one of us. Like Jasmine, some people are more vulnerable to this. In the absence of a sufficiently structured self, every Pied Piper can make believe whatever he or she wants.

Which feature makes Allen's characters, especially the female ones, so memorable, so easy to identify? Their humanity. They are full of contradictions, self-sabotaging drives united with vital thrusts and, I would say their characterising trait, tormenting vulnerability, the disquiet that comes from the *contrast* between a desire for realisation that appears to have become a right for everyone and an often disappointing reality. Jasmine, like all these characters, must grapple with this contrast. For her, such a contrast is so deep and based on so strong a denial that it becomes psychopathological: Allen's characters are always hesitant and subject to contrasting desires. (. . .) They are certainly unable to observe and analyse themselves. Rather, they seem to be bondless when they speak of themselves, their ghosts and their secrets. (. . .) Although they appear to self-analyze, they actually are not. In fact, their self-analysis does not allow them to solve their problems. (. . .) Thus, this self-analysis is nothing but a way to narcissistically confirm their certainty of being unique.

(Quilliot, 2011, p. 23, translated for this edition)

In *Blue Jasmine* Allen is not interested in denouncing society. Nonetheless, he depicts a woman who is so narcissistically frail that she cannot escape becoming the favourite prey of one of the worst myths of contemporaneity: the need to be seen. Appearing, showing oneself, in place of being. It seems trivial and obvious to refer to the myth of success and I find that it is only partly true. Success is also a value when it is the fruit of construction and work, keeping in mind that the contemporary myth does not consider success as an output of construction and work but as a gift of chance and a commitment to realisation in every manner, even without any talent or by stealing not only the money or goods of others but also their identities. The context in which Jasmine acts and lives before she flees to Ginger's house is a combination of the myth of the centrality of appearance and the contemporary disease of self-realisation at any cost, humiliating those who are excluded. Jasmine's self-sabotage is familiar to us: how many times have we found it in analysis in the form of repetition compulsion? How many times have we observed, in ourselves and in life, the incredible ease with which, for example, in romantic relationships, we fall back into the same phantom, we find the same object from which we want to escape? How many times have we seen people not graduate at the end of their university studies, sabotage a career, tell lies about themselves just as Jasmine does when she meets the new man at the party? The subject who, for a moment, had another chance, takes a step backwards, returns to the painful but sure terrain of repetition, of the identical. "It is as though his superego could not allow him to betray his negative ideals," (Green, 2011, p. 56). If we substitute the Ego Ideal with the Super Ego (or at least if we take the Super Ego into consideration), we arrive at Jasmine's drama.

Attempts to implement what we have seen to be the vital, creative and necessary side of the death drive (for example, searching for work or resuming studies) are fragile and inconsistent. Panic assails every attempt at change; the basic narcissistic defect prevents every confrontation and trial; fatigue renders abandonment inevitable, as in the past, in the face of such useless effort. It is much easier to wander around a party with a glass of champagne in hand and beautiful blue eyes greedily and stealthily looking around as if to recall objects of love – and, behold, yes, the invited object arrives. And here comes the lie, too. There is doubt, in certain moments, as to what the *quality* of such lies is. Lying is not always the same: sometimes we lie to survive, sometimes to protect others, sometimes to meet specific aims. No . . . Jasmine's lie is sadly different. It is a lie based on the mechanisms of negation ("I never was Janet, my husband was not arrested"), of self-deception (Jasmine seems to believe her own lies), of the unconscious/pre-conscious fictions and of the appeal to the paradoxical protection of the false self instead of a more authentic self. This authentic self is frail, helpless and unable to contain her in front of life's events.

We have seen, among the many aspects that we could focus on, what seems to me more pertinent to our theme: the repetition compulsion in a woman, not without talent and intelligence, but who cannot *not* repeat the ancient modalities through which she dealt with her early and recent trauma. In the case of Jasmine, these modalities can be summarised as *turn the other way*. Denial.

The story, tragic but not dramatic, leaves no way out. Sometimes repetition compulsion is resolved by repeating the same errors: in Jasmine's case, it opens the door to madness.

> It is a sweet madness. There are no screams, no noise as with panic or rage attacks. I think that the last few minutes of *Blue Jasmine* are among the best in contemporary cinema and can be better understood by poetry than by psychoanalysis: Jasmine welcomes almost like a gift of surrender (finally, a surrender!) the park bench as the coveted place of rest. Unable to see the world and the strangers around her, no longer needing to fight, to pretend, to beg for love. Madness appears to free her, at last . . .

> "What are you working on?" Mr. K. was asked. Mr. K. replied: "I'm having a hard time, I'm preparing my next mistake."
>
> (Brecht, 1965, p. 7)

A desperate vitality: Pasolini

> The more sacred the more wild is the world:
> without betraying the poetry,
> the original force,
> we are called to solve its mystery
> in human good and evil.
>
> (Pasolini, 1957, *L'Umile Italia*, in 2003a, p. 804,
> translated for this edition)

"The more sacred the more wild is the world."

What has not been said about Pier Paolo Pasolini? No Italian poet or intellectual has been as explored, revisited and praised even by those who tried to destroy him during his lifetime. Long after his death, he remains the subject matter of films, interviews and books in continuous publication, even in psychoanalytic ones, for example in Chasseguet-Smirgel's beautiful *The Body as Mirror of the World* (2003), in which the author compares Pasolini to other intellectuals such as Mishima and Foucault.

My point of view, followed thematically by the next chapter, will be partly different (although everything in psychoanalysis comes to correspond in the end): I will link Pasolini to a group of American writers who are generally little explored by psychoanalysis, not so much or only due to their relationship with the body and the death drive, but because they are emblematic through their work and life of this book's silver thread, death inside life. The death drive is active in the most vital, most libidinal and passionate personalities, especially Pasolini, whom it devastates, as I will show later. Is it plausible that too much vitality can lead to death? The aim of this chapter is certainly not to add something new. Rather, it is to offer some reflections on the link between art and the death drive and to try to identify a common denominator shared by a group of authors: for all of them, in particular Pasolini, death *really* lived inside life.

Pasolini's biography and immense interdisciplinary work testify to his love of life. He was enchanted by the *sacred*, in his very personal concept of sacredness as something that touches everything that is pure, poor and humble, uncontaminated by the monster of consumerism. He adored his closest friends, from Alberto Moravia to Elsa Morante and many other writers and intellectuals of his time; he adored the poets, including Attilio Bertolucci, Amelia Rosselli and the unfortunate Sandro Penna and Dario Bellezza, who he defended and promoted; he adored his mother Susanna. He loved to travel. His descriptions of India as a nostalgically lost pre-industrial world, full of poverty and poetry, are unforgettable and unsurpassed. He adored sensuality and having sex with street boys, the death drive leading him to physical death. But more than anything else, Pasolini loved Culture and Knowledge. Interviewed about his film *Oedipus Rex* (Pasolini and Halliday, 1992), he replies that, yes:

> (. . .) it is a pessimistic film. When Oedipus comes to understand, it does not matter anymore. Of course, we could reason on the hypothesis that, if Oedipus were not so deeply innocent and unaware, *if he were an intellectual and thus searching for the truth*, perhaps he could have modified reality. *The only hope comes from culture*, from being an intellectual. For the rest, I am certainly a pessimist.
>
> (Pasolini and Halliday, 1992, p. 146, my italics,
> translated for this edition)

His love of knowledge and truth led him to make many enemies, but for him it was better to be enemies of people than of truth. I find that to be one of his most important statements, one that I have always kept in mind during my long adventure with his work. Pasolinian discourse is deeply and psychoanalytically profound. He maintained a love for knowledge so intense and inexhaustible (perhaps Bion's +K) and pursued it in every moment of his life, from a precocious child poet in lonely Friuli to the first screenplays during his youth, to novels, films, theatrical work, unforgettable articles in Il Corriere della Sera newspaper, splendid reviews (*narratives of narratives*). Every aspect of his look at life and society, of which he was a harbinger and ahead of his time, cannot exist in someone dominated only by the Freudian death drive. We are at the opposite of Nirvana with Pasolini: it is the desperate epistemophilic drive, hungry for knowledge and hungry *for the love of bodies without souls*, as written in one of his most beautiful poems (*Prayer to My Mother*, 1964). Perhaps the Nirvana side, or the search for oblivion, in Pasolini can be seen in that *precise and momentary* mental state in which those "bodies without soul" should have given him orgiastic pleasure. It is an ephemeral and drugged mental state, split from daily reality and able to eliminate every tension, awareness and pain.

The authors I'm going to discuss in this chapter are in contrast to the *Sturm und Drang* stereotype, alone, depressed, overcome by misfortune and unsuccessful in life, affected by Baudelaire's romantic *spleen*. Indeed, these authors are successful, far from self-pitying (from Nobel Prize-winners such as Fitzgerald to the less famous such as Yates), published during their lifetime, translated in every language and, like Pasolini, *hungry for life*. They led confused lives, they married and divorced, had creative highs and lows, journeyed, invented new literary styles and artistic frenzies. Drunk on life and insatiable, they wanted to try everything and were anguished by their capacity to perceive too much. Prolific despite their life being brief, they left their overflowing passion on the written page, in the words they put down, words that partly saved them, partly not. Sublimation is by its nature partial and fragile and can turn to the death drive at any moment.

These authors were not depressed or melancholic, at least not in the psychopathological sense of the word. Indeed, their vitality, perhaps stronger than that of the average person, astonishes us when we read their pages. How is one able, in a life that is often so short, to produce so much, to live and think so much with such sharpness, such lucidity? Perhaps for the answer we return to what Freud, referencing the young Leonardo da Vinci, called the "pure" type of sublimation, the genius marked as a child by strong infantile sexual curiosity that is transformed to love for knowledge. But this answer seems true only up to a certain point. Leonardo led a quiet life without love or hate, solely dedicated to science, Freud tells us. Certainly he didn't stumble around the streets drunk like Yates or Fitzgerald or was found dead among animal carcasses on the beach at Ostia like Pasolini.

It must be said, however, that all of Pasolini's closest friends describe him as a meek man even when he was firm and passionate in defending those ideas that were widely criticised at the time. He was kind to everyone. As Moravia shouted at Pasolini's funeral, he was "(. . .) a deeply good, eclectic and bright man."

Few intellectuals in Italy or anywhere else represent the living testimony of death inside life quite like Pasolini does: his childhood curiosity about sex was the engine of genius, sublimated later in love for knowledge, but this is not enough to guarantee survival. We have seen it when we discussed sublimation: *sublimation does not protect us from anything, does not guarantee us anything.* As long as the two drives co-exist, under the positive influence of Eros, the objectivising and integrating function, integration, and, therefore, life, prevails. But when this mixture for some reason within Pasolini, with such complex, contradictory life forces, fails, the connection with life is lost.

What I want to point out with Pasolini and the other writers is that *there would not have been death if there had not been so much life.* There even exists the common impression, especially regarding young artists, that too much vitality is dangerous. As a young teacher who arrived in the Rome of the 1950s economic boom, Pasolini initially drank in the big city's vitality but he soon guessed that so much vitality and hunger for life would lead him to no good.

The young poet presaged that *too much vitality* is not compatible with a balanced life. In fact, living in Rome was not a simple move and relocation. With his passionate way of living every experience, for him Rome assumed a sort of physical, carnal and passionate dimension. In this sense, Pasolini had an important and intense love story with Rome. The following verses stress this point:

> I ran away with my mother, a suitcase and some delights that ended up being false,
> (. . .)
> I lived that page of a novel, the only one of my life:
> for the rest – you know
> *I have lived inside in a lyric poem, like every obsessive*
> (. . .)

> (Pasolini, 1967, *Poesia delle ceneri*, in 2003b, p. 1265,
> my italics, translated for this edition)

Like every obsessive . . . In this context, I will not deal with political analyses or considerations, with the many hypotheses regarding Pasolini's death, with any attempt to read his biography in psychopathological terms, with his homosexuality or with a literary assessment of his work. Let me say once more: as with films, an author is never a clinical case for me. What interests me is to grasp, in a *psychoanalytic* way, the essence of his poetry and life. First comes the text: the text always has its own strength, its truth that we must respect, I believe, before we make any interpretation, which is inevitably partial and limited. This is what Eco called the "intention of the text" (1994, pp. 44–63).

When I say that I am not interested in the sterile, in my opinion, polemics of Pasolini's death, perhaps a homicide or suicide, I am arguing that the death drive is the force that had consequences on his homicide or suicide. This is a quite underestimated aspect regarding Pasolini. According to Fernandez's version of the facts (1982, p. 33, translated for this edition), "Pasolini was killed by a hooligan who was forced by Pasolini himself to sink a rod into his chest." He committed suicide at the hands of another, one of the "bodies without souls" he loved and desired spasmodically. A suicide by proxy, Pasolini conferred young Pino Pelosi the authority to kill him. The unconscious logic seems to be, I commit suicide by someone I love, but I cannot possess in any way. According to Moravia, Pasolini's death:

> was surely provoked by the murderer's hatred for himself and by his identification with Pasolini at the moment of the crime. By killing Pasolini, the murderer wanted to punish himself; the homicide was thus a kind of dissociated and objective suicide.
>
> (Siciliano, 1982, p. 395)

This is a compelling hypothesis that does not change the basic issue of the death drive as a destructive force present inside the various characters. The young Pelosi may have killed his homosexual self. Nonetheless, I agree with Fernandez that on that night at the beach in Ostia, Pasolini *decided* to be killed by his beloved, interchangeable and never really possessed object. For him, love was something impossible to conceive outside of a deep, ancient and dark sadomasochism.

Let's take a step back. Pasolini was hungry for life in every cultural expression, including painting (he was an excellent painter himself). In his films, we can often find images of classical paintings, for example the magnificent body of the dead boy in *Mamma Roma* (1962) inspired by Andrea Mantegna's *Lamentation of Christ* (circa 1480). He was fascinated by a peculiar type of painting. As Chasseguet-Smirgel (2003) rightly notes, he liked paintings with lacerated bodies, with blood and death, with crucified bodies that he compared to every humble poor person being killed, dead bodies or living bodies facing death. He was interested in a particular painting by Caravaggio:

> I was immediately struck by the *young executioner and the elderly victim* (. . .). With his arms wide open, staring at the executioner bent over him searching for a point to plunge his long shining sword. (. . .) I continued to repeat to myself that it would take superhuman strength to not want to die thunderstruck by this *vision*.
>
> (Fernandez, 1982, p. 183, cited in Chasseguet-Smirgel, 2003, my italics, translated for this edition)

This is complex. Is it not perhaps a painting of his own death? Is Pasolini fascinated by it? He is not afraid of it. On the contrary, from such a vision one can die thunderstruck. A young executioner plunges his sword into the elderly victim's chest. It sounds like a premonition unconsciously pre-represented and pre-constructed.[2] The physical place of his death will be the one favoured for his nocturnal love affairs, which were robbed and stolen from his daytime self, split and painfully aware: Rome's slaughterhouses, Ostia's desolate beaches, the decaying suburbs. There is a harmful split between the nocturnal and the daytime intellectual:

> Even more excitedly I snuck into slaughterhouses. The big quadrilateral building occupied the area of the ancient Forum Boarium, the cow market where the Romans went to buy meat . . . This was the place for *sacrifices* and libations of blood (. . .). I should have confessed to myself a *turbid and irresistible curiosity* to make love there, in conditions that would have seemed horrible to anyone else. . . .
>
> (Fernandez, 1982, p. 226, in Chasseguet-Smirgel, 2003, my italics, translated for this edition)

Turbid and irresistible curiosity: every statement and every word is full of meaning, full of the co-existence of the opposing drives. Curiosity, one of the most vital feelings (let's remember Freud's idea of childhood curiosity for sex as the engine of genius), is associated with the adjective *turbid*, which refers to dark and deadly places. All of Pasolini's work is characterised by this. It is present in the work of many other authors, but not with as much force and continuity.

The unfinished film *Salò, or the 120 Days of Sodom* (1975) is Pasolini's last will and testament, not only cinematographic and poetic, but also political and personal. I do not intend to review it, but I want to stress that this film does not seem to deal directly with Pasolini himself: it was strongly criticised when it premiered and for many years it was misunderstood. I believe it is one of the purest and boldest films on sadism. The focus is certainly on "the eternal indivisibility between the Power and the Body" (Marramao, 2010, p. 116). It is an extremely complex work in which, through a political *universal* metaphor of mankind and power, Pasolini shows the deep connection between Eros and Thanatos. He was influenced by Freud but also by Marx and Nietzsche.

In a further step back, let's recall that Freud, upon discovering the death drive, argues that in psychoanalysis destructiveness occurs only when the connection between Eros and aggression is lost. Normal sexuality for Freud (and this can be inferred from our common sexual practices) always contains a certain amount of aggression, is "sadistic," but to a limited extent. It is only when the two drives disjoin themselves and Eros is free and banned from the instinctual world that Thanatos can freely act. Perhaps in history no other experience like the Holocaust has constituted the main proof of the existence of a pure death drive completely disjoined from Eros. *Salò* aims to be something similar in psychological rather than political terms (although the film is *intrinsically political*). Three years after *Beyond the Pleasure Principle* and the so-called turning point of 1920, Freud specifies even more clearly that:

> The sadistic component of the sexual instinct would be a classical example of serviceable instinctual fusion; and the sadism which has made itself

independent as a perversion would be typical of a defusion, though not of one carried at extremes.

(Freud, 1923, p. 41)

In *Salò* we see all these extreme consequences that, in her reflection on Pasolini, Chasseguet-Smirgel defines as:

> (. . .) a catalogue of perversions and a description of the progressive *appropriation* of the objects (by humiliating, dishonouring, mutilating and killing them) representing the sadistic appropriation having murder as the only limit. (. . .) The appropriation evolves in sadism.
>
> (Chasseguet-Smirgel, 2003, my italics, translated for this edition)

Chasseguet-Smirgel gives importance within sadism to the concept, borrowed from Paul Denis, of *appropriation*: not only is the aggressive drive uncoupled and free to annihilate the object, but it wants to possess it, appropriate it, strip it of its humanity and identity. In the deadly universe of *Salò*, no one has body or identity: the Power has stolen it. Chasseguet-Smirgel's reflections differ from mine – they focus on the body. However, there is no contradiction in any way because in Pasolini, more than in the other authors I will later discuss, body–power–death and drives are closely related.

Salò is the unrepresentable, the total loss of the symbolic. In order to represent it so effectively, so powerfully in this farewell manifesto, the profound content of *Salò* must exist deep within Pasolini, pulsating in his bowels, in his blood, before becoming a representation, like Caravaggio, a painter he admired so much: how can one represent the non-representable character of death that the unconscious cannot know, if we are not permeated by the death drive? But things are not so simple: death must ambiguously exist along with life and sublimation for the death drive to become art and even universal art: no form of art can be born from Nando's Nirvana-cradle. To sublimate the drive in an artistic form it is mandatory to live, but in the end death comes. This is the tragic paradox of Pasolini, without which we would not have his precious heritage: an extreme drive for knowledge, inexhaustible curiosity for life and at the same time a continuous acting out of the risks of the death drive. In spite of all of this, Pasolini remained insightful, to the end capable of representing the death drive through words, poems, narratives, images, metaphors. Perhaps, as mentioned, the only moments of Pasolini's Nirvana consisted of those mercenary orgiastic moments, squalid when seen through the eyes of the average person but essential for his Eros, which was so full of humiliation and risk, but also tenderness, a sort of poetic madness. Only the *bodies without souls* – the street kids, the beggars, the denizens of the working-class suburbs – were able to give him that orgasmic oblivion from everything, that ephemeral death of thought. In 1948 he writes from Casarsa to his friend Franco Farolfi:

For some years now my homosexuality has entered into my consciousness and my habits and is no longer an Other within me. I had had to overcome scruples, moments of irritation and honesty . . . but finally perhaps bloody and covered with scars, I have managed to survive, getting the best of both worlds, that is to say Eros and honesty.

(Pasolini, 1923, p. 41)

And again, to his friend Silvana Mauri 2 years later, barely having arrived in Rome:

Those who like me have been fated not to love according to the rules end up by overvaluing the question of love. A normal man can resign himself – that terrible word – to chastity, to lost opportunities; but in me the difficulty in loving has made *the need for love obsessive* (. . .).

(Pasolini, 1992, p. 257, my italics)

The obsessive need for love (note that he always speaks of love and rarely of sex) can be found for example in the 1964 poem *La ricerca di una casa* (The Search for a Home):

(. . .)
I am here,
at the bottom of the world
forced to feel different
having lost all of the loves of my youth.

(Pasolini, 2003a, p. 1105)

In Pasolini's work there are often references to what Bollas effectively calls "the homosexual arena" (1993, pp. 144–164), parks for cruising in which almost-dead selves gather to seek erotic salvation from their sad state. Inspired by John Rechy's novel *Numbers*, in which the protagonist "(. . .) migrates from darkened movie houses to parks in Los Angeles" as in "(. . .) a pantomime, (. . .) a frozen dream, a trance, (. . .) something dazed, traumatised, unreal (. . .)" (p. 147), Bollas describes the "arena" as substantially a place of death, a perturbing theatre where the participants, in search of that infinite love to which Pasolini refers, obsessively repeat a tragic ritual, "(. . .) the scene of death and annihilation" (p. 148). In her poem *Dialogue with the Dead*, the great poetess Amelia Rosselli, who was discovered by Pasolini, and who died by her own hand, gives voice to the "arena":

And the massacre turns into lust: and
lust into ecstasy contemplated in the
syphilitic wheat that coils around
my neck, worn out by too much abandonment.
To abandon oneself to empty sex and then think to be

unsoiled by the black pitch of
such petty doings of the poor.
Sex and violence were abandoned and
rediscovered sodden that glorious early
morning when all fell to pieces (. . .).

(Rosselli, 2012, p. 155)

Pasolini continues, in the heartfelt cry of love and presage of the death of his mother, *Prayer to My Mother* (1964):

(. . .)
You're the only one in the world who knows
what my heart always held, *before* all other love.
For this, I must tell you what is terrible to know:
in your grace was born my anguish,
And I don't want to be alone. I've an infinite
Hunger for love, for the love of bodies without souls.
Because the soul is inside you, it is you, but you
are my mother and your love's my bondage.
I spent my childhood a slave for this lofty,
incurable sense of immense commitment.
(. . .)

(Pasolini, 2005b, p. 89, my italics)

Before any other love, there is the love for the mother. It is difficult to imagine psychoanalytic words to better describe the impossible love for the primary object, a love that precedes every other miserable surrogate in for the bodies without souls, which Pasolini probably loved as the mother loved him, the child himself. Many are the poems about the mother or the mothers. His real mother, Susanna, lends the bony face of the older Mary in the film *The Gospel According to St. Matthew* (1964).

In the appendix of another poem, *The Religion of My Time* (1961), he writes:

(. . .)
As all around us fiercely dies
the good inside her never dies;
she has no idea that her humble love
– poor, sweet little bones of mine –

could make me die of sorrow and shame
in the comparison, how her confined
(. . .)
Nowadays everything, for her, the girl,
and me, the son, is over, has always been:
The only hope is that the end

will really come and stop the dogged
pain of waiting. Soon we'll be
together, *in that humble meadow dotted
with grey stones* (. . .)
(. . .) but ours won't be a quiet rest,
for it shall harbour still too much
of life lived without purpose.
Our shall be a paltry, laboured silence,
our sleep full of sorrow, allowing
no comfort or peace, but only yearning
and regret, the sadness of those who die
without having lived; (. . .)

(Pasolini, 2014, pp. 287, 289, 291, my italics)

Here Pasolini uses the plural: he and his mother are united in a common destiny
of death, although she will survive him in reality. They are forever fused. It is
a desire of fusionality, a Lacanian search for the One, an attachment to the primary object that can only lead to *jouissance* and thus to the deathly drive. Pasolini
knows that the love for his mother is not only something that will support
him for all his life but also something that will lead him to death; it is a form of
slavery. In these verses there is a continuous mixture between life and death: *but
ours won't be a quiet rest* because of the intensity of this bond and an erratic and
painful life.

The Religion of My Time is probably one of the saddest of Pasolini's lucid poems.
He says to his mother that they are one, an infinite tender object – *poor, sweet little
bones of mine*. This tenderness is the same that he places, without it being reci-
procated, on the street kids. She is a *little girl*, as they are kids, as he himself is
a kid who did not grow up or he grew up victim of a tragic split mechanism – a
precocious and extraordinary intellect and an immature affectivity, *destined to
solitude* because it is enclosed in the mother's body.

In the poem *The Diaries* (1950) Pasolini is also aware of the desire to remain
small, the libidinal (and deadly) fixity to be forever the object of maternal love,
forever a son who loves other sons:

Adult? Never, never – like life itself,
which never matures, forever green
from splendid day to splendid day,
I cannot help but remain true
to the wondrous monotony of mystery.
This is why, when happy,

I've never given up on myself – and why
in my anguish over all I've done wrong
I've never felt any real remorse.

(Pasolini, 2014, p. 138)

Pasolini's biographer and friend, Enzo Siciliano (1982), argues that the poet was "(. . .) extremely faithful to his own trauma" (p. 153). Is the biographer's happy and poetic expression "faithful to trauma" not another way to affirm that the repetition compulsion and the death drive are almost *necessary* for allowing the genius to access his own unconscious? So, Pasolini is fully aware of the tender and tormenting incestuous bond with his mother; but we know that the impossible return to primary love, the deadly seed of *jouissance*, is already enclosed in this bond, which in various poems he sings in sublime words: we will die together, he recites in his poetry, even if not historically true because his mother will survive him, but, in fact, it is as if the child died in her. As a little boy in Friuli, Pasolini writes:

> I squeeze my mother's arm tightly (indeed we're walking arm in arm) and bury my check in the modest fur coat she's wearing: in that fur coat I smell the odour of spring, a mixture of cold and warmth, of fragrant mud and of flower still without fragrance, of house and country. This odour of my mother's modest fur coat is the odour of my life.
>
> (Siciliano, 1982, p. 34)

Pasolini was not only familiar with psychoanalysis, he considered it the only discipline capable of understanding homosexuality.

In the above-mentioned *Oedipus Rex* interview, Halliday notes that Pasolini's free interpretation of Sophocles' tragedy focuses more on the parricide than on the incest. Pasolini replies that:

> (. . .) parricide and incest are complementary. In fact, we cannot have incest with the mother in parricide. (. . .) I was a rival of my father. I hated him. Thus, I was free to represent my relationship with him. The love for my mother has always remained dormant. I rationally understand it but I do not completely accept it. (. . .) For *Oedipus Rex*, I wanted to be as free as possible and I considered only my impulses and my instincts. In this sense, the hate of the father towards the son was an issue I felt much more than that of the relationship between mother and son. This is because such a relationship is not a historical or real relationship, but rather *a completely private and inner relationship, thus outside history and reality*. It is even meta-historical and thus not productive at the ideological level, whereas the engine of history is the hate-love relationship between father and son. (. . .) I felt a deep love for my mother. This love influenced all my work. It is an influence coming from the depth of my being (. . .). Thus, in *Oedipus Rex*, I put topics pertaining much more to psychoanalysis than to Sophocles' tragedy.
>
> (Pasolini and Halliday, 1992, pp. 142, 143, my italics, translated for this edition)

Who is Pasolini's Oedipus? What distinguishes him? He is a completely innocent and incompetent person.

As well as the naïve people, those innocent people living as preys of the life and of their emotions, he does not want to see into things. (. . .) There is a contrast among innocence, total ignorance, and the duty of knowledge. The focus is not that the cruelty of life leads to crimes but rather that those crimes are committed because people *do not try to understand the history, the life, and the reality.*

(ibid., p. 145, my italics)

Pasolini's *Oedipus* is the anti-intellectual. Oedipus is similar to Pasolini because he, too, is trapped in an incestuous relationship with his mother but he is completely different from him in his need for knowledge (let us continue to keep this in mind), an emblematic feature of Pasolini's life. Eros and knowledge come together: this is the Pasolini who is drunk with life. But Eros and the nostalgic love for the primary object no longer go together: this is the Pasolini who is drunk with death.

Our poet did not want to grow up. Pasolini was an eternal Oedipus, gifted with knowledge because adulthood and the time passing carry with them another consequence: Eros lapses, "Eros stripped bare becomes guilty" (Siciliano, 1982, p. 386). In the years of *Salò* and thus near the end of his life, Pasolini was unable to feel the joy of Eros and felt anguished. His mother was ageing: "Susanna showed few physical and health issues. Pier Paolo hugged her, whispered the tenderness of his passion: but he could see the trembling liquor of old age in her eyes. These were months of a tragic dawn" (Siciliano, 1982, p. 387). Pasolini hid his anguish behind intense intellectual work: it seems that he tried to invent a new life for himself, perhaps to return to painting, to abandon the deadly "arena." But, according to his biographer, "habits are hard to die, like his passions" (p. 387), even if in his last nocturnal roamings the drive had to have been stronger or the resignation to Italian society more desolate, and he was not afraid, not for himself. We have seen how in offering oneself to death there remains the contradictory relationship with a precociously and consciously accepted Eros and the profound repugnance that led Pasolini to be tortured day and night to the point of exhaustion. I agree with Siciliano that, perhaps even more tragically "it was an Eros that did not demand incest, and not even the fantasy of incest − perhaps it required punishment for the absence of this fantasy (p. 391)."

The boys are thousands.
I cannot have one (. . .).
I must defend this enormous and desperate tenderness that,
similar to the world,
I have since I was born.
(Pasolini, 1964, *La Realtà* [Reality], in 2003a, pp. 1112, 1113)

With Susanna's and Pier Paolo's ageing, Eros decayed. At the metapsychological level, this means that Eros released itself and set Thanatos (that never decays) free.

Habits, that is, the compulsion to repeat, to ever more dangerously engage in the arena, became more acute; lost pleasure, pure culture of the death drive. Although the intellect continued to have feverish ideas and projects, every sublimatory action was weak and at the mercy of the destructiveness of the subject, who was always fragile. The death drive won.

Life and work coincide, as with many authors, but here with authentic and disarming passion for the truth about himself. He put his life entirely into writing and writing narrates life, what he defined as the "(. . .) 'natural poetic quality of life'" (Pasolini, 2005a, p. 52), present in everyone, especially in the most humble.

Death was always present in Pasolini, I would say, always active in the details of life. It became the object of a poem *To Death: A Fragment* (1961). He was waiting for death, he knew it and he spoke to it:

> From you I come and to you I return,
> sentiment born with the light and the heat,
> baptized in a wail of joy, identified as Pier Paolo
>
> at the start of a frenzied epic:
>
> I walked in the light of history,
>
> but my being was heroic, always,
>
> *and under your sway, innermost thought.*
> (. . .)
> I'm in good health, the way you like it;
> my neurosis spreads all around me;
> exhaustion dries me out but
>
> hasn't beat me yet: beside me
> laughs the last light of youth.
>
> I've got all that I wanted, by now.
>
> I've even gone beyond
>
> some of the world's expectations: a hollow
> shell, *I've got you now inside me*, filling
> my time and our times.
> (. . .)

(Pasolini, 2005b, pp. 295, 297, my italics)

He surrendered: I have always been under your sway, you have always been inside me. This is a poetic and moving recognition of the death drive inside a life full of success, honours and controversy.

I chose Pasolini (in particular Pasolini the poet, omitting for the sake of space his ample writing on cinema, reviews, novels and articles) because I know his work very well and from it I perceive so much *passion for life* in all its expressions.

But, at the same time, I was not surprised by the way he died or by his passion for death.

David Foster Wallace, a great American writer who committed suicide in 2008, was tormented by the question of whether we can live with too much self-awareness, besieged by the ability to think and analyse (see Valdrè, 2017). It seems an anti-psychoanalytic paradox, but I believe that, yes, in particularly passionate and incendiary minds such as those of these writers, one can die from too much self-awareness.

We have seen, in part, the death drive that punctuates every word Pasolini wrote. But this is true also for the life drive or *passion*. It pulsates in every line. What kind of passion is this? A *tragic* one:

> (. . .) it corresponds with the painful awareness of an intellectual who *lives* in first person the contradictions of his times. However, it would be an error of perspective to focus only on the tragic aspect of Pasolini's style. (. . .) This is because the other tragic dimension is his excess of love for life. Thus, the passion is *joy*. The joy is the other dimension of the tragic dialectic of Pasolini's passions. Joy and suffering are the main players of a dialectic of passion. Passion is the love for conflict and Pasolini is able to "make the conflict dance."
>
> (Kirchmayr, 2010, p. 38, translated for this edition)

An explosive and dangerous joy for life (leading him to no good) and inexhaustible and always "outdated" search for truth coexisted with the inevitable end of everything, with caducity. "If the truth is fullness caught in the moment, it disappears in that moment" (Kirchmayr, 2010, p. 38, translated for this edition).

Ab joi is the expression Pasolini used to describe this particular fullness of joy. It is an expression coming from Provençal lyric poetry:

> Since I was young and since my first poems in Friulian dialect (. . .) I have used an expression of Provençal lyric poetry that is *ab joi*. It is the nightingale singing *ab joi*, for joy (. . .) perhaps it is the key term of all my poetic work. (. . .) I think that all my poetic work is marked by a *nostalgia for life*, by a sense of being excluded that actually increases and does not decrease the love for life.
>
> (Kirchmayr, 2010, p. 39, translated for this edition)

Can Pasolini's tender and nostalgic *ab joi* correspond to Eros, an Eros now tender, now furious, that coexists with the Thanatos of Salò, with the tragic death at the beach in Ostia? Yes, it is imaginable; but while digressing with these interesting conjectures, we must respect the mystery of art. What Pasolini (an exquisitely anti-contemporary character) was interested in is not the pursuit of happiness nor in finding ways to obtain it nor in escaping suffering: the charm and beauty of his poetics, accessible even to those who do not know him or his work very well, reside in his assimilation of life as joy and suffering. This is Derrida's *life death* discussed at the beginning. As psychoanalysis tells us, life can be conceived only as *nostalgia for life*. The object will be always a lost object. The phantasm of being excluded is inevitable in our unconscious. Nonetheless, for Pasolini *being inside while staying outside* was the essence of life. His words are now eternal and universal. He wanted a full life: but a full life does not mean a happy life. Being full of pain and in a *meta*-position from the exclusion, an exclusion that comes from the Oedipus complex, means to live a meaningful life. It means to believe in truth. In his brief and amazing *On Transience* (1915), Freud argues that beauty gives joy but is always transient. This transience increases and does not decrease the beauty, rather it highlights that life has a melancholic aspect that the artist can universally understand. Thus, beauty is transient: what is beautiful is what is never really possessed, lost forever and always searched for. Here, Pasolini offers us a clear and prophetic political vision, according to which consumerism and power kill what is beautiful, pure, simple and sacred. This can be found in a quite unusual poem of his, in which he touched upon many topics with moving tenderness: beauty, transience, the ephemeral and the deception of power. It is the poem dedicated to Marilyn Monroe (*Marilyn*, 1963), written the day after her death:

> (. . .)
>
> But still you remained a little girl,
>
> silly as antiquity, cruel as the future,
>
> while all the stupidity and cruelty of the present
>
> came between you and your beauty.
>
> Passively immodest, obediently indecent,
>
> you carried it always with you, like a smile behind the tears.
>
> (. . .)
>
> (Pasolini, 2014, p. 361)

It is perhaps beyond our scope but I want to remind us how, among many, Siciliano remembers the poet of "desperate vitality" immediately after his death:

> He was a generous and sweet friend: he had a mild look, his voice was gentle even when he got excited when debating his ideas vehemently. This vehemence gave him the certainty of solitude. His friendship seemed to come from far away: he was always able to tell you his thoughts in advance, even the reasons for his own murder. And this, for those who loved him, is an inconsolable torture. (. . .) It seems that Pasolini managed to make invention and reality coincide. (. . .) Now it is vain to relight the fire of his "desperate vitality." His writings, his verses remain: "I look in my heart, I am what my heart has inside."
>
> (Sicilian, 1978, p. 432)

The Lighthouse at the End of the World

The suicide of the writer: from Fitzgerald to D.F. Wallace to Yates, the American epic of hopelessness

> Inspiration contained a death threat. He would, as he wrote the things he had waited and prayed for, fall apart. Drink was a stabiliser. It somewhat reduced the fatal intensity.
>
> (Bellow, *On John Cheever*, 1983, my italics)

Saul Bellow, one of the great American writers, wrote these words on the death of his friend and colleague John Cheever. He argued that *true* inspiration always contains a threat of death. Although Cheever managed to write what he wanted to, he fell just the same. For the *fatal intensity* of some minds, alcohol is a terrible stabiliser. This is nothing but the profound psychological truth of all my arguments. Virginia Woolf used to say that writers are always unhappy.

There is much literature on the link between art and the death drive, on the ways through which artists use sublimation to write masterpieces but then suffer dangerous consequences. The myth of the doomed writer is always fascinating, although it is not always true; it shows that creativity can be very costly because of that dangerous *proximity* of life to death that sublimation entails. Being a vast topic, which I explored in part in a previous work, *On Sublimation* (2014), I have chosen to circumscribe the topic in this book by considering the life and work of some authors who share two features: an extreme and *fatal* intensity in thinking (Pasolini's desperate vitality) and the need for *addiction*, mainly alcohol (but the kind of substance is absolutely irrelevant), both for quelling this intensity and as a partially masochistic Nirvana expression of the death drive. I have chosen a group of writers I am extremely fond of: they represent the American genius, the universality of writing and a revolution in literary style. They were able to shift the paradigm of a generation of writers by openly talking about themselves directly or through their work. They lived between the 1920s and 1990s and some are well known, some not. I do not intend to discuss their biographies or specific work – that would require another book at least – nor do I intend to assess them as clinical cases. I will limit myself to a journey through some aspects of their lives and work by focusing on how so much vitality can coexist with evident expressions of the death drive.

In analogy with Chapter 2 and the female body as both a metaphor and terrain for a new (?) battlefield of death inside life, I have chosen male writers because men seem to be more vulnerable to substance abuse than women (although we can find examples of alcoholic female writers in Patricia Highsmith and Elizabeth Bishop, among others) and women to the so-called eating disorders more than men.[3] These authors, some very famous (Fitzgerald, Hemingway) and other less so (Carver, Cheever, Yates), who invented American Realism, often destroyed their successful lives. More recently, a different and unique case is David Foster Wallace, a paradigmatic example of *too* vital and energetic a mind. The fire of life was so strong in him that, to tamp it down, he first abused a stabilising substance and finally committed suicide. In other words, he had always felt the need to do something to stop all that excitement.

Bellow asks, perhaps unconsciously, the disturbing and fascinating hypothesis repeatedly taken up by Wallace: is it possible to tolerate too much vitality?

Is it possible to die from too much life drive? Many years before his suicide and after the success of *Infinite Jest*, Lipsky asked Wallace whether he conceived of "(. . .) a kind of toxic self-consciousness" (Lipsky, 2010, p. 25; see also Valdrè, 2017). Wallace agreed: for him writing was simultaneously necessary and toxic because it intensified that continuous excited state that he called *self-consciousness*. Referring to writing and the world of book launches and mundane events that his success required, he answered (exhibiting a certain awareness of the cause of his future death): "But this stuff is real bad for me, it makes me self-conscious. The more exposure I as a person get, the more it hurts me as a writer. (. . .)" "*But the self-consciousness is helpful to you, too?*" (Lipsky insists) "It's like everything else: It's real good up to a certain point. (. . .)" Wallace replies. (p. 25). "(. . . .) My brain does work that way, and it's in my interest to eliminate as many possible avenues of it. And you can see, I mean, I'm not a reclusive writer, I'm not saying no to this, I'm just trying *to be careful* about it" (Wallace concludes) (p. 26, my italics).

Wallace always wore a bandana. Few images represent more effectively the metaphor of a mind trying to contain itself. Lipsky asked Wallace about his bandana. Wallace explained that he started to wear one at his sister's house in Tucson to protect himself from the Arizona sun. Later he realised he *needs it to be always protected*:

> I started wearing it that year, and then it became a *big* help (. . .). And then I discovered that I felt better with them (the bandanas) on. (. . .) *Keeping your head together, you know?* (. . .) It's the recognition of a weakness, which is that I'm just kind of worried my head's gonna explode.
>
> (Lipsky, 2010, pp. 185, 186, my italics)

At various times, Wallace said that alcohol and substances were not important *per se*, rather they were temporary and interchangeable; they were like anaesthetics; they sedated not only the psychical pain, as it is commonly recognised, but *also* the psychical arousal, the excitement of thoughts and free associations and fantasies. It is impossible to always remain in this mental state, in spite of its creativity. For Wallace, even (and above all) television was so enthralling an anaesthetic that he had to do without it because if he turned it on, he would stay glued to it for hours.

All our writers are united by a peculiar and paradoxical use of the substance that will cause their death. This substance extinguishes life, the *excess* of vitality. We are on the opposite side of the Nirvana drive but the aim of the person is the same: to extinguish the fire of life. Long before his death, in one of his novels Wallace likened the depressed person who kills himself to someone who tries to escape from a burning building. I believe that the preconscious metaphor of the burning building represents his burning mind and not so much depression but its opposite, that manic state that beleaguers the minds of many artists (Jamison,

1996).[4] Suicide seems the inevitable answer when there are no more bandanas or anaesthetics and written pages can no longer provide any containment.

Why should we start this brief journey on the desperate vitality of our writers with Wallace? Because I believe that few contemporary writers are as good as he is at providing an *objective* and not subjective description of the downward spiral of drugs and the death drive at its source. He was not a substance addict: no anaesthetic worked better than writing (*hard working*) in his immense masterpiece that is *Infinite Jest*, where he dedicates page after page to describe, in the detail that was typical of his style, the life and mind of a person *addicted to* something that does not make him think:

> That most substance-addicted people are also addicted to thinking, meaning they have a compulsive and unhealthy relationship with their own thinking. (. . .) That it takes great personal courage to let yourself appear weak. (. . .) That no single, individual moment is in and of itself unendurable (. . .) That it's possible to smoke so many cigarettes that you get little white ulcerations on your tongue.
>
> (Wallace, 1996, pp. 203, 204)

These are some of the irreverent, dramatic and grotesque "discoveries" the author listed when he entered a rehabilitation centre. He explored the deadly dependence with neither modesty nor myth-making through hundreds of hyper-condensed words and phrases, each one containing its own truth. I place Wallace, who killed himself in his mid-40s, at the beginning of this part of the chapter because it is as if in his words, so tragically lucid and desolately contemporary that they spark immediate recognition (bringing to mind our patients), contain in hyper-modern terms the psychological truth of the American realists I'm going to discuss.

Cheever, Fitzgerald, Williams, Yates and others live and die in the environment that a few decades later Wallace, though stylistically different, described in detail. He knew alcohol and drugs inside out without being an alcoholic or a drug addict. Like his predecessors he fell "victim" to a precocious and powerful talent and had to resort to some form of anaesthetic (or bandana) to contain pain but also joy, ruin but also excitement. I think it is commonplace to link *addiction* to depressive, compulsive personalities and to the inability to handle suffering or the presence of trauma: it is often like that, but in most cases one *takes drugs for pleasure*. When we discussed Nando we spoke of Léthé: no other human pleasure, bond or sublimated form can remotely correspond to the ephemeral *pleasure* that drug addicts experience. The body retains the memory and searches repeatedly and past the point of pain until the subject is no longer able to manage life. The beginning may have been the search for non-thinking for Wallace, oblivion for Nando; either way, it is the search for pleasure.

None of these authors was, from what we glean from their biographies and work, "depressed" in the clinical sense; none of them was marked by a Baudelairian *spleen*; all of them loved life. The death drive of these gifted and tormented authors was impossible without their hunger for life. They lived passionate and exciting lives, unruly or methodical, with ups and downs, love, marriage, divorce, travel. Just like Pasolini's life, these lives could not combine creativity and quiet, libido and destruction. We will not follow their stories or work in a linear way, but we will pick up excerpts, ideas, suggestions. I will focus only on my argument, aware that I will exclude authors and topics that deserve a wide discussion. It is on the group, more than on the individual, that my reflection will focus – on the group or an eternal journey, in eternal escape.

There are many questions at stake at the metapsychological level: how to explain that sometimes, sometimes even suddenly, deadly drives are unbound and free to kill? What permits them to detach from the protective tangle? Why does the life drive become unable to support them, as if it were corroded from within, consumed in an unrivalled struggle? What was the role of compulsive alcohol abuse in this disentanglement? And what was the role of failure or of narcissistic frustrations in lives that otherwise flourished? It's impossible to answer: whatever the answer, it is hidden in these authors' minds. We can only agree with Bellow: creativity is *always dangerous* and always contains a threat of death – both in the artistic experience and at the metapsychological level. The same drives are always the source, the origin of creativity, and they can point to sublimation or perversion. This can explain the mystery that combines the sublime and the perverse in humans, often in the same subject. The border is razor-thin between desexualised/ deadly and de-sexualised/sublimated, between perverse outlets and creative ones, that nothing about this should surprise us. If all of this can have a meaning in the psychoanalytic theory of the drives, the mystery of art and genius remains a mystery.

Here, I am much indebted to the beautiful book by the essayist Olivia Laing, *The Trip to Echo Spring: On Writers and Drinking* (2013). Similarly to Knapp and Bullitt-Jonas' books, this book offers many psychoanalytic-flavoured reflections but is not a psychoanalytic work. It approaches familiar topics in a deep, original and bold manner. Just as Knapp and Bullit-Jonas experience the drama of eating disorders and only after having "travelled through" them manage to write about them, so, too, Laing, a British author, retraces the *physical* places in which this group of writers circulate and creates a new narrative genre – their moves, their travels, their many domiciles; as the title suggests, it's a journey through America.

Laing notes that all these extraordinary lives took "(. . .) the same dark trajectory (. . .)":

> I wanted to know what made a person drink and what it did to them. I wanted to know *why writers drink*, and what effect this stew of spirits has had upon the body of literature itself.[5]

(Laing, 2013, p. 6)

Four of the six American winners of the Nobel Prize for Literature were alcoholics and "about half of our alcoholic writers eventually killed themselves" (p. 7), she points out. We are used to thinking of a single author at a time – of the reasons for his life and death, of his childhood, his work, his demons. We are less used to thinking of something that I find of great interest in a psychoanalytic context: an overview, in this case, a sort of map of the movements of this group of men in America. We can conceive of it as a drama: individual drama that gifts us, the readers, with unsurpassed masterpieces. Would they have been able to achieve such splendour if they had been sober? It is another question without answer.

Laing focuses on another commonality: these authors were *relentless travellers*. Hotels, rentals, homes in several places, more often than not in the States but also in Europe. One, Fitzgerald, dies in a hotel, the crossing point *par excellence*; Yates's characters represent the many moves of his childhood due to his mother's vicissitudes and whims. It can be argued that mobility is an American characteristic; but I believe that the external, physical behaviours of these authors corresponded to an inner restlessness that led them to search for an elsewhere, a safe heaven, a peace, never found because it existed only within them, not outside themselves. Wallace did not like moving because he felt safely contained by his routine. In this way he was an exception among our writers, who were perpetually on the move: this helps to create a myth about them but I don't think that they found their constant movement so exciting. It was only flight, escape, running. These are men who were always missing a house – a home – both externally and intern-ally. They lived in hotels for long periods of time and the hotel becomes the temporary *house* of a mind full of demons. These long stays in different places in which they wrote and made memories form the basis of Laing's special journey, an adventure that recounts unexpected external and internal geographies, landscapes of the soul, disasters, joys, creative discoveries.

Almost all these writers, as is customary in the United States, taught or lectured at a university. For some of them, this constituted their only secure source of income but, more profoundly, life on a university campus, with its rules, rituals and colleagues, provided them with protection and structure. All our writers were heavy drinkers: some of them, for example, Carver (now considered a master among American minimalists), stopped drinking yet died early; others, such as Yates, lived a long life but went from one rehabilitation centre to another and at the end was too sick to write; others still, such as Wallace, Fitzgerald and Hemingway, killed themselves. In almost all instances, the death drive got the better of them.

Their biographies and the many testimonies of those who knew these writers testify to the fact that alternating between genius, with periods of pure dedication to writing and creativity giving way to clamorous and violent drunkenness, devastated their marital ties, social relations and physical health. Their public, their friends, their students and literary agents continued to love them and rarely abandoned them: they could not ascribe the writers' failures on alcoholism in the face of the writers' accolades and successes. They were loved by women who were often loyal to the bitter end even when faced with massive devastation.

Having shed light on the adult lives of our writers, we return to the repe-tition compulsion: they had dark childhoods. Childhood is that period of life from which we try to escape all our life, a period characterised by *intense loneliness* and *intense ignorance*, as Schreiner (1998) stresses. Childhood suffering is at the heart of alcoholism, flight, our authors' search for death – and pleasure is its driving force. I find Schreiner's definition sadly pertinent: no era, even if we do not remember it (or if we have defensively idealised it), can have the inconsolable solitude of childhood. Childhood makes unaware little Oedipi of all of us: unconscious, innocent yet already wounded, ignorant of life's facts and the future's events.

> Most of these six had – or saw themselves as having – that most Freudian of pairings, an overbearing mother and a weak father. All were tormented by self-hatred and a sense of inadequacy. Three were profoundly promiscuous, and almost all experienced conflict and dissatisfaction with regard to their sexuality. Most died in middle age (. . .). At times, all tried in varying degrees to give up alcohol, but only two succeeded, late in life, in becoming permanently dry.
>
> (Laing, 2013, pp. 9, 10)

Some of them were friends. The introverted and embittered Cheever and the young Carver taught at the famous Iowa Writers' Workshop at the same time. For the first, the University of Iowa was the place he left, in his early 60s, to be admitted to the hospital for delirium tremens; for the second, it was where he produced two works of poetry. Carver, who survived Cheever, later wrote that "he and I did nothing *but* drink" (Laing, 2013, p. 3). Hemingway and Fitzgerald, lovers of Europe, drank together at the same Paris café, companions, accomplices, drinking buddies sharing loneliness and excesses.

Tennessee Williams, perhaps the greatest American playwright, was found dead in a hotel on 54th Street near Broadway. He was 71 years old, unhappy, an alcohol and drug addict, paranoid, often admitted to hospital for delirium tremens. After the success of *A Streetcar Named Desire* (1947) and other work, he feared not being able to write or find work. His star was extinguished, perhaps because of alcohol, perhaps due to an unavoidable descent that alcohol accentuated. Creativity remains a mystery in its birth and in its death. It is not the death that, as he wrote years before in *Memoirs*, he would have liked: a child without a home who lived in various hotels in Manhattan (with the apparent justification of being near theatres), without warmth, he would have liked to die in Sicily, where he knew happiness, surrounded by peasants and simple people, outside the whirlwind of the literary world. Being loved for himself, no matter if recognised or not, was his demon: he longed for the warmth he found in faraway Sicily. He never experienced that warmth, literal and figurative elsewhere in his life: having produced masterpieces early in life, he was forced to try to meet the expectations that he himself and American culture placed on him. The narcissistic balance is always frail and propels the death drive to prevail over these men: if self-love is only linked to recognition, it is false, unstable, precarious. Alcohol becomes the anaesthetic of pain and happiness, because *too much* happiness can be unbearable. What will they demand of me *after this success*? Will I be up to it? Will I meet expectations? Williams was fully cognizant of these questions. Speaking of himself and another genius marked by alcohol, he writes:

> O'Neill had a terrible problem with alcohol. Most writers do. American writers nearly all have problems with alcohol because there's a great deal of tension involved in writing (. . .). And it's all right up to a certain age, and then you begin to need a little nervous support that you get from drinking. Now my drinking has to be moderate. (. . .).
>
> (Laing, 2013, p. 18)

The great unresolved trauma of Williams's life was the schizophrenia and subsequent lobotomy of his beloved sister Rose. Haunted by Rose's plight his whole life (perhaps because of his unconscious guilt for not having been sick in her stead), he kills himself with alcohol and drugs. The enormous success in the first part of his career does not make Rose's ghost disappear and, according to our hypothesis, forms the guilt at the basis of his determined death drive. He "lobotomised" himself because "(. . .) drinking might be a way of disappearing from the world (. . .)" (Laing, 2013, p. 18).

I believe that all of this is true. Just like the women whose eating disorder makes them skeletal or obese, so, too, alcohol or another substance makes one invisible to the world, a ghost. To the ghost of Rose, Williams responded with years of pure genius but eventually became a ghost himself. He hated his hometown of St. Louis, and started to drink at 17, like many teenagers today who would like to escape, "to disappear from the world." He took the opportunity, thanks to his grandfather, to travel to Europe (let's bear in mind that these are the years when the old continent holds great fascination for the most restless Americans and artists) and fell in love with the place, the always-sought elsewhere: he tasted his first French champagne and found it "really delicious" (Laing, 2013, p. 22). Here comes the balm and at first it is magical! But in Paris he also began to suffer acute anxiety, nightmares, paranoia that remained for the rest of his life. He tried to sedate himself with alcohol. He travelled to other French cities and to Venice. Alcohol became his only form of self-care, his preferred method of facing stress, fear and life.

On her journey, Laing visits the New York City hospitals to which the greatest minds of a generation were admitted – Williams, Cheever, Truman Capote. Medical reports seem stereotypical: anxiety, delirium, recovery, Alcoholics Anonymous meetings, relapse. Only Cheever, and later Carver, survived, but not for long. Yates survived, too. Laing does not write about him, but I think he deserves to be part of this group, both because he shares all the salient characteristics and because he has not been sufficiently recognised. In fact, although he is probably the greatest realist of his generation, he received few honours during his time and although his work has been recently re-evaluated thanks to the success of the 2008 Sam Mendes film *Revolutionary Road*, based on his debut novel, Yates remains in the shadows of fame. We will return to him and his work at the end of the chapter.

For all these writers, alcoholism provided double, ambiguous support, both positive (in particular at the beginning) and negative (and with the passage of time, devastating). But we cannot disconnect the genius of some early works from the "positive" effects of alcohol. It could be that alcohol produces dreams and nightmares and quells anxiety. The death drive arrives some time later (we have seen that only two of our writers are "saved") but because death is inside life we must recognise that the life drive may have been "helped" by alcohol: the subject would otherwise be dead, overwhelmed by anxiety. From the psychoanalytic perspective, these men are *not seeking* Nando's Nirvana or nothingness, the absence of tension. Rather, *at the beginning they try to manage the life drive*, to contain it, tame it. It is a form of self-care, not homeostasis. Personally, I am not of the (romantic) idea that genius and unruliness must necessarily go together but, as Wallace says, sometimes genius and excess of thought, the burning mind, may require the aid (the illusory aid) of the anaesthetic closest to hand, according to the customs of an era and a cultural milieu; or sometimes, on the contrary, creative approaches require stimulation. But this is only the other side of the coin.

The distinction, which I propose as pure hypothesis, is, in my opinion, important on the instinctual plane: the desire for non-desire, the death of desire, is one thing; and the need to *contain* desire, to tame it, is another. Only in time do the two processes coincide, both in the physical life of the subject and the drive: there is nothing but the death drive because it is stronger, more rooted, ancient, silent than the weak struggles necessary for being alive.

Returning to New York after his long journey to Europe, Williams had his greatest successes and his most profound mental breakdown; initially, the two went together. He speaks of "the blue devils" (Laing, 2013, p. 41), those demons that in the big city increase in number and must be calmed down with alcohol and promiscuity ("I evaded with drink and with sex") (p. 41). Not only anguished and sleepless, Williams also suffered from a paralysing shyness that disappeared only by drinking; but the price to pay for the balm of alcohol is difficulty in writing. When, in 1945, after his first great successes, he was catapulted into the New York scene as the writer of the moment, he experienced the same terror that Wallace described years later: "(. . .) success (is) terrible" (p. 45).

Perhaps Cheever is less famous but not less important than others in the group. Born to a family of modest origins, this "Chekhov of the suburbs" was, as mentioned, among the few who managed to recover from alcoholism ("to recover" is an important verb in Alcoholics Anonymous vocabulary because a person can never heal from addiction). Between the 1930s and 1940s, a feverish literary period, he, too, lived in New York. He admires Williams. Cheever is a master of the short story and his travel diaries from Europe are amazing. What tormented Cheever? At least from what we glean from his diaries and indirectly from the characters in his stories: the modest origins; an affective and overwhelming mother; perhaps, above all, the awareness of not being the most loved by his father, who preferred Cheever's older brother; and, when he was older and happily married, the tormenting doubt of being homosexual (this is an unanswered question). When his short story collections enjoyed a certain success and his name became known, the "formal" entry to the upper class to which he longed to belong, revealed that nothing is ever enough:

Cheever continued in the depths of himself to feel excluded (from paternal love? From a clear masculine identity?), someone marginal, never really belonging to the social group to which he now had the right to be a part. Indeed, he experienced this belonging as a sort of fraudulence, a deceit and theft, something not deserved: the lack of paternal love displaced by the desire to be part of a certain social circle that, when it comes true, ends up feeling like a fraud. We are talking about profoundly intelligent, deeply conscious men, even in their preconscious, then transferred to the written page of their destiny. With his perennial sense of *exclusion*, Cheever drank for many years. According to Laing, the greatest writers, even when honoured by society, remain a sort of *outsider*. She reports Cheever's words on this point:

> It was my decision, early in life, to *insinuate myself* into the middle class, *like a spy*, so that I would have an advantageous position of attack, but I seem now and then to have forgotten my mission and to have taken my disguises too seriously.
>
> (Laing, 2013, p. 55, my italics)

Like a spy, someone who insinuates himself: it is the experience of a fraud, a thief, a profiteer. What you did not have at birth, you will never have: in his characters, as we will see in Yates, we find this subtle sense of defeat, futility and dissatisfaction with every success achieved. However, in spite of these feelings and his uncertainty about his sexual identity in a period exalting the strength of the American male, Cheever continued to write (although he had never been prolific), stayed with his wife, attended Alcoholics Anonymous meetings and, when old and tired, was sober and maintained a certain modest, imperfect balance.

In Cheever's internal world, thanks to some combination or coincidence we do not know about, the life drive painstakingly prevailed over the death drive: sublimation was partially successful and he finally managed to accept himself and his uncertain identity and frail narcissistic structure. He came to understand that one starts to destroy himself slowly. In 1952, he writes: "When the beginnings of self-destruction enter the heart it seems no bigger than a grain of sand" (Cheever, 2008, p. 23).

However, Cheever always felt himself to be a failure. Again in 1952, he writes:

> As I approach to my fortieth birthday without having accomplished any one of the things I intended to accomplish – without ever having achieved the deep creativity that I have worked towards for all this time – I feel that I take a minor, an obscure, a dim position that is not my destiny but that is my fault, as if I had lacked somewhere along the line, the wit and courage to contain myself competently within the shapes at hand.
>
> (Cheever, 2008, p. 7)

Another common symptom of all our authors, but actually a sign of a deep anguish that they share and that I think is not disconnected from their creativity, is *insomnia*.

Alcohol disturbs sleep in many ways: at the beginning it facilitates sleep but later it has the opposite effect. A chronic alcoholic is often besieged by intractable and anxiety-producing insomnia (this is not a common aspect of all alcoholics, of course, but it is of all our authors). Williams, Yates, Fitzgerald and Hemingway suffered from insomnia. In one of his best short stories, *Now I Lay Me*, the latter writes:

> I myself did not want to sleep because I had been living for a long time with the knowledge that if I ever shut my eyes in the dark and let myself go, my soul would go out of my body.
>
> (Hemingway, 1955, p. 145)

The relationship with insomnia and its nightmares is *ambivalent* (as is the relationship with alcohol): is insomnia necessary for writing?

On the one hand, insomnia brings demons and nightmares, on the other hand a writer needs to be alert, *continually awake* in order to keep his demons and nightmares at bay. *Plenty of insomnia*, Hemingway writes, can illuminate the path and show us ground, the infernal terrain. Far from constituting a medical symptom of alcoholism or depression, the relationship writers have with insomnia forges a mysterious, complex and disquieting bond with creativity and the death drive that is always at its basis: does writing perhaps need this *nocturnal side* of consciousness, the negative, the shadow of life? We can only draw some conjectures from diaries, when they exist, the magic of the words.

Hemingway is another perfect example in our discussion: an extraordinarily vital man, who led an adventurous life, had many marriages, fought on the frontlines during war, changed countries, cities, houses and was surrounded by his dozens of cats in a sunny house in Key West, Florida, he killed himself with a gunshot to his forehead at the age of 62. Admired and beloved, considered the inventor of the American short story and of a dry and essential style, he was an alcoholic for almost his entire life. He seemed to have attempted suicide many times. He was wounded in war, but also later, his body battered by injuries, falls from small aircraft, accidents of all kinds, the literal scars of a lifestyle that challenged death and pushed everything *to the limit*. His last years were full of suffering: depressive and manic-depressive episodes, electroshock that undermined his memory and his capacity to write, diabetes, damage due to his many years of alcoholism, etc. The "active suicide," after a life on the one hand furiously vital and on the other hand typified by the ceaseless search for death, seems an inevitable consequence. As with Wallace (if he had lived longer perhaps he could have won the Nobel Prize in Literature), we are talking about uncommon people and ones united if not by the same suffering, then from the way they tried to manage that suffering or to *use* it creatively: alcohol. It is said that when in 1954, in the wake of *The Old Man and the Sea*, Hemingway was invited to the Nobel Prize ceremony, by then ill, he said "too late." He was completely different from the young man who in 1935 argued in the post-post-script of a letter to Ivan Kashkin:

I have drunk since I was fifteen and few things have given me more pleasure. When you work hard all day with your head and know you must work again the next day what else can change your ideas and make them run on a different plane like whisky? (. . .) Modern life, too, is often a mechanical oppression and liquor is the only mechanical relief.

(Hemingway, 1981, p. 420)

Even Fitzgerald, as we have said, the author of masterpieces such as The Great Gatsby and Tender is the Night, was haunted by insomnia. And then there was his relationship with his wife Zelda: beloved, she, too, an artist, united by the compulsion to travel and fantasise, protagonists together in a legendary life. Zelda became ill with a serious mental disease and remained hospitalised for the rest of her life. Fitzgerald, who never ceased to love and take care of her, was likely to find in this tragedy an additional reason to drink, although, candidly, he admitted that their life sailed between cocktails, literature and art even before her illness. "Zelda painting, me drinking" is a recurring expression in his European travel notes. Of Fitzgerald, the insomniac chased by nightmares and panic attacks, everything can be said but not that he was a dull or depressed man: his work is brilliant, acute, funny, in many instances he declared to love life and he demonstrated it in his tender bond with his daughter Scottie. In the last years of his life, when success had abandoned him, the words he writes to his daughter are sweet and full of hope, of interest in her and the things of the world:

A whole lot of people have found life a whole lot of fun. I have not found it so. But, I had a hell of a lot of fun when I was in my twenties and thirties; and I feel that it is your duty *to accept the sadness*, the tragedy of the world we live, in with a certain esprit.

(Fitzgerald, 1994, pp. 314, 315, my italics)

If Fitzgerald is a loving father and husband, can these be the words of a man haunted by death drives, Nirvana or self-destructive? The answer seems to be negative because he was also a successful writer and a star of high society. Then again he died of a heart attack at only 44. A friend says that he saved his wife from madness but destroyed himself. It is plausible. For him, too, like the other writers, insomnia was a double-edged sword: here is how he justified a delay to his editor: "I have drunk too much and that is certainly slowing me up. On the other hand, without drink I do not know whether I could have survived this time" (Laing, 2013, p. 72). A doctor would diagnose this as the usual ambivalence of the alcoholic and his reluctance to recognise the severity, the tendency to minimise ("I was drinking, intermittently but generously"), but the medical aspect is not what interests us here, rather, it is the complex relationship, mysterious and ambiguous, between what can potentially produce death (alcohol in huge quantities) and the need to be creative and tolerate life.

It is this trait, I repeat, which unites these writers and makes a unitary drive vision not easy, though fascinating. Longing for life, they consciously procured death; but it also seems that deprived of that substance of death, they would not have left us any masterpieces. "Drink heightens feeling. When I drink, it heightens my emotions and I put it in a story. But then it becomes hard to keep reason and emotion balanced. *My stories written when sober are stupid* (. . .). Drink is an escape. That is why so many people do it now" (Laing, 2013, p. 85).

Unlike his friend Hemingway, whose tolerance for high quantities of alcohol remains legendary, the young Fitzgerald, a thin and fragile boy, could not hold his drink. When drunk, he acted violently, to the consternation of those around him. What he drank, his friend Hemingway points out, seemed "*to stimulate him too much* and then to poison him" (Laing, 2013, p. 91). It's that stimulus, to escape his shyness, to paradoxically address his success – that's what Fitzgerald needed: that poison which, at the beginning, is pleasant and therapeutic for all our writers. Self-medication – that initial fuel necessary for writing, that an unparalleled pleasure – a succour that betrays: over time it loses its effect, creates dependence, kills the thought that at first exalted it, produces a vicious circle that requires more and more alcohol for ever-fewer effects. It's the same with the so-called *travel addiction* that hounded our group of writers: exciting at the beginning, then a ritual of forced and meaningless moves. The adult Fitzgerald (although it is difficult to imagine him as an old man) substituted the vital intoxication and the joy of youth with a sort of desolate, lucid Freudian meditation: humankind is not destined for happiness. In 1936 he writes: "So what? This is what I think now: that the natural state of the sentient adult is a qualified unhappiness" (Fitzgerald, 1945, p. 84).

The most recent of our group of writers is Carver. His short or very short stories are the subject of academic discussions and readings; his famous, ironic and bitter work, such as *Will You Please Be Quiet, Please?*, on the stolid and repetitive pain of married life, are small masterpieces. Although more recent than our other writers and one of the few among them who managed to escape alcoholism, his life and work are part of our discussion because they evince the main features of our topic: hunger for life, search for death, vitality and destructiveness.

Carver, who reached the peak of success in the 1970s and 1980s, was self-taught. Like his friend Cheever, he was born poor in Oregon, but he was not ashamed of his humble beginnings. His father was an alcoholic. Because of his parents' many moves, he could not have a regular education. Although he was not a good student, he was an avid reader. With his father going from one hospital to another, he married at just 19. He masterfully transferred to the page the precocious, immature experience of a young union, the struggle to support a family by taking many odd jobs, writing during snatched pieces of time. He and his first wife Maryann were the desolated characters who live in the suburbs, have many bills to pay and a girl to look after, angry for having stolen from one another the best years of their lives in that squalid house where they have dinner, accusations filling the acrimonious air:

Why don't you dance?

In the kitchen, he poured another drink and looked at the bedroom suite in his front yard. The mattress was stripped and the candy-striped sheets lay beside two pillows on the chiffonier. Except for that, things looked much the way they had in the bedroom – nightstand and reading lamp on his side of the bed, nightstand and reading lamp on her side.

His side, her side.

He considered this as he sipped the whiskey.

(Carver, 1981, p. 3)

Carver gave dignity to the drabness of everyday life, the bleakness of poor people who have nothing to say to each other, who live out their lives with the oppression of small everyday actions, a wife ironing and blabbering, a husband pretending to listen, a child screaming, a TV blaring . . . and life goes by. Yet, from his fulminating narrations there always shines a flash of light, as if from a window, the light of poetry.

Despite the enormous difficulties of the early years, he recognised, once he became famous, how much it influenced him, as a writer, to have had two children before the age of 20 – not so much the hardships such as having to write while they ate or wanted to play but, more deeply, over time, how early fatherhood abruptly introduced him to life and its responsibilities. Unlike Peter Pan, Fitzgerald's golden and eternal youth or Pasolini's *impossible* adulthood, Carver's young adult years were the hardest: the too-early domestic chores, the adapting to humble jobs, the late-arriving success, the alcoholism. The 1970s are the most difficult. Alcoholism made him paranoid and violent even towards his wife. Divorce followed. He lost his job in California. Years later, by now a successful author, remembering those hard years, but which are also the basis of all his most original narrative creativity, he says:

I was in my late twenties or early thirties. We were still in a state of poverty, (. . .) and years of hard work with nothing to show except an old car, a rented house, and new creditors on our backs. It was depressing, and I felt spiritually obliterated. Alcohol became a problem. (. . .) I suppose I began to drink heavily after I'd realized that the things I'd wanted most in life were myself and my writing. It's strange. You never start out in life with the intention of becoming a bankrupt or an alcoholic or a cheat and a thief. Or a liar.

(Laing, 2013, p. 274)

Like Cheever, he found some relief in Alcoholics Anonymous, first with varying degrees of success, then effectively. But it was perhaps too late: he died at 50 in 1988, at the height of his success as an "inventor" of short stories and of a new American realism, adored by readers and students, in his beloved house in the Pacific Northwest, where he had retired to write with his second wife.

There was nothing he loved as much as writing: writing saved his life, accorded him distance from the affective and material deprivations of childhood. Writing made him burn, as he recounted in his seminars and workshops. But, as for our other writers, writing was an ambivalent painful necessity: essential to life, but also the cause of excitement, exhaustion, a search that always runs alongside – remember the words of Bellow who opens our chapter – the death drive. Like the others, Carver was aware of his obsessions:

> There are certain obsessions that I have and try to give voice to: the relationship between men and women, why we oftentimes lose the things we put the most value on, the mismanagement of our own inner resources. I'm also interested in survival, what people can do to raise themselves up once they've been laid down.
>
> (Nesset, 1995, p. 27)

Some, for example, Kavaler-Adler (1993), speak of a "compulsion to create" in geniuses, in spite of their short lives. While understanding this basic instinct, I would not reduce it to "compulsion," placing it on the same level as an obsessive ritual. Rather, I propose considering it as a sublimative displacement of instincts and drives that otherwise would be destructive. In these authors the compulsion to create brings forth masterpieces but also parallels the compulsion to self-destruct.

Let us not forget that Carver, after all, was also a poet; like Pasolini, what does he seek at the end? Carver tells us In one of his most beautiful poems, *Late Fragment* (Carver, 1997, p. 294) to the question "And did you get what you wanted from this life?" his answer is simply "I did". His desire was to call himself and to feel himself beloved.

All of Carver's work can be conceived as focused on love in every form, from the highest to the lowest. "What do we talk about when we talk about love?" is one of his most famous short stories, after which a collection of short stories is named.

The deprived child, son of alcoholics, uneducated, found love as an adult thanks to his writing, his second marriage, his children, his readers. But, as with our other writers, everything seemed to arrive *too late*. Every act of reparation is certainly meaningful but comes after alcohol and other abuses have their devastating effects. I am always surprised every time I realise that so significant and universal pages, so able to reach our hearts, are written by people who were often in hospitals, on a bender, on the run. Just like Hemingway, Carver suffered various "accidents." Yet, the strength of talent, the urgency and the ability to express an inner world made universal by writing, kept those trembling hands on the keys for hours and hours, during endless sleepless nights, before reaching us.

I want to add Richard Yates to my discussion, although Laing does not mention him in her book, as I said, both because we find all our writers' characteristics in him and simply because I love him and all his work.

Unlike the other writers, Yates – who is identified with the mid-twentieth century Age of Anxiety in the same way in which Fitzgerald is identified with the Jazz Age – stays in oblivion for many years until the re-publication of his first novel and masterpiece, Revolutionary Road (Yates, 1961) only a few years ago, and the film adaptation, which retains the same title, completely faithful to the book. He remains, however, relatively unknown, although today he is considered a master of American realism and his other novels and stories are equally sublime (although not numerous, as there were gaps of several years between them).

It may be that, unconsciously, one of the reasons why he is not a household name, not even in his native United States, is his *constant unhappiness* and rejection of the American myth of happiness. This is how Nick Laird describes Yates in a 2009 article for the online version of *The Guardian*:

> Richard Yates spent the last years of his life living alone in a rented flat in Tuscaloosa, Alabama, stranded among brimming ashtrays and Salvation Army furniture. (. . .) That final apartment in Tuscaloosa was bare of decoration except for photos of his daughters on a wall and a quote from Adlai Stevenson taped above his desk – intended as an epigraph for his last, unfinished novel: "Americans have always assumed, subconsciously, that every story will have a happy ending."
>
> (Laird, 2009)

Only this (apparent?) absence of desperate vitality, of the frenzy of life, of dangerous and daring adventures, career zeniths and nadirs seem to differentiate Yates from the other writers in our group. Except for his drinking and his periods in psychiatric hospitals, where he was diagnosed with bipolar disorder (as was Wallace), Yates was an ordinary man, mild, sad. Inconsolably sad. He did not reach the ups or downs of success because he achieved little success during his lifetime, in particular as a critic or as a teacher; he did not travel romantically through Europe or go on Hemingway safaris. Still, early on he moved innumerable times from one apartment to the next, mostly in New York City to follow the restlessness and constant economic problems of his mother, the central character of his life. The bedrock of his death drive, of the creeping destructiveness even in the most serene periods, was alcoholism; although alternating between cures and long periods of abstinence, it never completely left him and it killed him in 1992 at 76, so, too, it formed of a sort of "fate neurosis" (Freud, 1920) which made things go bad for him, as if bad luck dogged him. He lived more than the others, but paradoxically with more death inside him.

He wrote a total of about ten books, mostly short novels (after his debut with the voluminous *Revolutionary Road*) and some short stories; the insecurity, the extreme perfectionism that never satisfied him, the depressive phases and the alcoholism, the teaching that he loved for its rules and containment and practical necessity for earning a living, all these elements delayed the publication of his writing and placed long intervals between one oeuvre and the next. His characters were mainly autobiographical; he found inspiration in himself and his mother, sister and wife. His parents divorced early. He did not enjoy a close relationship with his father and always lived among women. Perhaps this is why he accurately described his female characters at the psychological level. His female characters succumb to life even if often they do not realise it, so they continue to obstinately fight and, above all, to *dream*. His mother Ruth was the archetypal figure, the inspiration for his life and work. We find in many novels the eternal child who never grows up, who is both frail and determined; men and women who cannot free themselves from their initial mistakes, who trap themselves, who desperately long for success and love but do not get them or get them late or in all the wrong ways. They occupy "(. . .) the margin between expectation and reality" (Laird, 2009). In each character Carver writes of himself in a narrative mode so universal that it strikes at the heart of our quiet desperation, our every effort to emancipate ourselves from the pain of childhood – again, from the compulsion to repeat. The role of the mother is central here.

Ruth, left alone with two children after the divorce, never abandoned them and, indeed, relied on them, especially on young Richard, establishing a typical overturned relationship: his childhood was stolen. He was given no choice but to be a parent to his mother, the fragile, inconsistent and beloved dreamer Ruth. Eager to become a sculptor and to be part of the beautiful Bohemian world, she thought common work beneath her. So, pursued by creditors, she made her children constantly move. Having to make new friends every time and start a new school was traumatic for Yates. He found some solace in one of the moves, with an aunt, but until age 20 Yates was forced to chase, listen to and contain his mother's dreams. Ruth, herself a drinker, never achieved success but tenaciously clung to her dreams, like all of Yates's characters: split between the desolation of real life and the lustre of an imaginary future. Years later, Yates says of his mother:

> I knew she was foolish and irresponsible, that she talked too much, that she made crazy emotional scenes over nothing and could be counted on to collapse in a crisis, but I had come to suspect, dismally, that my own personality might be built along much the same lines.
>
> (Laird, 2009)

If, as Colette says, the requirement of a great writer is an unhappy childhood, Yates is kissed by fortune (Bailey, 2003).

When he recognised the identification with his mother, something intensified by the absence of his father or of other *third figures* offering alternative models, Yates left the maternal home (or homes), but he never freed himself of this internal object, loved and hated, intimate, for which he felt a poignant empathy. He grappled with it through drinking. There was nothing epic about Yates's alcoholism, unlike the daring adventures of Hemingway or Fitzgerald: it reflected the quiet desperation of his everyday life, it was a medicine for insomnia, it comprised part of a deadly and quiet routine. And yet, I do not believe that his novels are tragedies: the characters, very human in their weaknesses, are often ironic, neurotic, similar to those of Woody Allen who are always seeking an elsewhere that will never come yet do not give up trying. Laird (2009) finds some (unconscious) psychoanalytic material in Yates's writings (and for many years Yates himself was in psychotherapy, in which, alternately, he believed and did not believe):

> But the source of Yates's melancholy went deeper than anxiety over one's literary status. Despite his high-handed, Nabokovian dismissals of psycho-analysis (finally prescribed antidepressants, he gleefully remarks, "No more Sigmund Fucking Freud!"), he knew perfectly well where his problems began – in his disturbed and claustrophobic upbringing – and he circles this subject obsessively. Few twentieth century writers made more productive use of their own painful backstories. Family names survive only slightly changed (in *The Easter Parade* his mother Dookie appears as the only vaguely fictionalised Pookie) and real-life arrangements of sisters, husbands and wives and colleagues all find their too-perfect reflections, reappearing so com-pulsively that only a Freudian term can describe it: abreaction, the emotional release following the recall of a painful repressed episode. This leads to the usual law of diminishing returns: in the final, weaker novels, what fiction there ever was seems squeezed out of the frame by the push of repetition compulsion. Once, it appeared that the personal emotional release was the side effect of the fiction, but now you sense the weight of that dynamic shift. The characters become repeating versions of each other, following in the footsteps of their predecessors down a mirrored corridor of misery.
>
> (Laird, 2009)

All the more fascinating that Yates often argued that family is the main topic we can talk about. In fact, everything we will become in the future and all our pain suffered in the past comes from the family. This is true but implicit for every artist. But I chose to deal with Yates because he was extremely aware of repetition compulsion – one of the expressions of the death drive – and he was able to acutely, tenderly, indulgently write about it. His characters are always hunted and uselessly on the run. Countertransferentially we feel sympathy for Yates's characters, a reproduction of the mother, the sister (who married an alcoholic) and himself.

From the magnificent first sentence of *The Easter Parade*, a story of two sisters, Yates projects himself onto the poor sisters Sarah and Emily. He narrates (and perhaps *takes care of*) the childhood wound of his parents' divorce that left him without a valid paternal identification and at the mercy of a childish mother to take care of. Freudian "fate neurosis" occurs in various stages: every opportunity for happiness is rejected or not grasped or revealed to be illusory. Without knowing it, and indeed despite his scepticism towards psychoanalysis, Yates was, in my opinion, one of the most acute inquirers of the psyche. His, ours. His characters show not only fate neurosis and repetition compulsion, but also self-deception and deception, illusion and myth, a search for a love that never comes, a struggle for a lost youth, a wish for a success that cannot be achieved for lack of talent. It is a twisted way of looking at hope, an illusory hope to be sure. There is no way out of loneliness, dependency, economic trouble, failure, in these lives; yet there are no suicides, tragedies, twists. It is the ordinary Freudian unhappiness, the muteness of the death drive in the incessant return of the identical, in masochism, the phantom protagonist in Yates's books and life.

Alcoholism was his life's companion. Homes, cities, wives, editors changed but alcohol did not abandon him (except for short periods). Although he suffered from emphysema, he continued to smoke and in California, where he taught for a while, he set his apartment on fire and barely escaped unscathed. In a world divided by the contemporary myth of winners and losers, he was more interested in losers. Like unhappy families, they are more numerous, even if they are hidden or masked behind the myriad self-deceptions and defences that the mind manages to invent. Perhaps the novel that best describes the devastating effect of his alcoholism (though it is present in all his work) is *Disturbing the Peace* (2008), a tragic but silent epic of an ordinary man, which, perhaps because of this lack of epic pain, did not resonate with the public. It has another amazing opening: a man on a business trip phones his wife and tells her that he cannot return home to her and their son. When she asks why, he says: "You really want to know, sweetheart? Because I'm afraid I might kill you, that's why. Both of you" (p. 3).

The frankness of Yates's prose is disconcerting. The descent to hell (or to a psychiatric hospital) of John, the main character of *Disturbing the Peace*, is condemning and merciless. No surprise, it was Yates himself, the alcoholic son of alcoholics, who spent time at a psychiatric hospital, a place from which he drew inspiration for his novels. Like the two sisters in *The Easter Parade*, John destroys every possibility of change and recovery: "He had a steely dedication to destroying himself" (Bailey, 2003, p. 225).

John chooses to end his days in peace in a hospital, where he is no longer tormented by hangovers (the same happens to Yates during his manic phases) and does not have to tolerate his life or his wife. "(. . .) Most of us were in no real danger of dying – he noted in an early draft of 'Regards'– but our existence seemed clearly to be something less than life" (Bailey, 2003, p. 114).

I want to repeat that the peculiarity (and thus the *truth*) of the death drive inhabiting these characters is its *normality*. "His characters are the least heroic and romantic we can imagine. The full imperfection of their humanity is the most fascinating aspect" (Homes, 2004, p. 12).

The endings of Yates's books are as extraordinary as their beginnings. When John's ex-wife visits him at the hospital and, just to talk, asks if he has ever thought about what he will do when he gets out, he becomes confused and questions why he would ever leave.

How can we conclude? Every author discussed here deserves a tome all to himself. I chose them on the strength of two main and inseparable factors: the life drive and the death drive. The genius, which made Nobel Prize-winners and innovators of style out of some of them, seems to move in the delicate, mysterious balance between the two drives. Without the epistemophilic drive – deriving, as in Leonardo da Vinci, from the sexual curiosity of children and, I would add, from a certain dose of trauma in people who are particularly gifted at converting into sublimation – there would not have been that vitality which each of our writers expressed in his own way and all poured into wonderful pages. Without the death drive there would probably have never been that self-destruction that all these authors expressed with alcoholism, which led them to early and often squalid deaths, but allowed them to investigate the depths of human pain. How is it possible to *really write* about this pain without having experienced it? For all of them, from Pasolini to Wallace, Yates, Cheever, Carver and others, writing is *absolutely necessary*. *Working hard*, Wallace insisted, is the only thing that counts, the only protection from life and the death drive. According to Yates's greatest biographer, "life was always an excuse for writing." Confined to an unadorned room, one of the masters of American literature did nothing but write until his death, and only writing kept him hanging on to the frail thread of life. Alike and distinct, these brilliant and tormented writers often knew each other or at least they read one another's work, as if sharing a kinship in the same family. Yates said, "If there wasn't a Fitzgerald, I don't think I would have become a writer" (Bailey, 2003, p. 600). Alcohol was just the handiest anaesthetic, the real common trait of creativity and death. At the profound level of personality, Alcoholics Anonymous literature posits that *resentment* and *fear* are, even unconsciously, fundamental traits of the alcoholic, "a man on the run" (Coccioli, 1972) from unmanageable emotions: I do not need to struggle to imagine the immense resentment of Yates towards his mother, of Cheever towards his origins, Fitzgerald's fear of growing up, Wallace's too much self-consciousness. These are universal feelings which we all experience, but which some, for various constitutional and environmental reasons, try to combat with a poisonous potion rather than with the common baggage of defensive mechanisms. There is copious literature on alcoholism, above all from psychiatry and psychopathology, but I want to entrust, once again, the choice of testimony, the words of a journalist, Carlo Coccioli, who in the 1970s attended Alcoholics Anonymous meetings for many years in many countries without being an alcoholic himself. He intimately connected with many men and women he defined as fleeing: fleeing from what? I believe that that his reflections are worth more than any manual or psychiatric tome:

> The man on the run is a person who does not accept the world in which he lives, neither its form of time nor its form of space. (. . .) His terror (of space and time) has no explanation if we do not recognize that he has a different image of space and time. This image is a *memory*. A memory causing nostalgia and anxiety. It is similar to a strong desire for Paradise Lost, a world before the Fall of Lucifer. Thus, it is greediness to link with something *remote but not forgotten* again.
>
> (Coccioli, 1972, p. 32, my italics, translated for this edition)

This subject, in the throes of nostalgia, in search of the fusion bond with the primary object (common to all addictions, notes the author), identifies in alcohol the easiest way, the closest to hand and most inexpensive way:

> (. . .) to go elsewhere (. . .). An elsewhere, of course, that is similar to the peace of nothing, the rest of the not being, at last something very near to death.
>
> (Coccioli, 1972, p. 326)

This is the best way to conclude, that is, with the Freudian death drive. More ably than an analyst, Coccioli has experienced closeness, pity, sympathy and extreme empathy for the many alcoholics who welcomed him into their homes. He intimately grasped the essential and profound. The horror of the alcoholic is to be doubly "another:" other than the rest of the world and other than the part of himself that does not want to drink, that is, the vital part. To this division (clearly visible in all our writers), something more ambiguous and profound than ambivalence, the author gives the name "otherness," a state of mind "that does not completely coincide with strangeness" (Coccioli, 1972, p. 322), an even more painful, specific and complex situation. I would say that we can all experience estrangement in certain circumstances, even from ourselves, but only those who live in deep divisions can experience "otherness." The alcoholic is inhabited by this beast that steals part of the personality and isolates him in profound solitude. Coccioli rightly points out that this loneliness does not come from social alienation, but a self-alienation (hence the potentially healing power of groups). Self-induced loneliness, nostalgia for the primary bond with the lost and never possessed object, of the paradise *before the fall*, escape in the impossible elsewhere and search for deadly stillness are the features shared by all our writers, along with a desperate vitality.

The mystery remains, in my opinion, on the psychoanalytic and also human level because it is unclear why the mechanism of sublimation was not enough in these authors and did not pacify the drives and so was infiltrated by the death drive. Why do artists such as Renoir and Roth live for so long without becoming addicts? Did they perhaps have less painful childhoods, stronger life drives and thus more of a chance to invest in vital objects? We do not know. The question remains: even if deprived of the substance that destroyed them, would the authors discussed in this chapter have been just as brilliant? Was alcohol necessary to challenge death, to live with it continuously, in different ways, as it was for Pasolini; was alcohol the necessary ingredient for creativity?

All that remains is to return to Bellow's words: creativity always contains a threat of death. As Cheever points out:

> I must convince myself that writing is not, for a man of my disposition, a self-destructive vocation. I hope and think it is not, but I am not genuinely sure. It has given me money and renown, but I suspect that it may have

something to do with my drinking habits. *The excitement of alcohol and the excitement of fantasy are very similar.*

(Laing, 2013, p. 152, my italics)

It is also true, however, as the sculptor Louise Bourgeois aptly puts it, whose emotions are her demons, too much for her to handle which is why she transfers her energies to sculpture, that art is thus salvation (Bourgeois, 1998).

Notes

1. According to Jasmine's standards, of course. In fact, Jasmine tries to persuade Ginger that this man is not good enough for her and that she deserves a better life and a better man. Persuaded, Ginger starts a relationship with another man. It quickly falls apart.
2. Here I offer a cinematographic free association. The 2014 fatal overdose of the American actor Philip Seymour Hoffman in his New York apartment is perfectly represented in a scene in Sidney Lumet's *Before the Devil Knows You're Dead*, in which the actor starred in 2007. Andy Hanson (played by Hoffman) goes to his dealer's home to inject drugs and reach a Nirvana state of mind.
3. This is only partially true. In fact, today a disorder can occur both in men and women. The difference, as is proven by statistics and in Alcoholics Anonymous, is that women use food much more to attack themselves, whereas men use alcohol and drugs. Nonetheless, it is common for addicts to engage in addictions concurrently and to shift from one dependency to another, for example, from binge eating to binge drinking. This is proof of the presence of a basic compulsive personality or of biological dispositions.
4. It is interesting to note that in her essay *Touched with Fire* (1996) the American psychologist Kay R. Jamison uses a similar metaphor to describe mania and the deep link between bipolar disorder and art. She has a painful and direct knowledge of the subject, having burned for many years in the bipolar *fire*.
5. In a note, Laing explains that the origins of her interest in this topic are rooted in having grown up in a family of alcoholics.

References

Aulagnier, P. (2001). *The Violence of Interpretation: From Pictogram to Statement* (Trans. A. Sheridan). London: Routledge. (Original work published 1975).

Bailey, B. (2003). *A Tragic Honesty: The Life and Works of Richard Yates*. New York: Picador.

Bellow, S. (1983). *On John Cheever*. Retrieved from www.nybooks.com/articles/1983/02/17/on-john-cheever/.

Bion, W.R. (1965). *Transformation*. Heinemann: London.

Bollas, C. (1993). *Being a Character, Psychoanalysis and Self-Experience*. Routledge: London.

Bourgeois, L. (1998). *Destruction of the Father/Reconstruction of the Father. Writings and Interviews (1923–1997)*. Violette Edition: London.

Brecht, B. (1965). *Stories of Mr. Keuner* (Trans. M. Chalmers). City Lights Books: San Francisco.

Britton, R. (1999). Getting in on the act: The hysterical solution. *The International Journal of Psychoanalysis*, 80(Pt1): 1–14.

Carver, R. (1981). *What We Talk About When We Talk About Love*. Knopf: New York.

Carver, R. (1997). *All of Us: The Collected Poems*. W.L. Stull (Ed.). Harvill Press: London.

Chasseguet-Smirgel, J. (2003). *Le corps comme miroir du monde*. PUF: Paris.

Cheever, J. (2008). *The Journals of John Cheever.* First Vintage International: New York.

Coccioli, C. (1972). *Uomini in fuga.* Piccolo Karma: Milan.

Conrotto, F. (2012). Forme espressive della psicopatologia nelle società postmoderne. *Notes. Trasformazioni sociali e forme della psicoanalisi*, 0: 35–43.

Deutsch, H. (1942). Some forms of emotional disturbance and their relationship to schizophrenia. *The Psychoanalytic Quarterly*, 11: 301–321.

Eco, U. (1994). *The Limits of Interpretation.* Indiana University Press: Bloomington: IN. (Original work published 1990).

Fernandez, D. (1982). *Nelle mani dell'angelo.* Bompiani: Milan.

Fitzgerald, F.S. (1945). *The Crack-Up.* E. Wilson (Ed.). New Directions Publishing: New York.

Fitzgerald, F.S. (1994). *A Life in Letters.* M.J. Bruccoli (Ed.). Scribner: New York.

Freud, S. (1894). *The Neuro-Psychoses of Defence. S.E., 3* (pp. 43–61). Hogarth: London.

Freud, S. (1910). *Leonardo da Vinci, A Memory of his Childhood. S.E. 11* (pp. 59–137). Hogarth: London.

Freud, S. (1915). *On Transience. S.E., 14* (pp. 305–307). Hogarth: London.

Freud, S. (1920). *Beyond the Pleasure Principle. S.E., 18* (pp. 7–64). Hogarth: London.

Freud, S. (1923). *The Ego and the Id. S.E., 19* (pp. 3–66). Hogarth: London.

Green, A. (2005). *Key Ideas for a Contemporary Psychoanalysis: Misrecognition and Recognition of the Unconscious.* Routledge: London and New York.

Green, A. (2011). *Illusions and Disillusions of Psychoanalytic Work* (Trans. A. Weller). Karnac: London.

Hemingway, H. (1955). *Men without Women.* New York: Scribner. (Original work published 1927).

Hemingway, H. (1981). *Selected Letters 1917–1961.* C. Baker (Ed.). Scribner Classics: New York.

Homes, A.M. (2004). Preface. In R. Yates (Ed.), *Disturbing the Peace.* Minimum Fax: Rome. (Original work published 1975).

Ibsen, H. (1999). *A Doll's House* (Trans. N. Rudall) N. Rudall and B. Sahlins (Eds.). Ivan R. Dee: Lahnam, MD. (Original work published 1879).

Ibsen, H. (2005). *The Wild Duck* (Trans. D. Eldridge). Methuen: London. (Original work published 1884).

Jamison, K.R. (1996). *Touched with Fire. Manic-Depressive Illness and the Artistic Temperament.* Free Press: New York.

Kavaler-Adler (1993). *The Compulstion to Create. Psychoanalytic Study of Women Artists.* Routledge: London.

Khan, M.M.R. (1963). The concept of cumulative trauma. *The Psychoanalytic Study of the Child*, 18: 286–306.

Kirchmayr, R. (2010). Pasolini, gli stili della passione. *Aut Aut*, 345: 28–54.

Lacan, L. (1977). *The Function and Field of Speech and Language in Psychoanalysis. In Écrits: A Selection* (Trans. A. Sheridan, pp. 30–113). Tavistock: London. (Original work published 1953).

Laing, O. (2013). *The Trip to Echo Spring: On Writers and Drinking.* Picador: New York.

Laird, N. (2009). *Unhappily Ever After.* Retrieved from www.theguardian.com/film/2009/jan/17/revolutionary-road-richard-yates.

Levinzon, G.K. (1999). *A Criança Adotiva Na Psicoterapia Psicanalítica.* Escuta: São Paulo.

Levinzon, G.K. (2004). *Adoção.* São Paulo: Casa do Psicólogo.

Lipsky, D. (2010). *Although of Course You End up Becoming Yourself: A Road Trip with David Foster Wallace.* Broadway Books: New York.

Lisciotto, D. (2016). *Calpestio.* Alpes: Alpes.

Mann, T. (1990). *Black Swan* (Trans. W.R. Trask). University of California Press: Berkeley, (Original work published 1954).

Marramao, G. (2010). A partire da "Salò": corpo, potere e tempo nell'opera di Pasolini. *Aut Aut*, 345: 116–123.

Nesset, K. (1995). *Stories of Raymond Carver: A Critical Study*. Ohio University Press: Athens, OH.

Pasolini, P.P. (1950). *Roma 1950: Diario*. All'insegna del pesce d'oro: Milan.

Pasolini, P.P. (1992). *The Letters of Pier Paolo Pasolini. Volume I (1940–1954)* (Trans. S. Hood). N. Naldini (Ed.). Quartet Books: London.

Pasolini, P.P. (2003a). *Tutte le poesie. Tomo I*. W. Siti (Ed.). Mondadori: Miilan.

Pasolini, P.P. (2003b). *Tutte le poesie. Tomo II*. W. Siti (Ed.). Mondadori: Milan.

Pasolini, P.P. (2005a). *Heretical Empiricism* (Trans. B. Lawton and L.K. Barnett). L.K. Barnett (Ed.). New Academia Publishing: Washington, DC. (Original work published 1972).

Pasolini, P.P. (2005b). *Roman Poems* (Trans. L. Ferlinghetti and F. Valente). City Lights Books: San Francisco.

Pasolini, P.P. (2014). *The Selected Poetry of Pier Paolo Pasolini: A Bilingual Edition* (Ed. and Trans. S. Sartarelli). University of Chicago Press: Chicago.

Pasolini, P.P., and Halliday, J. (1992). *Pasolini su Pasolini: Conversazioni con Jon Halliday*. Guanda: Milan.

Quilliot, R. (2011). *La filosofia di Woody Allen*. Milan: Mimesis. (Original work published 2004).

Racalbuto, A. (2004). L'isteria dalle origini alla costellazione edipica: il "femminile" e il conflitto d'alterità. *Rivista di Psicoanalisi*, 1: 77–102.

Reza, Y. (2002). *Desolation* (Trans. C.B. Janeway). Vintage Books: New York. (Original work published 1999).

Riolo, F. (2005). Eidolopoiesi. *Psiche*, 2: 147–150.

Rosselli, A. (2012). *Locomotrix: Selected Poetry and Prose of Amelia Rosselli, a Bilingual Edition* (Ed. and Trans. J. Scappettone). University of Chicago Press: Chicago.

Schreiner, O. (1998). *The Story of an African Farm*. J. Bristow (Ed.). Oxford University Press: Oxford. (Original work published 1883).

Siciliano, E. (1982). *Pasolini: A Biography* (Trans. J. Shepley). Random House: New York. (Original work published 1978).

Valdrè, R. (2014). *On Sublimation: A Path to the Destiny of Desire, Theory, and Treatment* (Trans. F. Capostagno and C. Williamson). Karnac: London.

Valdrè, R. (2017). The End of the Tour – A journey into the mind of David Foster Wallace: A psychoanalytic and artistic reflection through the film. *The International Journal of Psychoanalysis*, 98: 909–925.

Wallace, D.F. (1996). *Infinite Jest*. Abacus: London.

Winnicott, D.W. (1960). Ego distortion in terms of true and false self, in *The Maturational Processes and the Facilitating Environment: Studies in the Theory of Emotional Development* (Ed. D.W. Winnicott) (pp. 140–152). Karnac: London.

Yates, R. (1961). *Revolutionary Road*. Little Brown & Co: New York.

Yates, R. (2001). *The Easter Parade*. Picador: New York. (Original work published 1976).

Yates, R. (2008). *Disturbing the Peace*. Delta Books: New York. (Original work published 1975).

Filmography

Cajori, M., and Wallach, A. (2008). Louise Bourgeois: The Spider, The Mistress and the Tangerine (1993–1997). Art Kaleidocope Foundation.

4

CONTEMPORANEITY

Is it really the Age of Sad Passions?

Despite being recent, I believe we are far away from the words of Imre Kertész in his assertion that the moral decadence rapidly devastating our age is caused by a profound desolation whose root is hidden in the refusal of historical experiences. He warns that a civilisation that does not declare its own values or abandons them, takes the road of decadence and of senile decay (Kertész, 2007, pp. 121, 129). Recipient of the 2002 Nobel Prize in Literature in 2002, he was a Hungarian Jew who lived through the twentieth century tragedy of deportation, internment in Auschwitz and imprisonment and who believed that the removal of the memory of history, the devaluation of life, is the tragedy of our time.

Totalitarian regimes are not historically distant; they are still present in certain parts of the world; new forms of terrorism have been possessed by evil; the death drive continues undeterred to the call of reason, bursting out in violence and destruction. Yet in the third millennium the overwhelming majority of Western people do not suffer because of this. They do not fight great struggles, if not the required ritual responses of various states to the new terror attacks, scattered and multiple, unpredictable and subtle; they have not *consciously* lost their memory. As our author maintains, but they seem to have lost it in the emotional, passionate sense. It is not a significant memory – with the exception of survivors such as Kertész – constantly invested with affections, even painful ones, as history passes them by; never have they been so well informed thanks to their *social networks* in real time. No, hyper-modern humankind does suffer from this. If there is persecution then it comes from *within*, the prison is self-induced and personal: we have seen women's bodies imprisoned in *addiction* and eating disorders, the search for new Nirvanas in contemporary clinical practices that even defy the same reasoning of the psychoanalytical statute. A new suffering, perhaps not so important as in the past, has made its appearance on the scene of contemporary humankind: disinvestment.

I know things, I am constantly kept informed, but it does not matter, it *does not touch* my life. Experiencing *passion* – that desperate vitality that killed our writers, as previously seen – is painful and difficult because we have seen how each passion contains a threat of death, or at least of destabilisation compared to the *status quo*. The risk of failure, so feared by the fragile narcissism of contemporary humankind, makes me stay away from investments that are too risky – a new company, a bond of affection, dedication to something – I could always lose, I would not be in control, I know I only invest in *safe* securities, I am a cautious saver because what would become of me if there were a collapse? And I also invest in *different* securities: as recommended by bankers, it is better to fragment assets into different investments, so as not to be laid bare facing a bankruptcy. Thus, investing in multiple objects that are relatively interchangeable – such as people, jobs, hobbies – ends up with *one thing being the same as the other*, the relativistic mantra of the third millennium. Nothing is really lost, if nothing is really gained. The objectives must be easy, the fatigue of one step at a time, of working your way up the ladder like our grandparents bores today's new eternal adolescents, and according to the *culture of law* (Valdrè, 2015) we all, regardless of values, efforts and talents, have the right to *happiness*, to *realisation*. Instead of being an incentive, this has paradoxically led to a flattening of passions and efforts that require toil, sacrifices, risks and pain. It is not I who has to commit myself, it must come *from outside*. The myth of well-being – as Lacan would say – and perfection (which is why I renounce *a priori* unless it is certain that that thing *will make me feel good* and that I will do it as best I can, without humiliating comparisons), the prevention (even health) of every evil before it occurs (Baudrillard, 1998), has led to a sort of "moral terrorism" (ibid., p. 151) for which, although born out of obvious good intentions, the abandonment of large investments, expensive for the drive economy, has led to a sort of life miniaturised on minimal objectives, concrete and close. At the top of the list is the body, the enclosed space of domestic life, the viscosity of bonds with one's own social groups with nostalgic identitary regurgitation, the perimeter of the known rather than the unknowns of the not-known. Where is it channelled, where does the aggressive drive end in all of this, am I perhaps painting too gloomy a picture? I do not think so. By definition, it never disappears, it only disguises itself, dons new attire.

> It turns out that this was a *fantastic mistake*. The whole antagonist aggressive drive, liberated at the same time, now no longer canalised by social institutions, surges back today into the very heart of the universal solicitude for the body [. . . .] in a total turnabout, this object becomes a threat that has to be watched over, reduced and mortified. . . .
>
> (Baudrillard, p. 120)

Contemporary man does not suffer from the remembrance of history, its valorisation or sublimation in art, the only process capable of "giving shape to this cultural negativity and getting to grips with it" (Kertész, 2007, p. 89), if not in authorial and specific cases. Instead he suffers from chasing after the lesser evil, the perfect image, the avoidance of unpleasant or tiring experiences (and sublimation *is* tiring and implies renunciation), shifting onto interchangeable objects (persons, things, virtual reality) so that he is never alone, alone with himself. All of this, and more, contributes to the complex phenomenon that, condensed into a single word, we call disinvestment.

Because adolescents are usually the barometer of an era's cultures, Benasayag and Schmit's 2003 essay *The Era of Sad Passions* enjoyed great success. Psychiatrists working with children and adolescents, the two authors wonder why there is a growing request for help by adolescents, on the one hand, and on the nature of this malaise, on the other, one that was not so common in the past. I believe their clinical-sociological interpretation extends beyond the adolescent world, although its diagnostic features are sharpest in teenage years, when young people are sick and suffer from what Spinoza calls the "sad passions." The opposite of the desperate vitality of our writers, the term sad passion appears to be a contradiction of terminology: there is no passion, the young are sick with the *absence* of passion. It is not precisely sadness in the evolutionary and transformational sense of the term given in psychoanalysis; and it is not precisely depression as it does not invest in a psychopathologic mourning dimension: it is *disinvestment*. A pervasive sense of powerlessness and uncertainty that leads us to withdraw into ourselves, to live the world as a threat, transferring all this to our children, unconsciously identified with our fears. In perennial waiting for a future *that will come*, what the authors call a secular redemption that our epoch has promised to everyone, having identified freedom with dominion over others and guided by the utilitarianism for which *you only do what you need*, life loses its quality, even the painful part of true passion, and acquires Spinozian notes of sad passion. If everything should serve for something, and I must do it immediately, we lose the ability of doing in a disinterested manner, the usefulness of the useless, the pleasure of cultivating our talents without an immediate purpose, the pleasure of what Woody Allen calls creative idleness, that the psychoanalytical setting has identified with free association, reverie and dream thought. *Disinterested doing and giving. The immense usefulness of the useless.* Without this dimension and this *investment*, life becomes sad in the Spinozian sense, not in the sense of traversing creative territories. Is this a form of death drive, a silent and pervasive expression arrayed for the contemporary scene? I think so. The polar opposite of extroverted destructiveness, and different from the introverted aggressiveness that expresses itself through suicide or its various anaesthetics, these forms obviously continue to exist but contemporaneity seems to be providing a fresh one: today the silent drive pervades many strata of society, youth in particular, and much of the contemporary clinic (as we will see in the next paragraph) in the form of the sad passion of *disinvestment*. Severe autism can be placed at the extreme end of the spectrum, passing through ever-more subtle and more socially justifiable withdrawals – "Why go if it is *useless*? Why invest if I am not guaranteed?" – all the way to the common and widespread flatness of so many lives, perhaps masked by the continuous race to do "useful things," with the collusion of a consumerist culture that encourages *consumption* in place of investment. Our life is full of inoperative bustle.

The pleasure of doing with disinterest, of the fertile utility of the useless, is a dimension that the contemporary world has in part lost, while psychoanalysis remains one of the last bastions. But not only this. *An ethics of boundary* must be reformulated, observe Benasayag and Schmit (2003), intended as a distinction between the possible and the not possible, an ethic of care for the other and concern, in order "not to resign ourselves to the dominant sadness of our societies" (ibid., p. 129). Boundaries, ethics, unpopular words. Boundaries are at odds with omnipotence – as seen with adolescents, but not only them – while ethics are considered as unnecessarily obsolete and true fertile sadness is unbearable.

Allow me to make a brief personal digression. To help me write some parts of this book on women's bodies regarding food *addiction*, and on writers and alcoholism, having noted that almost everyone, in particular Caroline Knapp and Katherine Bullitt-Jonas (see Chapter 2, last paragraph), had a lot of experience with Alcoholics Anonymous and Overeaters Anonymous,[1] I decided to attend some of their meetings, where anonymity is strictly observed, with the conscious, although confused, aim of collecting ideas, stories. In short, I wanted a greater understanding through case studies that are far more broad-ranging than our own studies and, as a common thread in this book, to collect first-hand *accounts*. By a lucky coincidence I found myself in these groups' home town, New York, where I had a vast amount of choice of meetings to attend, and so I went. Today, several months later, I do not know if that experience was of direct *help* to my book, because in the end I decided not to include any of those stories to which I listened directly. I made do with breathing in the particular atmosphere and letting the ideas move and associate freely within me, as if I were watching a film or dreaming. I said to myself that something would stay and something would emerge from it. Today I understand just how big a lesson I learned; none of those people – who had gone through painful tunnels, had made a partial recovery but were still fighting, too – were suffering from what Benasayag and Schmit had seen in their young people. Nobody was sad, in that sense. They all had one thing in common, over and beyond their personal recovery: their investment in the group, in helping others. Without expecting anything in return, no forced gratitude, whoever is better spontaneously goes to the rescue or welcomes those who are worse off. Listening is circular and *free*, you share without expecting answers or remedies, in a style not far from, but at the same time not overlapping, that of psychoanalysis. But what was more important is that all these people stop their *addiction*, or manage it, not through medical prescriptions or by following diets, but because *they do it deliberately without claiming that it is necessary, they do it for others*, or for themselves, practicing the magical art of *uselessness*. Someone was desperate, someone had a relapse, someone was recovered; but nobody was sad in the Spinozian sense. What kept them alive, and often what healed them, was *investment* in the group, just as a patient invests in an analyst, and sometimes with severe cases that is the only form of care.

Without expecting anything in return, says one of their many slogans, things will happen.

Without claiming to heal at *all costs and immediately*, you will be healed.

In the end, I was so much a part of the group atmosphere, that despite me being just a listener, as I did not have anything to say, I found myself putting the chairs out in a circle at the beginning of the meeting or doing other small practical things, as I did not have any other form of personal experience to pass on. But that unnecessary or *useless* doing, I now realise, would save our young people from the abulia of sad passion. With those small actions I was investing. A woman of a certain age, visibly very simple and modest, almost illiterate, told me that she had frequented the groups for 30 years and was now completely recovered from her disease, but she had continued to go, like many, simply to put out the chairs. Too uneducated to read the literature or talk on other levels, this woman from the Bronx had been putting the chairs out and then putting them away for thirty years, each time with the same grace, the same patience, the same gratitude. "I'm so grateful for this," she told me. *Grateful* is one of the words that circulates the most in these groups: how many times do we hear our teenagers say they are grateful? Everything is due to them; beauty, success (even when undeserved), the realization of oneself, even if it involves damage to another or the neglect of their own evolution, money. Gratitude, that *old-fashioned* word.

The act of putting the chairs out, for that woman and for me in that short time, had constituted an act of *sense*. I always went away from those meetings without any notes for my book, but feeling the priceless liberty of doing something as a disinterested person, without waiting, without expectations, without return, for others, with others that perhaps I would see again, perhaps not; it did not matter. It was magnificent, I understood the nature of their cure, when there was one, and of the absence of despair, when there was none: because despair does not derive so much or only from the disease, but from having something to invest in. Despite conduct, then, that had a brush with death every day, I did not sense a circular death drive in those rooms, as I have felt instead in other clinical and social situations.

It may seem like a feel-good sentiment, but I hope the profound human and psychologically useful nature of what has been said has been understood for its contrast with death: there is life where there is investment and not necessarily where there is health. The American surgeon Atul Gawande (2014), one of the most interesting contemporary medical writers, who has been working for years in rest homes, in his latest book *Being Mortal* posed an ethical dilemma that we rarely encounter in medicine: we have been taught how to repair bodies and save lives but not how to take care of lives *as they come to an end*. We believed that safety, cleanliness, care, treatment, the prolonging of existence would be enough, but from conscientious investigations and personal interviews over the years, he surmises that most elderly patients no longer wanted *more life* nor a more pristine and safe life: although they appreciated these objectives, what they wanted was *their* life. In the conflict between more "wellness" or more life, understood as the maintenance of interests, personal objects, habits, etc., they were all willing to live shorter lives but to remain bound to something personal in which they could recognise themselves: in a word, an investment.

> Human beings need faithfulness. It does not necessarily produce happiness, and may even prove to also be a source of suffering, but we all *need a devotion* for something other than us to make our lives bearable. Without this devotion, only desires remain to guide our way and they are by nature transient, fickle, unappeasable.
>
> (Gawande, 2004, p. 121)

Without a devotion, we are only left with desires. Therefore, pleasure follows and then the search to satisfy it, and then it starts all over again. Instead, devotion (which we call sublimation) tends to be paid for in self. In every age, then, the contemporary myth of the search for happiness at all costs, for fulfilment in any way, for an absence of conflict, has revealed itself to be a paradoxical source of unhappiness of disinvestment, of "unhappiness without desire" (as Handke reminds us in his well-known novel inspired by his mother, who committed suicide), where, instead of spick and span rest homes, the paying guests of the humanist doctor would have preferred the untidiness and the dirt of their little gardens and their cats. If an elderly person has a somewhat feeble voice of request, the whole weight of the contemporary requirement of well-being falls on the shoulders of the adolescent.

To return to the specific psychoanalytical sphere, you can match disinvestment with what we have seen Green call *unbinding*. Or rather, disinvestment follows unbinding:

> Ultimately, when the work of defusion carries the day, it is the destructive impulses that prevail and the forces of defusion that dominate. But when defusion prevails, the cohesion of the psychic structure is weakened, and the field left to destructiveness is increasingly extensive.
>
> (Green, 2010, pp. 67–68)

We are indebted to Green, whose elaboration on the death drive drew together all possible expressions, for the so-called work of the negative. The libidinal disinvestment of the object to which aggressiveness is directed, *aggression without libido*, is what constitutes the complex concept of the negative. What is the negative? The negative is not simply the opposite of positive, but rather its *refusal*, a radical refusal that leads to that desire of the negative that opens the doors to destructiveness, to unbinding, where "the relationship with pleasure, the relational dimension, the desire for the synthesis of Eros to prevail are replaced by unbinding" (Green, 2010, p. 170). Once established in the psyche, disinvestment, the negative, unbinding, acquire enormous strength, either silent or active, precisely because they weaken the psychic structure. This will become clearer in the next paragraph, how fragility must turn to repetition and therefore to coaction to repeat, constraining the whole psyche in a tragic rigidity.

But let us look at the socio–cultural aspect of the negative here. Within a unitary discourse, Green, in fact, distinguishes the individual forms of the negative, as we see in our clinics, from the *socio-cultural* one. The negative in the social sphere and in *Kultur* takes the forms described by Kertész and late Freud: the pessimistic waiving of the prevalence of goodness in man, the ineluctability of evil in its destructive, dictatorial, totalitarian forms and also in its *banality*, as illustrated so well by the tragedies of the twentieth century. The socio-cultural negative is nourished by ideologies that kill human values, those on which the birth of our civilisation is founded, to replace them with cultures of hatred. Nazism in the 1900s and the fanaticism of current radicalism all draw from the same destructive drive and death, killing recognition of the other, tolerance, alterity. Life. Green specifies that this is not interiorisation of the negative as may occur in an individual psyche, but "the result of a *power* that is violent and not shared. [. . .] An enforced coup has been established. It has replaced those who wished to state the right to speak in the name of a *fragile truth, changeable, questionable*" (Green, 2010, p. 181, my italics). In this coup of thought, in this kidnapping of truth at a collective level, aggression comes from outside and attacks interior reality, too. We see here the possible unitary connection between the negative on a socio–cultural level and the individual: in a society dominated by the negative, interior reality is massacred. With this coherent argument that I have synthesised, Green searches for a bond between the death drive, its enormous (and unresolved) social impact and the devastation it wreaks on the individual psyche. If one excludes some exceptional cases, such as Kertész or Primo Levi or others who managed to *give voice* to the unrepresentable, for most people, for the masses, the socio–cultural negative trans-lates into a pure killing of the psyche, in its ability to think and to create bonds.

This may be the main form of the negative in Culture but, to return to our title, we are reminded that the other, *sad passion* is less chaotic, less sensational, but in its silence is *the most characteristic* of our time. If destructiveness, hatred and fanaticism have always existed, sad passion seems to be a contemporary phenom-enon instead. Violence, dictatorships, tyrannies and predation on the lives of individuals, killings and mass murder little known in the West, wars and murders belong to the history of humankind that began with a murder, Cain's slaying of Abel; in some way the Nirvana search for zero tension through drug use has always existed as well – although not at the current levels of massification. What seems specific to the post-modern era is that the *sad passion* of disinvestment is not limited to individual personalities or an artistic and intellectual elite – this, too, has always existed – rather, it is a widespread phenomenon in *Kultur*. I use the term *Kultur* characterised in late Freud, to be construed in a broad sense as *civilisation and work of civilisation*, and not as specific cultural belonging; something in which we are immersed, even unconsciously impregnated and more than we might think, "La Culture nous enforme" (Séchaud, 2005). It forms us from within, it transforms us deeply and unconsciously and entwines with the internal drive world to a largely unknown extent, different in each individual but with common traits in all of us.

Leaving aside then the everted forms of the death drive, not because they are less important but because they are present in every era with different justifications and modes of expression, I would like to attempt an exploration of the contemporary silent drive that we identified with the broad term of *disinvestment*.

Contemporary evil in its everted form can be expressed in the form that Arendt (1963) was the first to advance as the *banality of evil*. You do not need large-scale massacres or carnage; the concept has its own intrinsic force that can be applied to an individual just as to a small group. We have said that, more than others, the barometer of symptomatic expressions of a *Kultur* are adolescents: how many crimes, acts of bullying and cruelty, from footling to striking cases that hit the headlines, express the adolescent hatred, the death drive in the form of a banality of evil? Young people who kill "without a reason," who harass those who are different, xenophobic or homophobic through boredom, in a quest for identity, in order to feel alive in comparison to perceiving dead zones, empty of self and of mind. This phenomenon is not exclusive to the adolescent, but I think that it is expressed in its maximum, shocking aridity in this age group.

Cinema has given testimony to great effect: masterpieces such as *Funny Games* (Haneke, 2007) or *Elephant* (Gus Van Sant, 2003) narrate the stolid, apparently unjustified violence on innocent random victims, where it is not even clear whether the subject derives a sadistic pleasure (only secondarily, I believe) or rather a confirmation of identity and a sense of vitality. I am more inclined to this second hypothesis that makes both the diagnosis and possible recovery very difficult: there is no fight impulse, which would leave the doors open to a transformation and donation of sense. We are in the land of the non-drive, the total lack of sense. If this form of violence has in all probability always existed, a violence justifying itself for the survival of a self felt as dead, that does not give drive pleasure or discharge, it may correspond to the evil side of the sad drives. In Arendt's reflections, absolutely "normal" people – but I would describe them, along with Bollas (1993), as "normotics" – can become authors of an evil "that is not radical or deep, but thoughtless and shallow [. . .] it spreads like a fungus on the surface of life rather than springing from any profound recesses" (McKenna, 2006, p. 161).

It can be understood how, for psychoanalysis as well as for any other "therapeutic" instrument, if it is already complex and often failing, any attempt to curb the forms of violence, faced with *this* kind of evil, unrepresentable, asymbolic and without meaning or drive, we are utterly powerless. The character who performs the banality of evil for the pure fascination that it exercises or, indeed, as a search for identity – better to have a bad identity than no identity at all – or to overcome the apathy of boredom, that is to say to win *disinvestment*, is now treading the boards of both cinema and great literature.

Withdrawal, lack of that passion for the useless that we have seen, flatness that does not develop into melancholy, narcissisms that use objects only for the maintenance of a fragile self, disinterest in life itself, others and the collective . . . How does the silent drive disguise itself today? With what voice does it speak? How did it manage to change its attire sufficiently to be able to masquerade, even subtly, in apparently opposite forms, in hyper-vital and efficient subjects, in micro-obsessiveness without which a person collapses? And, if it exists, what is the role of psychoanalysis, which representative of culture aims instead to promote vital investment in all this?

This, too – as proven by the success of Benasayag's book and the many studies on both the "new" clinic, narcissism, for example, as well as on the new social ills of post-modern relativism – has been amply spoken and written about, above all in philosophical, psychological and sociological terms. Less frequent, in my opinion, or completely absent, is any attempt to connect all of this, metapsychologically speaking, to the death drive, as in the previous example from Green (2018) and his most recent book, *Illusions and Disillusions of Psychoanalytic Work*. A complex scenario, so difficult to consider and even impossible to achieve, that we can only offer conjecture and food for thought.

Extensions of disinvestment and "crises" of sublimation (Valdrè, 2015), both in drive and observation terms, I believe are sufficiently parallel: having studied sublimation in depth, I have observed that the two phenomena are if not exactly overlapping then certainly close relatives. To sublimate is *the opposite* of disinvestment, even if superficially sublimation may appear as object desertification. The opposite is true: to be able to sublimate, either a little or a lot, in small or large parts, it is necessary to have renounced direct pleasure objectives in order to move the investment onto an other that is apparently non-sexual but in reality always has a sexual link. The object appears lost, but it is *the investment in its representation* that constitutes the heart of sublimation; a complex operation that therefore requires a subject that sublimates anyway, capable of elaborating mourning and, with Culture in mind, capable of representing an environment that approves, supports and recognises the efforts that sublimation entails for the subject. Having already discussed this (Valdrè, 2015), I will only refer here to its bond with contemporary forms of the death drive.

Benasayag's adolescents, who sometimes attend our practices, have no sublimation because there is no investment in objects or in parts of the self (if not apparent short-lived "aesthetic" investments), nor in things of the world, and certainly not in their representation. They do not put the chairs in a circle like the lady from the Bronx, they do not perform a *useless* service for which to be grateful. If they do anything, *it* must serve *them*. Patients of the contemporary clinic are characterised by pronounced difficulties in representation, free association and dreaming. The pieces of the puzzle seem to fit together. For the very young in particular, the erosion of the paternal referent – the much-discussed decline of the Father and the Oedipus, the crumbling of the metapsychic and metasocial guarantors who have always supported social life (Kaes, 2005), lead to what Assoun defines as:

(. . .) a paradoxical statute of modernity: a paradox of liberation of enjoyment in which, with Thanatos appearing as a pure principle of repetition, *aggressivity is turned on the subject* (. . .). At the same time, "narcissizing" strategies are developed which make the body an instance of "reparation" (. . .). All this testifies to a desymbolization of prohibition, which is paradoxically "compensated" through a quest for fresh forms of transgression and a sort of "*passion for the standard*" (. . .) As a result, the "social" component is no longer situated on the side of enforcement of prohibition, but on the side of incitement to enjoy as much on the side of rules: from which comes the *desire for the rules* which in our opinion sustains unconscious modernity.

(Assoun, 1993, pp. 247–249, my italics,
translated for this edition)

If there are no more Fathers, against whom or what can they rebel? Where is the physiological conflict that has always made generations collide and grow, if fathers are aligned with their children in an unprecedented, dangerous quest for *equality* – in my opinion, the consequence of these new fathers' terror of sustaining conflicts and terror of these new children's terror of investing in conflicts – where are we *all equal*? Aggressiveness can only turn itself against the self. We have seen it has many ways, many stratagems, conscious and unconscious and virtually unchanged since Freud's discovery: masochism (that young people know so very well, through drugs or self-harming – often in extreme forms), suicides masked as accidents, failures born out of repeating the school year or work. But the "passion for the norm," a well-chosen synonym of "sad passion" is a novelty: to aggregate, to want to be "normal" (according to whatever the definition of "normal" is at the time), *not to differentiate oneself*, to contribute in varying degrees to the sad passion of disinvestment. I do not expend myself, I do not distinguish myself, I adapt. Subjectivity, the purpose of individual life and successful analysis, even if never complete or obtained in full, cannot even be glimpsed at without the hard work and the risks of investment; as a consequence, the contemporary young person will risk being normal, but in a group, in a gang, not as a subject. As society, I believe, only works as a collection of subjects, collectively connected but distinct and thinking, if subjectivity is compromised then all the work of civilization and culture will be affected. How easy it is, then, to open doors to new terrorisms, to new groups scattered around the world in search of fanatical reasons to live.

Our age has been branded, especially in the past, as an age of individualism and narcissism; I believe there has been a degree of confusion here. If what is meant by this is the facile diminishing of responsibility (so nothing concerns me, someone else will deal with it), the lack of passions and altruism that expects nothing in return, or investments of a narcissistic nature that see in the other a self-object necessary for the confirmation of his own existence, then I agree that this is the era of individualism. But it is not to be confused with subjectivation, which on the contrary has as a condition that each person takes his own responsibility and that, as the subject, he is able to support investments, even when a return is not necessarily guaranteed or when there is a risk of failure. Here we touch on a crucial point: fear, the terror of failure. I believe that ultimately disinvestment – at various levels, from the bland to the profound – finds its roots in a fear, more acute than ever today, not only of not being the norm but of *failure, disappointment, being abandoned*. It is the famous metaphor of bank securities: why invest if there is no guarantee? Better to hoard the cash under the mattress. Every now and then we read about people who led miserable existences yet, after their death, a treasure trove is discovered hidden under their bed. The contemporary subject, victim of disinvestment, is a bit like those dead people who, for fear of loss, had hidden their treasure – the life drive, perhaps ending up by forgetting they have it, leading a life of poverty rather than "expending themselves" in the risky high seas of investments.

We see young people stuck in their studies, almost as if unconsciously fearing that the passage would bring them to *have to* invest in their future, or incapable of any affective relationship for fear of being abandoned or of not being liked, even unable to look for friends unless they are adhesively their equal, for the terror of comparison, of inferiority, incapable of cultivating and developing passions and hobbies, or of enjoying empty time as a time full of freedom. A patient of mine, in his thirties but psychologically a teenager, was pushed into therapy as a result of the loss (with his unconscious contribution as well) of an idealised group of friends to which he was extremely attached; since then, he decided that he would not become attached to anyone and that video games and televised sports would become his sole companions. At least they would never disappoint him or offend or abandon him.

If this, within certain limits, happens to everyone at some point in life, especially during those phases when the narcissistic balance is more at risk, such as adolescence and middle age, today the phenomenon is not limited to phases or oscillations of individual lives. Disinvestment as a shelter from narcissistic shocks has become the mark of an era, the disease of a generation, for the most fragile in particular.

Here, in my opinion, this broad discourse encounters narcissism, not so much as it being the era "of narcissism" in which, basically, everyone thinks of himself, but due to the risk of weakening precarious narcissistic positions that will lead to disinvestment.

It is not the age of narcissism, but of its lack and its precariousness. Kapsambelis (2011) aptly notes the recent forceful appearance, on the contemporary psycho-analytic scene as well, of a new ruling figure: narcissistic fragility. Although such a phenomenon does not exist in metapsychological terms, it has become a common concept in our studies as well as among people: so-and-so is fragile, certain factors or events are fragilising, and so on and so forth. Young people, but not only they, are the barometers of society and are *really* exposed to a phase of complex narcissistic configuration. They are its first victims: no longer helped by their Fathers, in both the physical and symbolic sense of passage, or by cultural guarantors, they are left to their own devices and today, like my eternal-teenager patient, they find a new ally in the activity of "disinvestment due to fragility" – technology.

Given that I do not consider it to be the cause of everything (tools are never the *cause*, they are indeed opportunities but only as instruments), technology provides and will increasingly provide its magic. When ever before now has a human being been able to access a relationship, virtually create it and destroy it, invent a nickname and all sorts of identities, with boundless freedom to enter and exit with a mere *enter* or *delete*? The instrument has endless potential and is extraordinarily useful but, in this case, its concrete contribution is to obscure the real investments with pseudo-investments, with fictitious creations that give an illusion of being free from life's rules, namely that I do not decide how far to enter into and exit a bond without confronting the other, that I possess an identity, this body and this face, even if I do not like them, and only in the virtual world can I invent myself as I would like, but in the real one I stay what I am. The magic of this all-powerful box is such that many people, and not just young people, live on this alone. Yet again there is ample literature on the subject and I do not intend to dwell on virtual reality, merely to flag it as an accomplice, with a contemporary contribution that deludes one into believing that so-called narcissistic fragilities, whereby *every investment is dangerous*, have been overcome. Perhaps at the beginning it does help, but in time it can become a prison. An interesting documentary in 2013, *Web Junkie* by directors Shlam and Medalia, focused on one of the 400 "treatment centres for internet addiction" that since 2004 have sprung up in China, a country that has been particularly hard-hit by this *addiction* and the first country in the world to classify it among pathologies to be treated with rehabilitation. The centres are geared towards adolescents who will spend some months there, working in parallel with their families, who are, as always, unaware and impotent. Before beginning rehabilitation, these young people never left their homes and spent their time connected to the internet, not for study or research, but to play games and to go on social networks, etc. Autistic with respect to the rest of the world, their entire universe is reduced to a piece of software. If we have said that, even clinically speaking, autism can be considered the highest form of disinvestment, these "new" autisms are anything but rare. They rarely reach our surgeries – as that would be the beginning of investment – and in their silence, in their not disturbing anyone and in a total absence of expressed aggressiveness, they represent one possible form of the death drive. Certainly subtle and close to the borderline with Nirvana, it could be argued that with this self-induced island young people are seeking oblivion, non-thought, an absence of any sort of tension. This Nirvana intertwines, however, with hatred, a fear and loathing of any investment and the killing of any curiosity. It seeks omnipotence and not just oblivion. It denies any "human" dependency while being paradoxically adrift in a dependency that needs treatment. Thus detached from the life drive – and what could be more vital than *curiosity*? – the untying has happened and the death drive, more silent than ever, circulates freely.

The generation of the so-called Millennials (or Generation Y, or the Net Generation), referring to people born between the early-1980s and mid-1990s, is characterised by its powerful co-existence with new technologies and, according to some authors, also displays certain narcissistic traits linked to our theme. However, the Net Generation diverges from adolescents who are absolutely enraptured by disinvestment, with its characteristics of ambition and ability to express significant expertise; nonetheless, on closer examination, it is not uncommon to see the terror of bonds or lasting investments in Millennials as well. Another paradoxical, corrosive phenomenon of our time, already mentioned in the chapter on women's bodies, is closer to the typology of the Millennials: too much freedom. Today as never before, the individual, young and equipped with online skills that connect him continuously to each byte of the world, is free to make his own choices: thousands of options, thousands of doors, are potentially open to these young creative minds . . . which one should they choose? Not infrequently the excess of options, unthinkable in the past, may be well exploited by some while for others it represents paralysis: too many choices, no choice. Opening a door denotes responsibility and implies the closing of other doors, to psychologically carry out mourning, something that many young people do not want to do. In the long term, this keeping *everything open* and waiting for the perfect opportunity ends up creating a sad stagnation that ultimately reveals other subtle forms of disinvestment, of death of the future. I have seen both in life and in literary and cinematographic figures, and not infrequently in my clinical practice as well, Millennials who are no longer as such, locked in an absence of choices because they have fantasised over *too many* choices, frightened of disappointing the image of self and the ideal of id, generally grandiose, who are stuck in a poverty of investments that, over time, has left them alone, depressed, in a swirl of jobs and displacements, devoid of passion: too much freedom is but two steps away from sad passions. The hypermodern individual is not only expected to live or survive, as in the past, but also has an ambitious task imposed on him by contemporary cultures: *be fulfilled.* Once an aspiration open to a few, mass culture has transformed it into one of the most painful imperatives of our time. Be someone, be fulfilled, stand out. Despite there being very little literature on this current phenomenon, it should be noted that not everyone agrees with this sad vision of the Millennials: while psychologists such as Twenge and Campbell (2012) hold that this phenomenon is on the rise, for others this generation appears to be more equipped with empathy and social sensitivity than past ones. In any case, the Freudian subject of the "unhappy century" was not free to experience everything he or she wanted; limits, super-egoic prohibitions, natural acceptance of differences led them to consider life, for the average person, as not being automatically happy. Happiness, now a standard word, is an imperative of our time. The task of being fulfilled, however, with the fall of the cultural guarantors and the eclipse of both the paternalistic society and the era of ideologies, *falls entirely on the individual.* If you do not succeed, you will be a failure, a word that contemporary man abhors. One possible consequence is to disinvest: marriages may fail, so what better way to prevent this than by not marrying. The freedom to choose from the many ways of meeting someone contributes to the postponement of any decision. The same applies for career choices and many other activities. It is true that, from a psychoanalytical point of view, this might all be considered as defensive and as such it has always belonged in the baggage of human defense strategies: in order not to suffer, I do not invest. Partners, jobs, interests will change, and I will always be free. Certainly, at an individual level it can be a defence, and only in the presence of analysis are we able to investigate; however I would like here to extend it to an attitude that prescinds from the individual, because its diffusion allows us to treat it as a collective defence, something that is part of the spirit of the time. *Everybody* today seems to deserve success; in his beautiful novel *Stoner*,[2] John Williams (2012), speaking of the character, a teacher and literature-lover who never becomes more than a teacher, writes: "Like many men who consider their success incomplete, he was extraordinarily vain and consumed with a sense of his own importance" (p. xiii).

We are terrorised by fear of risk, by thoughts of falling into the void; we fear that the traditional guarantors, although restrictive, are no longer there to contain us:

Leap, and the net will appear.

(Julia Cameron)[3]

It would be of some psychoanalytical and anthropological interest to investigate the presence or, rather, the expression of the death drive in other cultures. Its presence as a human drive is unquestionable; its expression has perhaps been more the subject of anthropological than psychoanalytic studies. As far as I know, there is the work of Dominique Cupa (2006), who studied the impact on the psychic apparatus of some sects in totalitarian or micro-totalitarian regimes and in suicide-bombers. The psychic apparatus would be destructured, capable of reasoning but denied the possibility of criticism and discernment (as in every form of totalitarianism); the super-ego is silenced so that the subject remains exalted and prey to an ideal of the pathological and grandiose ego activated by powerful and evocative external forms. The limits of such works, although very interesting, as Doninotti (2011) notes, are that they are still speculative observations because we will never have an Islamist terrorist or a suicide-bomber on our couch, nor will we understand the nature of his childhood identifications and his ideals. As Freud says, studying a psychic apparatus must be done "live."

In conclusion and in contrast, we can study "live," in the analysis room and then broaden out into speculation, the many forms of *sad passions* that represent, in my hypothesis, a contemporary expression, corrosive and silent as befits it, of the death drive. Forster (2005) also observed how the soul is tired and fears losing the little that it understands so it retreats to the permanent lines dictated by habit or chance (p. 232): the death of gratuitous interest and of the joy of the useless, the death of risk, the death of subjectivation because it is itself a risk, the death of the bond in so far as it can be lost, and it is fallacious and frustrating; the death of sublimation.

The silent clinic of disinvestment

> The dead mother had taken away with her, in the decathexis of which she
> had been the object, the major portion of the love with which she had been
> cathected before her bereavement: her look, the tone of her voice, her
> smell, the memory of her caress. The loss of physical contact carried with it
> the repression of the memory traces of her touch. She had been buried alive,
> but her tomb itself had disappeared. The hole that gaped in its place made
> solitude dreadful, as though the subject ran the risk of being sunk in it, body
> and possessions.

(Green, 1983/1996, p. 154)

Michael Stone, a dull middle-aged husband and a "salesman" with a certain
amount of success, goes to Cincinnati for one night to give a speech on his book
about how to become a brilliant salesperson. Persecuted by nightmares, depression
and memories of a love that had finished without him understanding why, a
joyless marriage, distressed by a sense of the unbearable solitude, in the hotel he
meets Lisa, a shy young woman who has a slight physical disability. On this
unique, magical night he falls in love with her, but the next day everything returns
to its ordinary alienation. A contemporary fable about love as an anomaly, an
episode of breakage that can only be placed in passage, in transit, as symbolised by
the hotel, *Anomalisa*, the delightful and discerning film by Charlie Kaufman (2015)[4]
portrays the contemporary desolation of disinvestment better than any treatise.
There are few characters and they are not actors but completely realistic stop-
motion figures; their bodies and faces are "masks," the hotel a tangle of corridors,
the voice is just one voice, Lisa's. After the only night of their shy love, the
awakening is already different: Michael is irritated by a gesture Lisa makes, he goes
to present his book, both go back to their lives. Extremely original in its stylistic
language, in my opinion, the film perfectly depicts a human world where desire
fights to survive (the anguished search through the hotel corridors), but the
difficulty in investment brings the character back, in the end, to the monotone
routine of the desert that is each day.

Love exists, but as an anomaly and it always has *a defect*, even just a slight one
like Lisa's face. Love is unbearable. Its commitment and surrender to the other
who demands it means they do not manage more than the brief period of one
night together. Michael returns to the normalcy and ordinariness of a family life
that is perturbing yet so human in its senselessness. The decision, certainly not
random, to use animation makes the characters even more mechanical and soulless,
and the labyrinth of the hotel corridors depicts a mind, a universe in which
humankind has lost its bearings.

Even if only love, contact with the other, has a discordant voice – indeed,
possesses a voice at all, Lisa's voice – that escapes from the silent death drive, in the
end desertification and the reassuring repetitive will prevail.

Anomalisa, far from representing the stylistic "game" of a bold experimenter
such as Kaufman, in my opinion, is a brilliant *tranche de vie* of our debate: the

difficulty of investing in objects. Not only in love, as seems clear, but also in more vital parts of self, to be explored and unknown, in risk, in the future, in change. Michael Stone could lie down on one of our couches: a typical contemporary urban subject, going through a so-called middle-age crisis, he has reached a good position but takes no joy from that, feels that his work, *sales*, is meaningless and his home a prison to which he returns, while anxiety and panic continually torment him.

Perhaps Michael Stone carries inside him, in his unconscious, that complex psychic constellation Green (1996) defines as "the dead mother." We must return to Green, not because I intend to pay homage, but in investigating and reviewing the death drive in an attempt to find a synthesis with the object, I think he is the author who has given the broadest and most extensive contribution to the silent drive clinic in the mutant light of the contemporary. The "dead mother" can also be physically alive in the external reality but is, so to speak, psychologically dead in the inner reality. She may have been a depressed mother, herself deprived of vital investments, and the child will not be abandoned in reality but left psychologically and emotionally alone in an internal world that is desertified on the one hand and full of anguish on the other. The trauma of the child, so frequent in our clinics, may be twofold: to have been *disinvested* from a maternal function that is not sufficiently alive for it to be an object of investment or, in an overturned relationship, for him to have to take care of and keep alive, with his concern, the dead mother (a traumatic situation that is not uncommon in those who choose to become psychoanalysts). Not only does maternal depression prevent or restrict each and every empathy with the needs of the child but above all, as far as our topic is concerned, if this psychic constellation is installed in a lasting manner, then the pathological identifications will prevail and they will prevent any vital and vitalizing investment: we will virtually have the *interiorisation of the negative* (Green, 2010, p. 171). Let us not forget that Green was initially Lacan's pupil, and it is thanks to him and the post-Lacanian generation that was later to be emancipated, that the review of Freud was so completely and profoundly formulated and synthesised. It is the concept of *lack* that Green derives from Lacan: the narcissism of death corresponds, in a Lacanian sense, to the continuation in the child of a falling in love with *One* who denies the *Other*. If this autarchic state of pure primary narcissism persists, then the conditions are created for a horizon of sense autistically folded towards itself. The lost Thing is denied, as it is otherness, and replaced through the eroticisation of its own image in the mirror. Clinical work shows that in some circumstances the subject develops a perverse awareness: to desire oneself offers shelter from dependence on the *Other*. "One must do without the object which is the object *of lack* /in the object becoming a sign that one is limited, unachieved and incomplete" (Green, 1996, p. 133).

The subject lives an impossible relationship with the *phantom* of the dead mother who, as in Alfred Hitchcock's renowned *Psycho*, conditions the existence of the son, shaping his inclinations, decisions and desire. It is no longer the One who lives but the deceased Other in him: the individual tries throughout his whole existence to build a fortress capable of withstanding the internal attacks of a *malignant Otherness*, introjected and *forgotten* but who lives in him, in his place, just like Norman Bates' mother. In analysis the symptom is shown in terms of feelings of affective-emptiness especially evident in the subject's discourses that invariably accuse the mother without an apparent reason. [. . . .] The intellectual narcissism that often characterises this type of existential condition performs the function of a defensive barrier against the deadly drives that tend toward the inanimate originated by what has become a present *Absence* that is able to colonize the unconscious space. The introjected absence produces an abyss on a "structure" that enlivens with *non-sense* the production of the sense of a "*narcissist of death*" whose "thought image" is empty, devoid of affective tones.

(Milazzo, 2014, translated for this edition)

We will see how all this approaches without completely overlapping, in my opinion, the concept of white psychosis.

In the previous paragraph we have discussed two types of negative, the sociocultural and the personal; here, in the prevalence of primitive pathological identifications dominated by disinvestment, we have the personal negative, that complex psychic that *negatively* marks the lives of many of us and of a multitude of contemporary clinical cases. In such cases:

> [. . .] the mind has introjected these defensive primary reactions as a mode of unconcious defense, altering the psychical organization and preventing it from developing along the usual lines of the pleasure-principle. In other words, the mind escapes the models of behaviour dictated by positive experiences. The outcome has made it *lose its flexibility* [. . . .] What has happened, then, with the internalization of negative, is that the manifestation of the negative have become identificatory introjections that are not so much *chosen* as obligatory, they have become what might be called *second nature*, artificially grafted on to a mind that has been precociously modified by pathology and its defensive reactions. The latter become so deeply rooted in the subject who has been subjected to them, [. . .] forming part of an innate nature.

(Green, 2018, pp. 173–174)

Green does not fail to emphasise the aspects constituting the child as well, different in each of us. It is certain that the dead mother, with her disinvestment, has *taken away* any capacity for future vital investment, just as if the root has been chopped off: love, passion for things, that risk we talked about earlier at a collective level. The film is so astute in not neglecting one aspect (obviously still remaining within our conjectural metaphor), namely that investment is impossible or impossibly *enduring* (fleeting investments are almost always possible for everyone), but the desire remains. The dead mother has not taken desire away as well, thus relegating the child's future to an even more tragic destiny: to desire, and to fail to have; to desire and to fear; to desire and to disinvest the morning after.

I would like to emphasise how I believe disinvestment is not the same thing as destruction, although clinically the effects can coincide: our Michael *has not* destroyed Lisa, who boards the coach to take her home with a slight smile of gratitude towards a memory that will accompany her throughout life (even the flawed girl had a little love!). No, he has destroyed himself, denying himself investment in a new object. The clinic of destructiveness and the clinic of disinvestment are, in my opinion, often parallel because there is only one mind and everything coexists with everything, but while the collective destructiveness has always existed, it is disinvestment that is pathognomonic of our times. The Michael Stones are the post-modern subjects. Furthermore, destructiveness is deafening, disinvestment is silent.

It is clear that between this chapter and the previous one there are ample intersections.

Obviously the consequences on analysis technique are not negligible. It is true that the mere act of going to a therapist shows that the disinvestment is not total (if the patient comes of his own initiative and not like certain autistic, withdrawn adolescents, who are pushed by their parents), but some breach, even minimal, is open and the person is usually suffering from a sense of emptiness, of futility, or more actively produces symptoms such as the anxiety of Michael Stone, that lead them to seek help. Where disinvestment is total and all-encompassing there is no push to cross the threshold of analysis and start on the bumpy path of transference, analysis's elective investment, onto the figure of another human being, the analyst. But if the patient does come, the analyst will be investigating into the inner world of the patient and where pathological identification has been totalising, the unbearable anguish of psychic death will resurface in the course of sessions the moment in which the pathologic core is approached. In this regard, notes Green (2010), the risk the analyst runs is of collusion, counteracting the immobility of the patient by "doing." Or by "too much investment": to balance the patient's scant investment, his drive mutism, we can unconsciously be induced to compensatory countertransferential reactions, in order to feel alive in the opaque climate of the sessions, such as talking too much, supporting, in an attempt to inject life, research, curiosity. If the analyst is aware, it may prove to be a useful tool for countertransferential understanding, and some patients, within certain limits, *really do* need someone to help them to invest, to not surrender to the simple call of the silent drive, even when they are not aware of having come for this. Remember that for Nando, the mere realisation of my possible expectations, made him fall back into the safe limbo of negative therapeutic reactions.

I remember a moment of my analysis with G., a young woman who was extremely committed to her profession as a business woman, apparently the opposite of a person deprived of investments, the opposite of our Michael Stones; her life was full of initiatives, her diary filled with appointments and research to enhance her career. G. spoke about everything except about us; her relationship with me never came up if not, in time, in some dream. I realised there was an unusual countertransferential reaction: if the patient spoke a lot, I spoke a lot, too, as happens more commonly with silent patients. Why, with such a chatterbox, did I feel the urge to make comments, to "keep up with" her torrent of words? Because they were what Lacan would call *empty words*, something I realised over time, working within myself and from the analysis of the first dreams: G. spoke about everything so she could talk of nothing. Her investments in her profession (before a boyfriend appeared on the scene, where she managed to make a genuine, demanding investment) covered a substantial lack of passion, of genuine interest. With my excessive talking, I had unconsciously captured this vacuum and I would reply filling it, as if watering parched land. Hers was saying without saying. The progressive understanding of all this in the analytical process ultimately led G. to recognise this "empty feeling," to be terrified, that deep down nothing mattered to her; the same had happened with her previous boyfriends, all of whom were virtually idealised but none actually loved until she met L., the first real investment that analysis was able to unlock in this young woman's life.

I quote this brief and extremely partial memory of G.'s analysis to emphasise that the type of patients we are talking about do not necessarily appear clearly as empty, without interest, essentially narcissistic or poor; this may happen but the opposite may also occur. Many are the covers, the disguises, the defences that can deceive us, as in G.'s case; I would say that only careful analysis of our counter-transference, and the aid of dreams if they appear, may enlighten us. Patients of this type, in fact, can be particularly inclined, in the sea of words, to pseudo-free associations and can maintain this sort of analytical false self even for a long period. In short, the silent drive can occur even in its opposite disguise, such as an excess of words, but disinvested ones.

Let us return to the examples that art offers. We mentioned the intertwining with narcissism (that I will not dwell on as ample literature already exists) that I feel has a complex relationship with real disinvestment. The term has acquired dimensions that are far too sweeping and extensive, just as with "fragility" to which it is often also terminologically paired, narcissism, too, can be found every-where. Here I am referring to those narcissistic situations – and even these have always existed but they are deemed pathognomonic of the "new" clinic – of patients unable to foster real investment in objects. They can appear, clinically speaking, in different forms: reticent and solitary people or quite the opposite, centralised and seductive, what they have in common is a sort of emotional desert, of those "devotions" to something the surgeon Atul Gawanda talks of, an absence of investments that covers a spectrum that ranges from more subtle situations to cases verging on sadism due to the marked indifference to the other. With cinema's help, I find an example in the character of Stéphane, the protagonist of *A Heart in Winter* (*Un cœur en hiver*, Claude Sautet, 1992). A masterpiece on disinvestment narcissism, Stéphane (beautifully portrayed by Daniel Auteuil) could be another classic, potential patient of our time. The plot is incredibly simple: Stéphane,

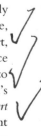

reticent and solitary, is a refined lutist together with his extrovert colleague Maxime, who is temperamentally his exact opposite, his alter ego. The two complement each other and work in harmony until a new girlfriend comes into Maxime's life, the lovely Camille, a violinist played by Emmanuelle Béart. Lone wolf Stéphane's charm gradually attracts Camille; his silences, his reticence, some mild seductive signs are mistakenly interpreted by Camille as signs of love, of interest, while they actually contain a mere half-convinced vanity of winning her. Not to have her with him, not even out of any particular rivalry with his colleague – who truly loves Camille – but out of a pure, empty, narcissistic attitude. Apart from his lute, an inanimate object that he handles with great artistry, nothing matters to Stéphane, not anyone, let alone Camille. He is a man without needs, without passions, the typical Narcissus who can find his way into the heart of many women who are subject to charm's snare. Instead, passion grows in Camille, a young, passionate woman who not only does not hide her having fallen in love from Stéphane, but in a central scene of the film humiliates herself before him, crying out her love. But having now understood the illusion and deception, she is faced with a Stéphane who is completely indifferent, frozen. His was a heart in winter. A frozen heart. Although certain criticism of the time saw virtually "a hibernation" in Stéphane's reticence, a hibernation of the desire not to expose him to the wear and tear of satisfaction (which would be, however, of a narcissistic mould), I tend to see here a perfect example of the inability to invest in any human object, bond, risk or emotion. Without suffering or remorse, Stéphane leaves everything, Camille and even his dear lifelong colleague, Maxime, as they cause too many complications now. Everything ends. Without an apparent reason, without pain. Camille will mourn and Stéphane leaves the scene and only music, perhaps the sole libidinal movement he is capable of, is preserved. The film is not recent, but I have never forgotten the icy, expressionless, inanimate gaze of Stéphane, his indifference to Camille's suffering, his skillful initial seductiveness, the coldness of a reticence that does not cover any shyness, on the contrary it attests to the whole of his arrogance.

Like all great films, it is not deliberately "psychological," but we can assume a probable dead mother complex in Stéphane's inner world. An ancient freeze that protects him from any possible pain as well as from any possible pleasure; pleasure, in Freudian terms, consists of avoiding pain, and perhaps secondarily in assisting the other who succumbs, Stéphane sees his own power confirmed. However, there is no triumph in Stéphane's hibernated gaze. The film's keen perspicacity lies precisely in its ability to relate the winter of disinvestment, not the run-of-the-mill cruelty in relationships: not even Stéphane is happy. Stéphane may well represent a patient of our times, able to put the analyst's resistance to the test that may, once more as with G., my patient, fall into different scenarios: to fall for the fascination and seduction of someone dark and handsome as Camille did, maintaining the illusion that the patient has entered into the analytical process and that, in his own way, is moving it forward, with the risk of stagnant and interminable analysis; or that the analyst ends up frozen by infection together with the patient, who thus has supremacy while the analyst becomes unproductive, with scant capacity for thinking, dreaming and producing reverie. Or a wrathful aggressive countertransference could be triggered in the analyst, as in Camille, faced with an intelligent but ungrateful patient who does not respond to any stimulus nor reciprocate our love. Depending on the personality, on the climate of the analytical couple, on the cultural orientation of the analyst, there can be many developments and constructions in the analytical field in these difficult situations that if not understood tend to stall, to be glaciated which is exactly what the patient intends to project onto the analyst, in the unconscious hope, in the best of cases, that he will make it his own, understand and cure it.

There is only one remedy to the daily tragedy of disinvestment: love.

As Kertész says (2007, p. 250), which we cited in reference to the Holocaust:

The only solution is love.

(quoted in Green, 2010, p. 181)

Only the libidinal drive, capable of fostering investments in objects, contrasts the dark force of disinvestment. In the poetics of *Anomalisa*, love resists one night in the symbolic passage of the hotel, a place of passage *par excellence*, but then it decays; in my patient G., maniacal defensive coverage is reduced only with slow, sincere investment in analysis and in a new object, dissimilar to her many appointments and interests; while for Stéphane of *A Heart in Winter*, disinvestment prevails instead. With realistic bitterness, the film has not sweetened a situation that is so frequent both inside and outside the analysis room. Things are dead, finished.

A beautiful documentary by the Austrian Nikolaus Geyrhalter (2016), with the provocative and ironic title of *Homo Sapiens*, shows, with an original style and ingenious reading, a world emptied of human investment. In the absolute silence of the absence, with no music or words, the camera goes around the world – the one that was formerly the world of human intelligence – and shows all the abandoned places that bear the sign of human presence that at a certain point disinvested from them, as if a future inhabitant of another planet happened on Earth and saw the *remains*: houses, schools, theatres, public places . . . Places where homo sapiens built life and culture, submerged by weeds, snow and rain, because while everything that is human, if disinvested, is fleeting and dies, nature continues with its incessant, stolid circularity. When I saw *Homo Sapiens*, I thought there could not have been a more artistically successful representation of disinvestment. If we do not look after objects, frequent them, live in them, if they are not objects that have life *per se*, then human intelligence has counted for nothing. Only love counts; that is to say that human intelligence is fruitful and will not be reduced to a land of desolate remains if we only maintain investment in things and in people. A child disinvested from birth, dies, if not physically then psychically. And so this applies to every bond, to every activity. Such frequent recourse to artistic examples, as well as representing my personal taste, was necessary for me, I realised as I wrote these pages. How can disinvestment be described? It is, by its very nature, indescribable, unutterable. Analytical reconstructions are arduous and fruit of our countertransference collages (and patients of this kind are not easy analytic frequenters). Art therefore remains, in my view, the most powerful form of representing the un-representable: *Homo Sapiens* needs no words and is, indeed, dumb, like the death drive. It is we who inhabit the objects of this world and who make it alive, this is its powerful message, just as the subject of the subconscious *is not by nature a given guarantee*, it is not an essence-subject, but it is the task of psychoanalysis to make it exist (Recalcati, 2010, translated for this edition): I would also add, to make it *resist*.

Does this psychopathological spectrum we are talking about overlap with the Greenian concept of "white psychosis" (*psychose blanche*, Green, 1990)? I think here it is worth mentioning the concept of "white," as it approaches, without overlapping, our underlying theme. Differentiation is not simple, and perhaps arbitrary: the concept, an inner core to the irreducible psyche both to neurosis and to psychosis, the "white" state characterises borderline subjects above all or, rather, the *états-limites*. A "psychosis without psychosis," without an overt or symptomatic expression necessarily in the traditional psychotic sense. White is an emptiness (while classic psychosis is not necessarily empty, indeed, with delirium significance can be inflated), a structural emptiness of thought. For thought to be there, processing is required of mourning, of the depressive position and of frustration; if this does not happen or only partially takes place, the mind remains as if with holes, as we have seen with the transgenerational in Ilany Kogan (*psychic hole*) and, in Green's words, *white*. If the subject refuses frustration, there is no thought. It is in the failure of the transitional area and in the attack of thought, bringing together the thinking of Winnicott and Bion, that Green identifies this particular and today extremely widespread and silent form of psychopathology. It should be noted that, for Green, unlike in real psychosis, in white psychosis there is a certain quota of Oedipus and triangulation; however, identification and subjectivisation via desire are lacking, because:

> The object refuses frustration, there is from their symbolic function [. . .] and reduced to a pair of subjects regulated by the criteria of good–bad and present–absent. The problem is that the good is always absent, idealized, out of reach, inaccessible, whilst the bad exerts an obsessive and intrusive presence on the subject.
>
> (Recalcati, 2003, p. 118, translated for this edition)

The behavioural outcomes can be quite similar, indistinguishable from more generic situations that, in this chapter, I wanted to describe more as a *climate* rather than as specific pathologies. An *état-limite* patient may at times show a paralysis of thought, a hole in his mental activity, an attack on thought in the sense intended by Bion, with consequent complaints due to an inability to be content, to produce and so forth and, certainly, also to create bonds and invest. But, indeed, what is highlighted here, on a psychoanalytical level and not from external observation, is *the attack on thought* rather than disinvestment as an effect of the deadly drive. Borderline patients, in fact, although with violent love-hate ambivalences, know how to temporarily invest objects. Of course, ultimately the outcome may be similar, one clings to the thought (a clinically more serious act) or one disinvests the world for fear of suffering. Thought *is* suffering. Another outcome, frequently encountered in Nando's history and in writers, is drug addiction, where the substance gives shelter from frustration, abolishes thought and kills any possible transactional area, any expectation, giving the illusion of obtaining without ever losing. The contemporary Nirvana, if we assume addictions – all of them are interchangeable – as the archetypal psychopathology of our time, responds to a death drive that branches off into simple oblivion, Léthé, disinvestment, a clinic of white and empty, attack on thought, enjoyment.

I would even go so far as to say that the contemporary clinic *is* a clinic of the death drive.

Not on the everted aggressive and destructive side, which does exist but there have perhaps been even more destructive eras in the past, but on its silent, Nirvana side: an anthropological mutation has quietly taken place under our very eyes.

The nothing of white – the term itself is strongly evocative – the desert of disinvestment impoverishes life but preserves – or gives the illusion of preserving – by suffering. However, while a borderline patient is capable of bonds and strong bonds of hatred (love/hate), the age of sad passions does not foresee passions, neither of love nor of hate, and it is therefore right, in my opinion, not to mix them up. A similar panorama, "psychosis without psychosis," is described by Recalcati (2010) in what he defines as "man without unconscious": dominated by the need of enjoyment and no longer by removal and oedipal limits, hypermodern man is particularly exposed to the death drive. The contemporary clinic, increasingly disengaged from desire and conflict and inhabited instead by enjoyment and the avoidance of frustration, is a clinic that is incredibly close to second topography Freud and, in my view, it is metapsychologically oriented to the death drive.

> The dissipative enjoyment of the death drive, structurally antagonist and alternative to that of desire, drags the subject into an autistic drift that separates it from the Other.
>
> (Recalcati, 2010, p. XIII, translated for this edition)

The terms change according to the orientation, but the underlying concept is the same: white, enjoyment, sad passions, attack on thought, absence of symbolic . . . is this what awaits contemporary man, is this what especially the weakest among us are already living?

And does psychoanalysis, which has the unconscious as its elective place, and contemporary psychoanalysis in particular, faced with these challenges, still have a role? Can it survive and have something to say to *a man without unconscious?*

Have we lost the object of our discipline? Or do we need to find it, to flush it out in other forms, in the exhausting business of maintaining psychoanalytic identity while adapting it in the light of a human world that has become so different and susceptible to constant threats to thought and the forms of representability and significance? The roots of the so-called crisis of psychoanalysis lie deep down and are not merely attributable to the current economic situation or to changes in the rhythm of life. I have previously explored (Valdré, 2015) the role of the contemporary subject's diminished ability to sublimate and the lower value that *Kultur* places on a psychic experience that is already difficult in the drive economy as possible contributions to the "crisis," but I believe that nevertheless, and not just nowadays, the extension of the death drive, in its various forms of appearance over the ages and in personal contexts, definitely distances patients from analysis which is sublimatory and vitalising by nature. If at one time approaching psychoanalysis aroused conflict, as the age of conflict has passed, I believe that today it has been replaced by a disillusionment, a disenchantment, a disinterest, as if the malignant force of disinvestment has invaded interest in looking after ourselves as well. Most people, if not scared by it, are simply not intrigued by it, which, in my opinion, is far worse. What Green called *Illusions and Disillusions of Analytical Work*, in a reasoned and relatively bitter review of his entire life's work, I believe principally draws on the tenacious resistance and the obtuse and ugly force of the death drive in a human being.

> If not as failures, he writes, at least as ones that involved patients who were particularly resistant to, or rebellious against analytic work. However, the worst is not always bound to happen and, as long as the analytic work continues, the result is not necessarily unfavourable. After analysing the various outcomes that can potentially occur, things sometimes turn out less badly that one thought they would. Above all, I have learnt to nuance my opinion. With respect to certain patients, I have told myself they have tried to fight against their suffering as best they could.
>
> (2010, p. 171)

The wisdom of his years, the vastness of his experience, the Freudian teaching that has always reined in facile enthusiasm, his observation of life outside the analysis room, can but make me agree with these assertions.

Personally, I would take an open but realistic view; as already said, the mere fact that the patient crosses our threshold is a sign of hope. What is then played for, once through the door, may be the result of a thousand compromises to keep the death drive and its crazed thrust at bay, not to eliminate it. In analytical work, I find it essential that the patient *recognizes it*, as must the analyst. He must look it courageously in the face. In the cases I have recounted, this happened in part with Nando, whose compromise consisted in a useful escape to a world, Thailand, that did not ask too many adult responsibilities of him. In Jade, the degree of awareness was more profound: four years after the end of analysis, she returned with an explicit request to be helped "not to destroy." The new relationship, born with the analysis and with completely different characteristics to the preceding ones where she was destructive, placed her in a serious dilemma: if I can no longer be the one to be got rid of by the malice of the other, will the return of aggression on myself lead me to destroy? Some signs had quite rightly alarmed her: unjustified criticism of her partner, unleashing of quarrels in which she recognised as being completely spurious, "cornering" him just as once used to happen to her. Jade *saw herself*, she saw the rumblings of the drive destroy precisely what she valued most, and she asked for help. I have mentioned this case, an analysis in two *tranches* that gave not just me but both of *us* a great deal as people and as an analytical couple, because I think that, when this occurs, it is the best we can hope for in our work: not magically or maniacally to eliminate or give the illusion that death does not exist in us, but *to learn to recognise it*. Can a human being do more?

It never ceases to amaze me, despite twenty years of clinical activity, of reading, reasoning, observing the relational swirl around me, how the death drive is expressed in the most insidious, painful of forms, damaging precisely what we hold most dear. Jade loves her partner, but she is led to wear him out to the point of destruction, with her work and her studies, after so much effort to obtain them; the most precious relationships are put at risk. This is so common that, even as analysts, we end up by not questioning overmuch what I think is a fundamental human tragedy; psychoanalytically speaking, it is included as coaction to repeat, certainly, but perhaps it is a nuance, a *coté* that is yet more dubious and subtle.

Blue Jasmine, who has not come through the analysis room door, destroys precisely that second *chance* that could have saved her life, with her coaction to the lie; *Anomalisa's* Michael, oppressed by a life that he feels is useless and empty, allows himself the possibility of salvation for just one night, and then he ruins it; and Stéphane of *A Heart in Winter*, in destroying Camille's passion also loses his best friend and lifelong colleague. We don't rage against strangers, it is, indeed, not uncommon that care be taken towards superficial relationships or mere acquaintances; no, we tend to destroy those we love, what we love. It is also true that this has always happened, it is as old as humankind, but it is not to be excluded that contemporaneity has made its contribution by depriving the individual of those guarantors, ideologies or religions or ethical values that at least apparently and as pure cover provided a brake or a barrier to giving free rein to destructiveness. Catholic values unconsciously handed down over generations made people tolerant in marriages, that were to be saved *anyway*, and the spectre of the loss of a possible paradise put a brake on things, a threat of punishment for evil doing.

Far from feeling any nostalgia for the past, I note that contemporary man must add, in addition to the intrinsic and inevitable death drive that dwells within him, a greater freedom to operate it.

John Wilder, the protagonist of the already mentioned *Disturbing the Peace* by Richard Yates (2008),[5] feels he is a failure in his profession and in his conjugal life. Like all of Yates's characters (and most of us) he is not actually persecuted by evil, but it is as if something within himself is set on destroying him.

He has some chance of success as a screenwriter in Hollywood. He encounters a young woman with whom he has a passionate affair, his artistic projects playing their part. But he never stops drinking, he has incredible outbursts of anger and changes in mood: everything he held most dear is destroyed.

Is this an unconscious fear of illusion and disillusionment in Yates the ex-child, who knows that his mother will never stop changing homes, and thus prevents disasters by procuring them by himself? It is not uncommon to see this in analysis: patients who leave before analysis has ended, or before the holidays. Is this pure death drive, directed exclusively towards the self in a sort of almost knowing masochism?

Let us take a step back and return to the dead mother complex that I find, in this vast psychoanalytic speculation, certainly not exhaustive but in these cases most indicative. The patient, as with all those named so far in the guise of literary characters, does not display strictly depressive symptoms, but it is the transference that enables you to discover that:

> The feeling of impotence is evident. Impotence to withdraw from a conflictual situation, impotence to love, to make the most of one's talents, to multiply one's assets or, when this does take place, a profound dissatisfaction with the results.
>
> (Green, 1996, p. 148)

In each story we have outlined, in my clinical practice or from writers or in films, there is *always* an original maternal depression. Green lists several situations in which such depression may speak; in fact, the child will be disinvested, and there will remain "a cold core, which will eventually be overcome, but which leaves an indelible mark on the erotic cathexes of the subjects in question" (Green, 1996, p. 150). And the father? An inaccessible father.

It is interesting to note how the trauma is early but not that early: photos show a cheerful, happy baby who felt loved; only *subsequently*, in later photos, does the sadness of the child show. In his memories Nando had been a lively child, before the breakdown; there had been life, fortunately. "As with the disappearance of ancient civilizations . . . nothing is left but ruins," notes Green in this splendid metaphor (ibid., p. 150). *Homo Sapiens.* We do not have psychosis, in fact the subject lives, is in contact with reality, but disinvests objects or, once invested, unconsciously acts so that everything will be destroyed. It is not uncommon to hear these stories in analysis and in life: "I had everything, I could have . . . ," "I ruined everything, I made him/her escape . . . ," "I left a job half done, and yet I wanted it . . . ," these situations frequently occur: where the wound, the cold core, taps into a talent but we might have had an artistic if not commonplace unhappiness without glory. It is typically in middle age, once the expectations of youth and self-deception, that the deadly core manifests itself:

> In middle age there is mystery, there is mystification. The most I can make out of this hour is *a kind of loneliness*. Even the beauty of the visible world

seems to crumble, yes even love. I feel that there has been as some mis-carriage, some wrong turning, but I do not know when it took place and I have no hope of finding it.

(Cheever, 1990, p. 3)

The majority of patients today, I find, come with this desert, this *kind of loneliness*, in the words of the author. If in adolescents, according to Benasayag and Schmit, it is easier for the silent drive to brood in the silence of passions, in boredom and substance abuse, in middle age, as one takes stock, the subject is more likely to bring to the analyst, in the best of cases, his ruins and destruction. It seems to me that the awareness of their role in all of this, of their own responsibility, the choice of possible compromises between living and dying is one of the outcomes that is humanly possible in a clinic that is now distant from the neurotic symptomatic translation of conflict – which certainly exists but not as in Freudian times. Therefore my vision, while realistic, is not bleak: a certain disillusionment belongs to life, and it would be surprising if our work was exempt. If the patient sees his ruins then he can do something: Jade has seen them and has returned, writers have transferred them onto the page, *Blue Jasmine*, denying herself access to the truth, collapsed, Michael Stone and Stéphane remained frozen, prisoners of the cold core.

The game is played in analysis and in life, in the drive interweave of the two drives, between the binding and unbinding, investment and disinvestment. We have repeatedly referred to isolation. I would like to make a distinction between this and *loneliness*: the contemporary word "empty" creates regrettable semantic confusion, but they are quite different instances in the psyche. Michael Stone is isolated, but lives among people, has a family, speaks in public, is not *alone*. The hypermodern subject has a horror of solitude, but like the *Web Junkie* kids he can live 24 hours a day isolated in a room with a videogram inside his head. Disinvestment could, in literary terms, result in that feeling of *boredom* that leads to a horror of loneliness and the search for the gregarious, a typically adolescence resort, but it is a deceptively conformist trait that characterises our times. Disinvestment therefore translates into isolation, not necessarily physical but also of thought, a psyche without movement; while loneliness is a difficult conquest and caused Dickinson (1998) to say "*It might be lonelier | without the Loneliness*," a complex integrative movement, which requires and avails itself of the company of internal objects that must be sufficiently good enough not to become persecutors, that draws on sublimations, requires effort, makes no compromises, gives valuable contacts with themselves, but the price to be paid is high. Isolated but eternally connected, isolated but never alone, never in silence, the subject of sad passions has also disinvested the bond with himself, with those parts of self to be enjoyed in solitude, and squanders it and wastes it in the Nirvana of substance abuse. Even gregarious adaptation and conformism are Nirvana substitutes and contain, in my opinion, quotas of death drive, as they do not make you think but rather dispense oblivion, extinguish subjectivity and are therefore always to be looked at with a keen psychoanalytic eye. Where there is no subject, nothing good can be expected.

Isolation and loneliness can stay in diametrically opposite places, the former representing the first symptom of sad passion, and the latter one of its possible cures.

But let us we close the parenthesis on loneliness *versus* isolation and let us return to our drive interweave:

> In short, the closer the state of fusion is, the more the death drives are bound by the life drives, and the more unbinding is neutralized. It is illusory to hope for a total suppression of the effects of the death drive; the ambivalence one always discovers, which never disappears completely, is proof that they will never be completely suppressed.
>
> (Green, 2010, p. 68)

The ambivalence, we could say, although painful for the subject who feels it, is basically a lifesaver; it makes living difficult, exposes us to coaction to repeat, to the slips and self-boycotting that we have seen, but if it were less so, the subject deprived of conflict, in the hands of the death drive alone, then only suicide would remain or, if the instinct is extroverted, murder. Having made use of artists and clinical cases we have certainly come across more death drives toward the self: some of our writers committed suicide. I do not mean to subtract importance from destructiveness and the everted death drive, but rather I have considered its investigation less interesting because it has already been the subject of many studies and reflections, both psychoanalytic and not. Its deafening noise cannot be avoided, while the silence of the silent drive towards the self leaves its mark on most human suffering and characterises the contemporary clinic, and its masking, also due to lifestyles that have changed over time, may pass completely unnoticed. Well before Freud, in the 1920s, discovers the existence of a death drive that dwells in life and makes the theoretical systematisation we have dealt with here, art preceded him. I have referred to more recent literature and filmography, but does the death drive not reign supreme in the adverse destinies of nineteenth century heroines Madame Bovary and Anna Karenina, or in a crime as purely drive driven, without purpose, such as the pure aggressive discharge in *Crime and Punishment*? On the other hand, Freud has never denied his debt towards the poets, the absolute superiority and precocity of art in sensing and reading human things:

> Creative writers are valuable allies and their evidence is to be prized highly, for they are apt to know a whole host of things between heaven and earth. . . .
>
> (Freud, 1906, p. 7)

Notes

1. An association founded in 1960, 30 years after AA and based on the same, maintaining its principles, objectives and tools, but replacing the word "alcohol" with "food." Both started in the United States and are now widespread throughout the world.

2. Originally published in 1965, reissued by Vintage in 2003.
3. An American author, journalist and filmmaker who now lives in New Mexico, she was married to Martin Scorsese. The quote is from her most famous book, *The Artist's Way: A Spiritual Path to Higher Creativity.*
4. Presented at the 2015 Venice Film Festival.
5. See Chapter 3.

References

Arendt, H. (1963). *Eichmann in Jerusalem: A Report on the Banality of Evil.* Viking Pres: New York.

Assoun, P.L. (1993). *Freud et les sciences sociales.* Paris: Armand Colin.

Baudrillard, J. (1998). *La Société de consommation. Ses mythes et ses structures* [The Consumer Society. Myths and Structures]. London: Page Publications. (Original work published 1974).

Benasayag, M. and Schmit G. (2003). *Las pasiones tristes. Sufrimiento psiquico y crisis social.* Editorial Siglo XXI: Buenos Aires.

Bollas, C. (1993). *Being a Character. Psychoanalysis and Self Experience.* London: Routledge.

Cheever, R. (1990). *The Journals of John Cheever.* New York: Knopf.

Cupa, D. (2006). Psychanalyse de la destructivité. EDK: Paris.

Dickinson, E. (1998). *The Poems of Emily Dickinson* (R.W. Franklin, Ed.). Cambridge, MA: Harvard University Press.

Doninotti, E. (2011). *Psychoanalysi della distruttività. La Pulsione di Morte.* Padova, Italy: Domeneghini Editore.

Forster, E.M.R. (2005). *A Passage to India.* London: Penguin. (Original work published 1924).

Freud, S. (1906). *Volume IX Jensen's Gradiva and Other Works.* London: Hogarth.

Gawande, A. (2014). *Being Mortal. Medicine and What Matters in the End.* New York: Metro-politan Books.

Green, A. (1990). *La folie privée. Psychanalyse des cas limites.* Gallimard: Paris.

Green, A. (1996). *On Private Madness.* London: Karnac. (Original work published 1983).

Green, A. (1999). *Le travail du negatif* [The Work of the Negative]. New York: Free Association. (Original work published 1993).

Green, A. (2010). *Illusions and Disillusions of Psychoanalytic Work.* London: Karnac.

Green, A. (2018). *Illusions and Disillusions of Psychoanalytic Work.* London: Routledge. (Original work published 2010).

Kaes, R. (2005). *Transmission de la vie psychique entre générations.* Paris: Dunot.

Kapsambelis, V. (2011). La "fragilité narcissique," une clinique contemporaine. *Revue française de psychanalyse,* 75(4): 1097–1112.

Kertész, I. (2005). The Unhappy 20th Century. In *Imre Kertész and Holocaust Literature.* West Lafayette, IN: Purdue University Press.

Kertész, I. (2007). *Il Secolo Infelice.* Milan: Bompiani.

McKenna, A. (2006). Fellini's crowds and the remains of religion. Contagion: Journal of *Violence, Mimesis, and Culture,* 12/13: 159–182. Retrieved from jstor.org/stable/4192 5289.

Milazzo, F. (2014). *La ferita dell'assenza. Sulla "madre morta" di André Green.* Retrieved from psychiatryonline.it/node/5374.

Recalcati, M. (2003). *Introduzione alla psicoanalisi contemporanea.* Milan: Mondadori.

Recalcati, M. (2010). *L'uomo senza inconscio. Figure della nuova clinica psicoanalica.* Milan: Mimesis.

Séchaud, E. (2005). Perdre, sublimer . . ., *Revue Francaise de psychanalyse*, 69: 1309–1379.

Twenge, J. and Campbell, K. (2012). Generational differenences in young adults' life goals, concern for others and civic orientation 1966–2009, *Journal of Personality and Social Psychology*, 102: 1045–1062.

Valdrè, R. (2015). *On Sublimation: A Path to the Destiny of Desire, Theory and Treatment.* Karnac: London.

Williams, J. (2012). *Stoner.* London: Vintage. (Original work published 1965).

Yates, R. (2008). *Disturbing the Peace.* London: Vintage Books. (Original work published 1975).

Filmography

A Heart in Winter. (1992). Claude Sautet, France.

Anomalisa. (2015). Charlie Kaufman and Duke Johnson, USA, (Winner of The Grand Jury Prize for best animated feature film at the 2015 Venice Film Festival).

Elephant. (2003). Gus Von Sant, USA (Winner of Palme d'Or at the 2003 Cannes Film Festival).

Funny Games. (2007). Michael Heneke, Austria.

Homo sapiens. (2016). Nikolaus Geyrhalter, 2016, Austria.

Web Junkie. (2013). Documentary by Shosh Shlam and Hilla Medalia, USA-Israel (Sundance Film Festival 2014 World Cinema Grand Jury Prize: Documentary; distributed by many TV broadcasting companies but not in every country).

CONCLUSIONS

Conclusions are impossible. We close with questions and with two of my own suggestions. Is it therefore legitimate to call our era, among the many other definitions, the era of sad passions and to endorse a new clinic of disinvestment in place of, or more broader than, neurotic conflict?

The characteristics we have outlined, that certainly do not give the full picture as that will be for History to decide, allow a hypothesis to be made that yes, third millennium humankind coexists more with disinvestment than with the ambivalent passion of conflict, more with unbinding than with a struggle towards bans that in fact have been expunged and that the individual must give to himself – or search in external idealised forces, as in the overturning that occurs in new radicalisms. All of this can make death inside life particularly seductive, an easy solution "to the horror of time and space" seen with Coccioli, escaping to the borders of human categories through substance abuse, use of the body, nirvanic isolations. In any case, there is no doubt that with respect to neuroses, destructive drives – both towards the subject as well as archaic mechanisms of defence – today carry far greater weight and challenge the analysable concept itself.

We have retraced the strong Freudian theoretical structure from *Beyond the Pleasure Principle* with the 1920 watershed and subsequent contributions that, in my opinion, with the exception of André Green, have not added significant elements to the Freudian way. We have gone over some clinical cases, given prevalence to the value of living testimonies through the stories of those who have step by step, for the whole of their lives, danced with the death drive, sometimes succumbing, sometimes surviving. I find the value of these first-hand accounts sincere and admirably authentic, invaluable, like a particularly long session. We have moved in the world of art, through writers, from Pasolini to a group of well-known American authors, some particularly famous and others less so, all sharing troubled lives, desperately vital, exuberant and suicidal. We have revisited

contemporary films, documentaries, confident that nothing like the language of art, with its universality, with or without words, manages to transversely recount human drives – their eternity, their strength but also their grasp of the tacit and fleeting change in time, often anticipating it.

If we can draw any conclusion then I would say it is this: the contemporary clinic is *above all a clinic of the death drive*.

From here, in my opinion, whether one "agrees or not," shares it or not (inverted commas because, given the size of the problem, I find worrying about the school of thought really laughable) the extraordinary modernity of Freud in having intuited that there exists a *beyond* to the pleasure principle, that does not make life faithful to Good but, in the coaction to repeat, *faithful to the trauma*: a clinic beyond the pleasure principle is the contemporary clinic. I agree with Recalcati (2010) and others in discerning the new paradigm in the spectrum of *addiction*, and I agree with Conrotto (2012) in preferring a distinction between removal/rejection, that is to say, between the basic mechanisms, rather than between the now all-embracing diagnostic definitions of borderline or narcissism. It is well understood, rereading all this, how still today the perturbing hypothesis of death inside life has raised so much opposition, although mentioned by many, and transformed into the more easily understandable aggressiveness. Freud was not interested in the mystery of death nor in any mysticism bound to it, but as if it were inside of life – as subsequent biological-immunological discoveries have confirmed – not only does death start and produce but the organism "chooses" its own death as in an extreme, last bastion of freedom.

It is this Freud, not the one of the discovery of the unconscious and dreams, it is the Freud of *Beyond the Pleasure Principle* who continues to keep open a Pandora's box of irreducible, indigestible questions; it is not the death that comes from outside that interests him, it is the death that comes from inside.

If we may draw another conclusion, it is that the greatest and most powerful and tragically irreducible expression of the death drive is *the coaction to repeat*. Think of it as the assassination of time. This is a book about the coaction to repeat. Human tragedy lies not in the presence of Evil, not in the presence of trauma, but in the fact that the subject himself who undergoes it will subsequently *repeat it himself*, sometimes on himself, sometimes projectively on others. So simple and shocking a discovery illuminates, on its own, the whole mystery of human destiny.

Of the three forms with which Freud actively sees "death at work," the negative therapeutic reaction is largely observable in the therapeutic context. I must confess that primary masochism remains, despite everything, a shadowy area of theoretical-clinical mystery. The coaction to repeat every day dismantles a lot or a little of the enormous efforts of our lives. It does not expect any dramatic turn of events, it quietly waits for middle age, when the choices seem to be well advanced, the worst mistakes avoided and the return of the removed comes back to visit us with all that baggage we thought we had left behind us. Certainly some will be more fortunate, but we all have a little Jasmine in us, without going crazy; because infinite are the ways in which we survive. A patient once asked me how it was possible, after so much evil, repeated evil, that he was still there, that he was still alive. I think I replied that I did not know, but that it was interesting, just to observe this thing. He would not have appreciated an ode to being alive, nor am I particularly adroit; we both had a sensitive and painful awareness of the strength of the coaction to repeat, we had never hidden this, never related how it is said, and I think that was a fatiguing but fairly good analysis. I believe that the patient does less harm to himself than before.

How we kill ourselves. How we damage our lives, by our big and little choices. How we neglect the objects and the passions that are dearest to us. How we get sick in body, sometimes, cutting out the encumbrance of the mind. How we fall asleep with drugs of any kind, or the drugs of disinvestment. Despite having lived in the Short Century (Hobsbawm, 1994), permeated with the fervours of great ideologies and of future falls that Freud will not see, the intuition contained in *Beyond the Pleasure Principle*, if reviewed today seems to illuminate the contemporary clinic – the sad passions – with more secular and farsighted acumen than most of post-Freudian psychoanalysis or other psychological theories. Although relying on the criticised labile drive concept, to be reviewed for as long as you wish, the death drive in Freud as originally formulated, resumed at a later time (as stated in Chapter 1) only in part by Klein and Lacan with completely different paths, has been the subject of this book. We have deliberately neglected its everted forms, aggressiveness and destructiveness, because they have already been widely studied and well documented. An unequivocal attempt to talk again about the death drive in the Freudian sense, that is not declined in the easy act of aggression, is much more difficult to find both due to the skepticism which it has aroused as well as its *silence*. If it is silent by definition, how can it be talked about? As a consequence, we have had to resort to art, to the fine mesh of the clinic, and I have had to rely on my imagination.

Freud believed in humankind, this animal dependent beyond time on the primary object and extremely fragile, but he did not believe it to be *essentially good*, essentially aiming at good. With a perturbing counter-intuitive hypothesis that spikes the guns of the contemporary myth of the "struggle for life and happiness," it is precisely with *Beyond the Pleasure Principle* that I believe we have a canvas of the clinic and of contemporary suffering. There is no need to go further and look elsewhere.

If *Beyond the Pleasure Principle* is the object of death into life, and of *silent* death, that does not appear or show itself, that would be to surrender our weapons and conclude that not psychoanalysis, but rather only faith and religions, can provide comfort to a person from the battle against the death drive. Instead, we believe that as never before psychoanalysis plays a very precise role, not to *be confused* with the "psychologies," not abdicating its *other* paradoxical position that it *holds within while remaining out* of Culture's dictates and fashions, but being most definitely a participant (Valdrè, 2015), revaluing the so-called, and in my view misunderstood, Freudian pessimism regarding human nature in that empathetic "disillusion" that does not leave the field, but enhances the possible compromises to the patient's drive world and, without succumbing to the countertransference urge of "doing," collects and orchestrates the fragments of the life drive that exist in every patient.

Why do I eschew psychologies with some insistence in my writings? We must be careful: in a clinic of disinvestment, where you navigate in sad passions, where subjectivity is obscured and isolation is confused with loneliness, the lure of a clinic of the obvious is strong; a clinic of pure relationality of confirmation, of response, of pure effort to promote investments, contacts, to impose life and vitality as the supreme goods, with the danger of obscuring other ways, other modes that *that* individual may more creatively find in itself.

Richard Yates did not necessarily want to be happy; he had given that up. He understood, even without analysis, that you could not be saved from certain childhoods; he wanted to write and that saved him. It is preferable to define it as without unconscious, dominated by a psychotic foundation that does not correspond to real psychotic psychopathology (Recalcati, 2010) but a widespread lack of interior dimension, or the "age of psychopathy" (Eigen, 2001) with the absence of the normal guarantor of the super-ego, with the consequent "psychopathy" of everyday life in all of us, we are certainly in a clinic of Evil. Because only the unconscious, with its instances of desire and prohibition and, let us repeat, these should *not be taken for granted*, and only Ethics, as a limit and Oedipal boundary, allow the drive fusion to head towards more sublimative outlets, more binding, more vital, more caring for the other.

Even if nothing ever disappears completely in the psyche, the era of symptom translation is in decline. Today it is precisely in *Beyond the Pleasure Principle* that the match is being played: with the new nirvanisations, with the hundreds of people I have met in AA and OA[1] meetings who went there and not to us, and here is not the place to discuss why. We need not fear the perturbing assumptions that death dwells inside us, that we carry it inside ourselves; some people – not many – manage to give it an artistic form; more people coexist badly with it; others pacifically proceed in drive play discharging aggressiveness on the other; the more balanced attain a certain fortunate integration that, however, as we have seen with sublimation, is never constant and should never be taken for granted once and for all. The drive world lives in turmoil and so it seeks the quiet.

I would not talk of the struggle of life against death, understandable but now a very contemporary slogan of the fashion for wellness, but I would return to the Derridian *life death* with which we opened the book that at best coexist, compulsory guests of the same mental home as the "neither with you nor without you" spouses of Carver's stories, the most possibly conscious in the subject, the most possibly conscious in Culture as a whole and in the analyst. Every phantom kicked out of the door, we know, will return through the window to claim his right. I would also like to stress that I do not believe that there is in Freud or in my rereading any apology of suffering, any ode to death. Clinical Freud observed certain phenomena. They took him by surprise, they seemed paradoxical to the pleasure principle until then the pillar of his theory and they mixed up the cards that he had to take account of from there onwards: pleasure has no primacy over psychic life. Pleasure occurs only in the absence of displeasure. We are the bearers of a remains, an excess and this must never be forgotten. Freud the speculator derived the strongest, the most current of his theories from this. There is no love of pain in itself; only, more prosaically, one realises that displeasure comes first, then, by subtraction, pleasure is given. It is a realisation, not an opinion. Ricoeur was right when he said:

To suffer is always to suffer too much.

I would end these impossible conclusions by returning to art, with a poet who is very far from the drive universe of death that we have tried to chart. Wisława Szymborska was anything but morbid, anything but apparently sad. She will always be remembered for her unique style, her bitter humour, grace, irony, her vital and rebellious spirit; she was able to wonderfully observe the details from the depths of her journey through a difficult life. She knew hatred and persecution, victim of the Communist regime in Poland; she never allowed herself to become infected by hatred, but she did dedicate just one of her many splendid poems to it:

Hatred

See how efficient it still is,
How it keeps itself in shape –
our century's hatred.
How easily it vaults the tallest obstacles.
How rapidly it pounces, tracks us down.

It is not like other feelings.
At once both older and younger.
It gives birth itself to the reasons that give it life.
When it sleeps, it's never eternal rest.
And sleeplessness won't sap its strength; it feeds it.

[. . .]

Justice also works well at the outset
Until hate gets its own momentum going.
Hatred. Hatred.
Its face twisted in a grimace
of erotic ecstasy.

Oh these other feelings, listless weaklings.
Since when does brotherhood draw crowds?
Has compassion ever finished first?
Does doubt ever really rouse the rabble?
Only hatred has just what it takes.

Gifted, diligent, hard-working.
Need we mention all the songs it has composed?
All the pages it has added to our history books?

All the human carpets it has spread
over countless city squares and football fields?

Let's face it:
it knows how to make beauty.
The splendid fire-glow in midnight skies.
Magnificent bursting bombs in rosy dawns.
You can't deny the inspiring pathos of ruins
and a certain bawdy humor to be found
in the sturdy column jutting from their midst.

Hatred is a master of contrast – between explosions and dead quiet,
red blood and white snow.
Above all, it never tires
of its leitmotif - the impeccable executioner
towering over its soiled victim.

It's always ready for new challenges.
If it has to wait awhile, it will.
They say it's blind. Blind?
It has a sniper's keen sight
and gazes unflinchingly at the future
as only it can.

(December 2016)

Note

1. The already mentioned groups of anonymous groups of alcoholics and food addicts.

References

Conrotto F. (2012). Pulsionalità tra azione e simbolizzazione, in *Notes. Trasformazioni sociali e forme della psicoanalisi* (Eds. F. Munari and E. Mangini), 0: 35-43.

Eigen M. (2001). *Damaged Bonds*. Karnac: London.

Hobsbawm E. (1994). *The Age of Extremes 1914–1991: The Short Twentieth Century*. Michael Joseph: London.

Recalcati M. (2010). *L'uomo senza inconscio. Figure della nuova clinica psicoanalitica*. Cortina: Milan.

Szymborska W. (2000). *Poems, New and Collected 1957–1997*. Harcourt: New York.

Valdrè, R. (2015). *On Sublimation: A Path to the Destiny of Desire, Theory and Treatment*. Karnac: London.

INDEX

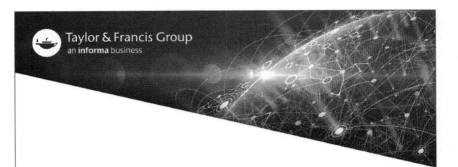

Made in the USA
Middletown, DE
24 April 2022

64721256R00115